ODD *girl* OUT

ODD *girl* OUT

the

hidden

· culture of

aggression

in girls

RACHEL SIMMONS

HARCOURT, INC.

new york
san diego
london

Requests for permission to make copies of any part of
the work should be mailed to the following address:
Permissions Department, Harcourt, Inc.,
6277 Sea Harbor Drive, Orlando, Florida 32887-6777.

www.HarcourtBooks.com

Library of Congress Cataloging-in-Publication Data
Simmons, Rachel, 1974–
Odd girl out: the hidden culture of aggression in girls/
Rachel Simmons.—1st ed.
p.   cm.
ISBN 0-15-100604-0
1. Aggressiveness in children.   2. Girls—Psychology.   I. Title.
BF723.A35 .S56 2002
302.5'4'08342—dc21   2001006864

Text set in Galliard
Book design by Kaelin Chappell

First edition

K J I H G F E

Printed in the United States of America

To my parents,
Claire and Luiz Simmons,
whose constant faith, love,
and support made this book possible
and
To Jane Isay:
heroine, world changer, and friend,
who believed, and believed, and believed.

contents

introduction   *I*

CHAPTER *one*   the hidden culture of aggression in girls   *15*

CHAPTER *two*   intimate enemies   *39*

CHAPTER *three*   the truth hurts   *67*

CHAPTER *four*   she's all that   *103*

CHAPTER *five*   the bully in the mirror   *129*

CHAPTER *six*   popular   *155*

CHAPTER *seven*   resistance   *177*

CHAPTER *eight*   parents and teachers   *203*

CHAPTER *nine*   the road ahead   *231*

conclusion   *261*

notes   *271*

bibliography   *277*

acknowledgments   *287*

index   *291*

When I was eight years old, I was bullied by another girl. I remember very little about that year. My memory is fractured by time and will. I was in the third grade, wore pigtails, and had a lisp. I was known to my teachers as a "rusher," the girl who tore through long-division worksheets and map quizzes, making careless mistakes I was told I could avoid. But I loved to finish first.

So did Abby. She was my popular friend, not a particularly close one. I still don't know why she did it. First she whispered about me to my best friend, who soon decided she'd be happier playing with other girls. When we went to dance class after school at the local community center, Abby rounded up my friends and convinced them to run away from me. Into the center's theater I would sprint after them, winded and frantic, eyes straining in the sudden darkness. Down over rows of slumbering chairs and up on the stage, I would follow the retreating patter of steps and fading peals of laughter.

Day after day I stood in half-lit empty hallways, a stairwell, the parking lot. In all of these places I remember standing alone. In the early evenings before dinner, I cried to my mother while she cooked.

The sorrow was overwhelming, and I was sure I was the only girl ever to know it. This is what I remember most.

Sixteen years later, I was attending graduate school in England. It was raining the day I rode my bike to the library in search of answers about what had happened with Abby. Exactly what pulled me there is hard to say. Something about the memory seemed terribly off-balance to me. On the one hand, I could remember few details. On the other, the anguish of being abandoned by all of my friends and of losing my closest at Abby's hand felt real and raw. It was something that never receded gently with the rest of my childhood memories. I wanted—I needed—to fill in the blanks.

That day, I carried with me the memory of a late night at college, when a casual midnight snack led to six of us confessing that an Abby haunted our past. It was exhilarating to discover we'd all been through the same ordeal. Like me, my friends had spent years believing they were the only ones.

Armed with that knowledge, I pedaled carefully along the slick streets, certain there would be volumes of books waiting to explain how and why girls bully each other. When my first few computer searches turned up next to nothing, I chalked it up to rusty research skills, or rushing. Then I called the librarian over for help. As it turned out, I'd been doing just fine on my own.

In a sea of articles on boys' aggression and bullying, there were only a small handful of articles about girls. There were no accessible books. No guides for parents. No cute survival manuals for kids. As I sat reading the articles, I could not see myself or Abby in what most of these researchers called bullying. I was first surprised, then frustrated.

I sent out an e-mail to everyone I knew in the States and asked them to forward it to as many women as they could. I asked a few simple questions: "Were you ever tormented or teased by another girl? Explain what it was like. How has it affected you today?" Within twenty-four hours my in box was flooded with responses from all over America. The messages piled up as women told their stories into

cyberspace with an emotional intensity that was undeniable. Even on
the computer screen, their pain felt as fresh and unresolved as my
own. Women I never met wrote that I would be the first person ever
to hear their story. It would be a long time before I knew it was because I was the first to ask.

Silence is deeply woven into the fabric of the female experience. It is
only in the last thirty years that we have begun to speak the distinctive truths of women's lives, openly addressing rape, incest, domestic
violence, and women's health. Although these issues always existed,
over time we have given them a place in our culture by building public consciousness, policy, and awareness.

Now it is time to end another silence: There is a hidden culture of
girls' aggression in which bullying is epidemic, distinctive, and destructive. It is not marked by the direct physical and verbal behavior
that is primarily the province of boys. Our culture refuses girls access
to open conflict, and it forces their aggression into nonphysical, indirect, and covert forms. Girls use backbiting, exclusion, rumors,
name-calling, and manipulation to inflict psychological pain on targeted victims. Unlike boys, who tend to bully acquaintances or
strangers, girls frequently attack within tightly knit networks of
friends, making aggression harder to identify and intensifying the
damage to the victims.

Within the hidden culture of aggression, girls fight with body language and relationships instead of fists and knives. In this world,
friendship is a weapon, and the sting of a shout pales in comparison
to a day of someone's silence. There is no gesture more devastating
than the back turning away.

In the hidden culture of aggression, anger is rarely articulated,
and every day of school can be a new social minefield that realigns itself without warning. During times of conflict, girls will turn on one
another with a language and justice only they can understand. Behind a facade of female intimacy lies a terrain traveled in secret,
marked with anguish, and nourished by silence.

This is the world I want the reader to enter. It is where, beneath a chorus of voices, one girl glares at another, then smiles silently at her friend. The next day a ringleader passes around a secret petition asking girls to outline the reasons they hate the targeted girl. The day after that, the outcast sits silently next to the boys in class, head lowered, shoulders slumped forward. The damage is neat and quiet, the perpetrator and victim invisible.

Public awareness of bullying has grown in recent years, propelled by the tragedies of youth gun violence. The national conversation on bullying, however, has trained its spotlight mostly on boys and their aggression. Defining bullying in the narrowest of terms, it has focused entirely on physical and direct acts of violence. The aggression of girls, often hidden, indirect, and nonphysical, has gone unexplored. It has not even been called aggression, but instead "what girls do."

Yet women of every age know about it. Nearly all of us have been bystanders, victims, or bullies. So many have suffered quietly and tried to forget. Indeed, this has long been one of girlhood's dark, dirty secrets. Nearly every woman and girl has a story. It is time to break the silence.

I set out to interview girls between the ages of ten and fourteen, the years when bullying peaks. On my first day, I worked with several groups of ninth graders at a coed private school on the East Coast. My plan was to encourage an informal discussion guided by a list of questions I'd written down. Standing before each class, I introduced myself, explained my own history with bullying, and told the girls what we'd be discussing. Without fail, the girls would do a double take. *Talking about* what? *During class?* They snickered and whispered.

I started each session with the same question: "Do you think there are differences between the ways guys are mean to each other and the ways girls are mean to each other?" The whispering stopped. Then the hands flew like streamers. Suddenly, they couldn't talk fast enough. Their banter was electric. The girls hooted, screeched, laughed, snorted, and veered off into personal stories, while notes flew around the room, accompanied by rolling eyes and searing and knowing glances.

It was exhausting. My carefully organized list of research questions grew stale in my hand.

Not a single one of my group discussions that day went according to plan. This, it turned out, was a good thing. I quickly understood that trying to box the girls' voices into my prearranged questions would make them think I was an authority figure, and this was the last thing I wanted to be. I wanted *them* to be the authorities. After all, they were living what I was trying to understand. It wasn't a tactic so much as an instinct.

The girls responded in kind. Over the months that followed, we traded e-mail and instant message handles, talked about music groups, new shoes, summer plans, and crushes. They showed and told me things their teachers and parents couldn't know about. We sometimes strayed from the topic at hand to talk about the pressures of school and family.

Over time, however, I realized there was another reason for the ease we felt with one another. Most people who talk to kids about bullying approach the issue with the same message: Don't do it. Be nice to each other.

I came from the opposite place. My assumption was not that the girls ought not to be mean, but that they were; not that they should be nice, but that they weren't. I was there not to stop them, but because I wanted them to help other girls find a way to deal with it. If they wanted to participate in the group discussion, fine; if they didn't, they had to sit quietly and they couldn't bother the ones who did. Either way, I told them, they'd get a free snack out of it.

More often than not during the sessions, a girl would tell her own story of victimization. She might begin by replying to one of her classmates' remarks, and then, as though taken by surprise, slide into a slow, tearful remembering of her pain. Although I knew I was in the classrooms only to conduct research, I was overwhelmed by feelings of protectiveness toward these girls.

For this reason, I adhered to an informal discussion format, going with the girls where they wanted to go. Like the women I met on the Internet, many of the girls had never been asked about this part of their lives. Like me, they seemed to feel that they were all alone, the only ones to have gone through this. I met their sadness at the level of my own. They had chosen me to hear their stories, and I wanted to honor their voices. I also wanted them to realize it happened to me and plenty of others. It felt inhumane to move over and through their pain and on to the next question on the list. Sometimes I got through all my questions, sometimes I didn't. If my work suffers in any way, the responsibility is mine, and it's one I am happy to take.

During this period, I was guided by the work of psychologists Lyn Mikel Brown and Carol Gilligan, to whose pioneering research with girls I owe a huge intellectual debt. With a group of colleagues, Brown and Gilligan developed a "Listening Guide" to use in their interviews.[1] The method emphasizes flexibility and harmony with the interview subject, and it discourages orthodox interview protocols. Instead, researchers are to "move where the girls [lead]" them. The method is especially important to girls who might otherwise stay quiet in the presence of an interviewer who appears to have an agenda. Staying with the girls' voices, rather than emphasizing one's own, "can help girls to develop, to hold on to, or to recover knowledge about themselves, their feelings, and their desires," according to Brown and Gilligan. "Taking girls seriously encourages them to take their own thoughts, feelings, and experience seriously, to maintain this knowledge, and even to uncover knowledge that has become lost to them." With such an emotional issue as girls' bullying, this seemed more than appropriate.

As I sought out more schools to work with, I got mixed responses from administrators. Most were relieved to have me talk with their students. Staff had been mystified by the intensity of the girls' anger toward one another. They were bewildered and overwhelmed by the episodes unfolding around them.

The smaller towns and some private schools were less welcoming. Their refusal to grant me access, though never explained, seemed to me a sign of anxiety that the truth would be discovered about their girls: that yes, indeed, they *were* capable of being mean. In a society raising girls to be loving and "nice," this was no small exposure.

Because of the sensitive nature of the discussions, I made another decision. To get a comprehensive account of the problem of girl bullying, I had originally planned to travel to as many different cities as I could. After a few intensive sessions with the girls, I knew this would be impossible. To earn their trust, and the faith of their teachers and parents, I would need to become a part of their communities. For this reason I chose to stay in three parts of the country for extended periods. I was rewarded with almost unconditional access and support by many of my host schools. Two schools even reversed their policy of not permitting researchers on campus to allow me to work with their girls.

In exchange for their generosity, I promised to change the names of the girls, staff members, and schools. Other than giving an economic and racial profile, I use very few details to describe each school. I worked with a total of ten over a period of one year. In a major middle-Atlantic city, I visited three schools: the Linden School, a private school with mostly middle-class students, 25 percent of whom are minority; Marymount, a private all-girls school with a predominantly middle-class population and about 20 percent students of color; and Sackler Day School, a suburban middle-class Jewish day school. In a second Northeastern city, I visited Clara Barton High School, an alternative high school, and Martin Luther King Elementary; both schools had predominantly black, Puerto Rican, and Dominican populations. I also worked at the Arden School, a laboratory school with a mostly middle-class population that is 20 percent minority, and Sojourner Truth, an all-girls school with a majority black and Latina student body. Finally, I spent several weeks visiting the elementary, middle, and high schools in Ridgewood, a small town in northeast Mississippi.

At each school, I conducted group and individual interviews with students and interested staff and parents. At some schools, interviews took as many as three or four hours. At other schools, where time for the interviews was more limited, the meetings were shorter. At two of the urban schools, I struggled to connect with some students and parents. The families were mostly poor, and some did not have telephones, although I am sure my presence as a white, middle-class woman deterred an unknown number of others. Some students and parents expressed interest, then did not return my call or meet me at the appointed time. At every school I was disappointed, though not surprised, to find no parent willing to discuss a daughter who bullied.

In addition to girls and their parents, I interviewed approximately fifty adult women by phone and in person. I include their stories because time and therapy have given them broader, more nuanced perspectives on their ordeals. Their voices present a marked contrast to the stories of young victims and bullies.

Although I sought guidance from the methods of Brown and Gilligan, this book is not the product of a formal research experiment. In it you will not find statistics or scientific conclusions about girls and aggression or information about boys. Few would argue that boys have access to a wide range of ways to express their anger. Many girls, on the other hand, are forced to cut themselves off from direct aggression altogether.

Odd Girl Out is the first book devoted exclusively to girls and nonphysical conflict, and it tells the stories of perpetrators and victims of what I call "alternative," or unconventional, aggressions.

In no way do I want to imply that only girls behave in these ways. Boys most definitely engage in alternative aggressions, though reportedly at later stages of childhood than girls. Nor am I suggesting that *all* girls do it. Although I set out to map the hidden culture of girls' aggression, it was always clear to me that not all white middle-class girls lock conflict out of their relationships. Overwhelmed by what I was discovering, I neglected to talk with more girls who do feel comfortable with anger and conflict. I regret that.

I will use the term "girl bullying" throughout the book to refer to acts of alternative aggression. Yet I am arguing not that girls *feel* angry in fundamentally different ways than boys, but that many girls appear to *show* anger differently. Girls' aggression may be covert and relational; it may indeed be fueled at times by a fear of loss or isolation. That does not mean, however, that girls do not want power or feel aggression as passionately as their male peers.

In their important book *Best Friends, Worst Enemies: Understanding the Social Lives of Children,* Michael Thompson and colleagues point out that every child wants three things out of life: connection, recognition, and power. The desire for connection propels children into friendship, while the need for recognition and power ignites competition and conflict. My point is that if all children desire these things, they will come to them, and into learning how to acquire them, on the culture's terms, that is, by the rules of how girls and boys are supposed to behave.

When I began this journey three years ago, I wanted to write so that other bullied girls would know they were not alone. As I spent more and more time with the girls, I realized I was also writing to know that *I* was not alone. I would soon discover that the bullying I endured in third grade was only the tip of the iceberg. I discovered that I harbored pain and confusion over many relationships in my childhood.

Around the circles of girls I met with, I could see I wasn't the only one who felt this way. The knowledge that we shared similar memories and feelings, that someone else understood what we had previously held inside, was amazing. The relief was palpable, and it opened unexpected doors that we were able to enter together. If we began the journey at the memory of bullying, we ended up asking, and answering, more questions about the culture we live in, about how girls treat each other, and even about ourselves than we had ever thought to imagine alone.

What little research exists on alternative aggressions is buried in academic journals. It has gone unnoticed in the recent media frenzy over bullying. Public commentary suggests that bullying is most dangerous between boys or when it culminates in physical violence. In chapter one, "The Hidden Culture of Aggression in Girls," I summarize current research on girls. I explore what may be unique about girls' aggression and analyze school attitudes toward girl bullying.

This chapter also examines the phenomenon of covert aggression between girls. A great deal of girls' anger flows quietly beneath the radar of teachers, guidance counselors, and parents. It is not, as one woman told me, "something you find in your child's drawer." Girls, ever respectful, tend to aggress quietly. They flash looks, pass notes, and spread rumors. Their actions, though sometimes physical, are typically more psychological and thus invisible to even an observant classroom eye. There is the note that is slipped into a desk; the eyes that catch, narrow, and withdraw; the lunch table that suddenly has no room. Girls talk to me in this chapter about how and why they act in secret.

The barbs of a girl bully go unnoticed when they are hidden beneath the facade of friendship. In chapter two, "Intimate Enemies," I explore dynamics of bullying and emotional abuse between close friends. The importance of relationship and connection in girls' lives, along with the fear of solitude, leads many of them to hold on to destructive friendships, even at the expense of their emotional safety. Perpetrators, on the other hand, are hurting the close friends they appear to love.

Although I set out to understand severe episodes of bullying between girls, I quickly discovered that everyday episodes of conflict can be just as harrowing. In chapter three, "The Truth Hurts," girls answer the question, "When you are angry or upset with someone, do you tell them about it?" They unpack their fears of direct conflict with one another and explore the indirect acts they choose instead. Girls dissect the politics of how and why they gang up on each other. They explore how repressing anger and avoiding confrontation can lead to disastrous consequences.

Of all the insults girls can hurl at each other, one of the worst is getting called a girl who thinks "she's all that." In the chapter of the same name, I ask girls why they can't stand it when someone appears conceited or full of herself. If this is indeed the age of girl power, why would someone else's success bother them? The girls open up about why they keep jealousy and competition secret from one another, and along the way introduce me to a code they use to communicate uncomfortable feelings.

I count myself among the many women and girls who have demonized the girl bullies in their lives. At some point, I began to wonder what it would be like to see Abby today, and I imagined the questions I might ask her. In chapter five, "The Bully in the Mirror," several former and current bullies talk about why they hurt and betrayed their friends. Listening to their stories, I consider my own past, wondering why so many of us are quick to separate ourselves from the "mean girls," and how this may affect our ability to address the problem of girl bullying.

The culture's socialization of girls as caretakers teaches them they will be valued for their relationships with others. In chapter six, "Popular," I challenge some of the current research on what makes girls popular. In particular, I look at how the politics of girls' relationships can lead to mistreatment and aggression. I explore why some girls may be nice in private but mean in public and why other girls simply abandon their friends.

Not all girls avoid conflict. Aggression may be biological, but the face of anger is learned. Although I found alternative aggressions most severe among white middle-class girls, I spent time in other communities where assertiveness and direct conflict are valued in girls. In "Resistance," I explore the history and practice of direct conflict and truth telling in African American, Latino, and working-class communities. Although girls from these specific communities are at the center of this chapter, the reader should not take this as a sign of their exclusion from others. *Odd Girl Out* focuses on life under rules of feminine restraint that all but refuse girls open acts of conflict. Those girls are primarily, but certainly not only, white and middle class.

The attention shown victims and perpetrators of bullying often means the situation parents face is overlooked. Parents and guardians of victims harbor intense feelings of shame and helplessness, yet they are as isolated from one another as their daughters. Often they can only watch as their daughters come home crying day after day. Called at work because of a stomachache that doesn't exist or watching their girl's increasing isolation, they are embarrassed that their child is scorned. Some blame themselves, while others are angry at their daughter's passivity. Girls, if they confide the problem, often beg their parents not to intervene, fearing retribution.

In chapter eight, I explore how parents find themselves thrust into a world not unlike their daughters'. They want to help their children but fear making things worse. They are first torn, then muzzled, by their own confused feelings. Even as they struggle to help their child, they fear confrontation with another parent. Some choose to wait for the problem to pass or the phase to end.

At the end of every one-on-one interview I conducted, I asked women and girls to tell me what might have been done to make their lives easier during their ordeal. In group sessions, I asked girls why so many refuse to talk to their parents about bullying. I asked teachers to tell me their secrets for dealing with the issue, or what they would need to deal with it at all. Chapter nine, "The Road Ahead," is a collection of their responses, including a veritable laundry list of everything girls hate to hear when they're in social trouble with their peers. After three years of living and breathing the issue of girl bullying, I include some of my own suggestions for how girls can enjoy more protection from alternative aggressions at school.

Are girls' problems with conflict confined to friendship and bullying? In the conclusion, I visit girls at a leadership workshop and discover unexpected parallels between their identities as girlfriends and girl leaders. Remembering the girls of chapter two, I explore links between girls' behavior in abusive friendships and the trauma of relationship violence. Finally, I consider the loss of self-esteem that besets girls around adolescence. Since alternative aggressions explode between girls around this time, I suggest potential connections between the two.

———

Because I wanted the girls to feel comfortable saying anything, teachers almost never joined my interview sessions. At one woman's insistence, I allowed her to sit in the back of a classroom I was visiting. Thirty minutes into a lively discussion about the ways girls are mean to each other, she was sitting stiffly, her face tightening in anger. Finally, she raised her hand.

"You know," she said, "not all girls are mean. Girls are wonderful! Women are the most important friends you'll ever have, and I don't think it's fair to talk only about the bad parts of girls." Although I could not agree with her more, the remark haunted me. It would be a grave mistake for the reader to interpret this book as a condemnation of girls and women. Nothing could be further from the truth.

Our culture has long been accustomed to celebrating the "niceness" of girls. The stories of *Odd Girl Out* may therefore unsettle some readers. But my attempt to name the aggression of girls should not be read as an attempt to disparage them. For the purposes of this book I interviewed only girls who identified as perpetrators or victims. Not all girls bully, nor do they inflict injury in such severe ways.

I want to make clear that my deep affection for girls and women has guided this project every step of the way. Throughout my life, women and girls have nourished me with strength, wisdom, and care. I credit a great deal of my own success to older women mentors, many of whom were invaluable in helping this book come to life. And without the women closest to me, I would never have had the courage to arrive at many of the personal insights I share in this book.

Writing this book changed my life. I was astonished to find how many of my own fears and questions about relationships were echoed in the girls' remarks. Their stories forced me to look hard at my own fears of conflict, especially my need to be a "good girl." It is my hope that readers will be able to confront their own fears and pose their own questions. Such a journey of reconnection is certainly not easy, but it is well worth the trip.

CHAPTER ONE

the hidden culture of
aggression in girls

The Linden School campus is nestled behind a web of sports fields that seem to hold at bay the bustling city in which it resides. On Monday morning in the Upper School building, students congregated languidly, catching up on the weekend, while others sat knees-to-chest on the floor, flipping through three-ring binders, cramming for tests. The students were dressed in styles that ran the gamut from trendy to what can only be described, at this age, as defiant. Watching them, it is easy to forget this school is one of the best in the region, its students anything but superficial. This is what I came to love about Linden: it celebrates academic rigor and the diversity of its students in equal parts. Over the course of a day with eight groups of ninth graders, I began each meeting with the same question: "What are some of the differences between the ways guys and girls are mean?"

From periods one through eight, I heard the same responses. "Girls can turn on you for anything," said one. "Girls whisper," said another. "They glare at you." With growing certainty, they fired out answers:

"Girls are secretive."

"They destroy you from the inside."

"Girls are manipulative."

"There's an aspect of evil in girls that there isn't in boys."

"Girls target you where they know you're weakest."

"Girls do a lot behind each other's backs."

"Girls plan and premeditate."

"With guys you know where you stand."

"I feel a lot safer with guys."

In bold, matter-of-fact voices, girls described themselves to me as disloyal, untrustworthy, and sneaky. They claimed girls use intimacy to manipulate and overpower others. They said girls are fake, using each other to move up the social hierarchy. They described girls as unforgiving and crafty, lying in wait for a moment of revenge that will catch the unwitting victim off guard and, with an almost savage eye-for-an-eye mentality, "make her feel the way I felt."

The girls' stories about their conflicts were casual and at times filled with self-hatred. In almost every group session I held, someone volunteered her wish to have been born a boy because boys can "fight and have it be over with."

Girls tell stories of their anger in a culture that does not define their behaviors as aggression. As a result, their narratives are filled with destructive myths about the inherent duplicity of females. As poet and essayist Adrienne Rich notes,[2] "We have been depicted as generally whimsical, deceitful, subtle, vacillating."

Since the dawn of time, women and girls have been portrayed as jealous and underhanded, prone to betrayal, disobedience, and secrecy. Lacking a public identity or language, girls' nonphysical aggression is called "catty," "crafty," "evil," and "cunning." Rarely the object of research or critical thought, this behavior is seen as a natural phase in girls' development. As a result, schools write off girls' conflicts as a rite of passage, as simply "what girls do."

What would it mean to name girls' aggression? Why have myths and stereotypes served us so well and so long?

Aggression is a powerful barometer of our social values. According to sociologist Anne Campbell, attitudes toward aggression crystallize sex roles, or the idea that we expect certain responsibilities to be assumed by males and females because of their sex.[3] Riot grrls and women's soccer notwithstanding, Western society still expects boys to become family providers and protectors, and girls to be nurturers and mothers. Aggression is the hallmark of masculinity; it enables men to control their environment and livelihoods. For better or for worse, boys enjoy total access to the rough and tumble. The link begins early: the popularity of boys is in large part determined by their willingness to play rough. They get peers' respect for athletic prowess, resisting authority, and acting tough, troublesome, dominating, cool, and confident.

On the other side of the aisle, females are expected to mature into caregivers, a role deeply at odds with aggression. Consider the ideal of the "good mother": She provides unconditional love and care for her family, whose health and daily supervision are her primary objectives. Her daughters are expected to be "sugar and spice and everything nice." They are to be sweet, caring, precious, and tender.

"Good girls" have friends, and lots of them. As nine-year-old Noura told psychologists Lyn Mikel Brown and Carol Gilligan, perfect girls have "perfect relationships."[4] These girls are caretakers in training. They "never have any fights...and they are always together....Like never arguing, like 'Oh yeah, I totally agree with you.'" In depressing relationships, Noura added, "someone is really jealous and starts being really mean....[It's] where two really good friends break up."

A "good girl," journalist Peggy Orenstein observes in *Schoolgirls,* is "nice before she is anything else—before she is vigorous, bright, even before she is honest." She described the "perfect girl" as

> the girl who has no bad thoughts or feelings, the kind of person everyone wants to be with....[She is] the girl who speaks quietly, calmly, who is always nice and kind, never mean or bossy....She reminds young women to silence themselves rather than speak their true feelings, which they come to consider "stupid," "selfish," "rude," or just plain irrelevant.[5]

"Good girls," then, are expected not to experience anger. Aggression endangers relationships, imperiling a girl's ability to be caring and "nice." Aggression undermines who girls have been raised to become.

Calling the anger of girls by its name would therefore challenge the most basic assumptions we make about "good girls." It would also reveal what the culture does not entitle them to by defining what *nice* really means: *Not* aggressive. *Not* angry. *Not* in conflict.

Research confirms that parents and teachers discourage the emergence of physical and direct aggression in girls early on while the skirmishing of boys is either encouraged or shrugged off.[6] In one example, a 1999 University of Michigan study found that girls were told to be quiet, speak softly, or use a "nicer" voice about three times more often than boys, even though the boys were louder. By the time they are of school age, peers solidify the fault lines on the playground, creating social groups that value niceness in girls and toughness in boys.

The culture derides aggression in girls as unfeminine, a trend explored in chapter four. "Bitch," "lesbian," "frigid," and "manly" are just a few of the names an assertive girl hears. Each epithet points out the violation of her prescribed role as a caregiver: the bitch likes and is liked by no one; the lesbian loves not a man or children but another woman; the frigid woman is cold, unable to respond sexually; and the manly woman is too hard to love or be loved.

Girls, meanwhile, are acutely aware of the culture's double standard. They are not fooled into believing this is the so-called post-feminist age, the girl power victory lap. The rules are different for boys, and girls know it. Flagrant displays of aggression are punished with social rejection.

At Sackler Day School, I was eating lunch with sixth graders during recess, talking about how teachers expected them to behave at school. Ashley, silver-rimmed glasses snug on her tiny nose, looked very serious as she raised her hand.

"They expect us to act like girls back in the 1800s!" she said indignantly. Everyone cracked up.

"What do you mean?" I asked.

"Well, sometimes they're like, you have to respect each other, and treat other people how you want to be treated. But that's not how life is. Everyone can be mean sometimes and they're not even realizing it. They expect that you're going to be *so* nice to everyone and you'll be *so* cool. Be nice to everyone!" she mimicked, her suddenly loud voice betraying something more than sarcasm.

"But it's not true," Nicole said. The room is quiet.

"Anyone else?" I asked.

"They expect you to be perfect. You're nice. When boys do bad stuff, they all know they're going to do bad stuff. When girls do it, they yell at them," Dina said.

"Teachers think that girls should be really nice and sharing and not get in any fights. They think it's worse than it really is," Shira added.

"They expect you be perfect angels and then sometimes we don't want to be considered a perfect angel," Laura noted.

"The teacher says if you do something good, you'll get something good back, and then she makes you feel like you really should be," Ashley continued. "I try not to be mean to my sister or my mom and dad, and I wake up the next day and I just do it naturally. I'm not an angel! I try to be focused on it, but then I wake up the next day and I'm cranky."

In Ridgewood, I listened to sixth graders muse about what teachers expect from girls. Heather raised her hand.

"They just don't..." She stopped. No one picked up the slack.

"Finish the sentence," I urged.

"They expect you to be nice like them, like they supposedly are, but..."

"But what?"

"We're not."

"I don't go around being like goody-goody," said Tammy.

"What does goody-goody mean?" I asked.

"You're supposed to be sitting like this"—Tammy crossed her legs and folded her hands primly over her knees—"the whole time."

"And be nice—and don't talk during class," said Torie.

"Do you always feel nice?" I asked.

"*No!*" several of them exclaimed.

"So what happens?"

"It's like you just—the bad part controls over your body," Tammy said. "You want to be nice and you want to be bad at the same time, and the bad part gets to you. You think"—she contorted her face and gritted her teeth—"*I have to be nice.*"

"You just want to tell them to shut up! You just feel like pushing them out of the way and throwing them on the ground!" said Brittney. "I wanted to do it like five hundred times last year to this girl. If I didn't push her, I just walked off and tried to stay calm."

Try as they might, most girls can't erase the natural impulses toward anger that every human being knows. Yet the early research on aggression turned the myth of the "good," nonaggressive girl into fact: The first experiments on aggression were performed with almost no female subjects. Since males tend to exhibit aggression directly, researchers concluded aggression was expressed in only this way. Other forms of aggression, when they were observed, were labeled deviant or ignored.

Studies of bullying inherited these early research flaws. Most psychologists looked for direct aggressions like punching, threatening, or teasing. Scientists also measured aggression in environments where indirect acts would be almost impossible to observe. Seen through the eyes of scientists, the social lives of girls appeared still and placid as lakes. It was not until 1992 that someone would question what lay beneath the surface.

That year, a group of Norwegian researchers published an unprecedented study of girls. They discovered that girls were not at all averse to aggression, they just expressed anger in unconventional ways. The group predicted that "when aggression cannot, for one reason or another, be directed (physically or verbally) at its target, the perpetrator has to find other channels." The findings bore out their theory: cultural rules against overt aggression led girls to engage in other, nonphysical forms of aggression. In a conclusion uncharacteristic for the strength of its tone, the researchers challenged the image of sweetness among female youth, calling their social lives "ruthless," "aggressive," and "cruel."[7]

Since then, a small group of psychologists at the University of Minnesota has built upon these findings, identifying three subcategories of aggressive behavior: relational, indirect, and social aggression. *Relational aggression* includes acts that "harm others through damage (or the threat of damage) to relationships or feelings of acceptance, friendship, or group inclusion."[8] Relationally aggressive behavior is ignoring someone to punish them or get one's own way, excluding someone socially for revenge, using negative body language or facial expressions, sabotaging someone else's relationships, or threatening to end a relationship unless the friend agrees to a request. In these acts, the perpetrator uses her relationship with the victim as a weapon.

Close relatives of relational aggression are indirect aggression and social aggression. *Indirect aggression* allows the perpetrator to avoid confronting her target. It is covert behavior in which the perpetrator makes it seem as though there has been no intent to hurt at all. One way this is possible is by using others as vehicles for inflicting pain on a targeted person, such as by spreading a rumor. *Social aggression* is intended to damage self-esteem or social status within a group. It includes some indirect aggression like rumor spreading or social exclusion. Throughout the book, I refer to these behaviors collectively as *alternative aggressions*. As the stories in the book make clear, alternative aggressions often appear in conjunction with more direct behaviors.

beneath the radar

In Margaret Atwood's novel *Cat's Eye,* the young protagonist Elaine is seated frozen in fear on a windowsill, where she has been forced to remain in silence by her best friends as she waits to find out what she had done wrong. Elaine's father enters the room and asks if the girls are enjoying the parade they have been watching:

> Cordelia gets down off her windowsill and slides up onto mine, sitting close beside me.
>
> "We're enjoying it extremely, thank you very much," she says in her voice for adults. My parents think she has beautiful manners. She puts an arm around me, gives me a little squeeze, a squeeze of complicity, of instruction. Everything will be all right as long as I sit still, say nothing, reveal nothing....As soon as my father is out of the room Cordelia turns to face me.... "You know what this means don't you? I'm afraid you'll have to be punished."

Like many girl bullies, Cordelia maneuvers her anger quietly beneath the surface of her good-girl image. She must invest as much energy appearing nice to adults as she will spend slowly poisoning Elaine's self-esteem.

Some alternative aggressions are invisible to adult eyes. To elude social disapproval, girls retreat beneath a surface of sweetness to hurt each other in secret. They pass covert looks and notes, manipulate quietly over time, corner one another in hallways, turn their backs, whisper, and smile. These acts, which are intended to escape detection and punishment, are epidemic in middle-class environments where the rules of femininity are most rigid.

Cordelia's tactics are common in a social universe that refuses girls open conflict. In fact, whole campaigns often occur without a sound. Astrid recalled the silent, methodical persistence of her angry friends. "It was a war through notes," she remembered. "When I wouldn't read them, they wrote on the binding of encyclopedias near my desk, on the other desks; they left notes around, wrote my name on the list of people to send to the principal." This aggression was designed to slip beneath the sight line of prying eyes.

Most of the time, the strategy works. Paula Johnston, a prosecutor, was dumbfounded at the ignorance of her daughter's teacher when Paula demanded Susie be separated from a girl who was quietly bullying her. "[Susie's teacher] said, 'But they get along beautifully!'" Paula snorted. "I asked her to move Susie, and she moved one in front and one behind! She would say, 'Everything's wonderful; Susie's adorable,' and meanwhile, Susie's in the library hiding."

A Sackler sixth grader described her attempt to expose a mean girl to her teacher. "[The teacher] said, 'Oh my gosh! You in a fight? How can that be!'" At every school I visited, I heard stories of a teacher being told of a girl's meanness, only to respond, "Fight? She'd never do that!" or "I'm sure that's not true!" or "But they're best friends!"

Covert aggression isn't just about not getting caught; half of it is looking like you'd never mistreat someone in the first place. The sugar-and-spice image is powerful, and girls know it. They use it to fog the radar of otherwise vigilant teachers and parents. For girls, the secrecy, the "underground"[9]—the place where Brown and Gilligan report girls take their true feelings—are hardly unconscious realms. In the film *Cruel Intentions,* Kathryn cloaks her anger in syrupy sweetness. In a bind, she decides to frame another student because, she purrs, "Everybody loves me, and I intend to keep it that way." Later, surreptitiously snorting cocaine from a cross around her neck, Kathryn groans, "Do you think I relish the fact that I have to act like Mary Sunshine 24–7 so I can be considered a lady? I'm the Marcia-fucking-Brady of the Upper East Side, and sometimes I want to kill myself."

In group discussions, girls spoke openly to me about their intentionally covert aggression. When I visited the ninth graders in Ridgewood, they threw out their tactics with gusto, prompting the semicircle of bodies to lean forward, nearly out of their desks, as eager affirming cries of "Oh yeah!" and "Totally!" filled our fluorescent white lab room.

Walk down the hallway and slam into a girl—the teacher thinks you're distracted! Knock a girl's book off a desk—the teacher thinks it fell! Write an anonymous note! Draw a mean picture! Roll your eyes! Send an instant message with a new username! Steal a boy-friend! Start a rumor! Tell the teacher she cheated!

"You step on their shoe. Oops!" Jessie squealed in a girly-girl singsong voice. "Sorry!"

"You walk past someone and you try to bump them. You say, '*Excuse you!*'" The girls laughed in recognition.

"The teacher says she didn't mean it, she just bumped into her," Melanie explained, "but the girls, they *know* what it is because it happens so much."

"Girls are very sneaky," said Keisha. "Very."

"We—are—sneaky!" Lacey crowed, emphasizing every word.

The next day, the Ridgewood sixth graders met. The freight of the good-girl image still weighed heavily upon them, and they lacked some of the boisterous energy and sarcasm of the ninth graders. Their voices were hesitant and halting. Amy was brave.

"The teachers don't say anything. They don't expect it. They don't think we're doing anything, but . . ." She paused.

"But what?" I asked. I was getting used to sentences abandoned midway.

She was silent.

"The teachers think girls behave better," Elizabeth explained.

"Does that make a difference in how people get in trouble?" I asked.

"Some people call each other names and stuff and the teacher wouldn't believe it. They would say, so-and-so did this to me, and the teacher would say, 'No, she didn't.' Some teachers have pets, and you say, 'She called me a bad name,' and the teacher says, 'No, she wouldn't do a thing like that.'"

Leigh said, "Some girls act real good around the teachers, and then when they do something bad, the teachers don't believe it because they never seen them do it."

"Boys don't care about getting into trouble. They think they're all bad and don't worry about it. They don't care if they got in trouble, but girls don't want anyone to know they got into trouble,"

Maura said. "Girls worry about how they're going to look. They have more of a nervous system than boys." The room tittered.

Tina raised her hand. "A girl in my class passes notes and never gets in trouble for it. Around the teacher she acts all sweet and stuff."

"Everybody writes notes," Sarah Beth added. "Teachers are so stupid. They don't get it. You can see it. It's easy."

Kim said, "Girls can be passing notes during class and the teacher will find out about it. She won't get them in trouble because they're like one of her best students. Most of the girls in her class are but the boys usually aren't."

Torie sat up on the back of her chair, elbows on her knees. "If girls are whispering, the teacher thinks it's going to be all right because they're not hitting people. If they punch, they get sent to the office. Teachers think they're not hurting you," she said, looking cautiously at her classmates, "but they are."

At once I was reminded of scary movies in which only children can see the ghost. The adults pass through the same rooms and live the same moments, yet they are unable to see a whole world of action around them. So, too, in classrooms of covertly aggressing girls, victims are desperately alone even though a teacher is just steps away.

Sixth period was about to end. Jenny's stomach clenched harder with each loud click of the wall clock. She never jumped when the bell rang. Although she prided herself on her good grades, Jenny stopped paying attention five minutes before class ended. Still, at 1:58 her heart started to race. By 1:59 she was short of breath.

Through the cracks between her straight brown hair she watched the other seventh graders get up. As usual, she pretended to be slow and preoccupied. She shuffled her pencils noisily in the cool metal air inside the desk, buying time. In a moment she would be free to leave.

Ever since Jenny arrived two months ago from San Diego, the popular clique at Mason Middle School had decided two things: first, that she was a major threat to their status, and second, that they were going to make her life miserable.

She had moved reluctantly with her family to the small ranching community in Wyoming four days after the end of sixth grade. In San Diego, Jenny had gone to a huge city school and had mostly Mexican friends. She spoke fluent Spanish and loved the warmth and friendship of Mexican culture. She never minded being one of the only white students in school.

That everything was different in Mason was an understatement. There were eight hundred white people in the whole town. Everybody knew each other's business, and outsiders were unwelcome. So it didn't matter to Brianna and Mackenzie that Jenny's entire family had grown up right in Mason. Even though Jenny spent her summers riding tractors through their families' fields with her grandfather, the town alderman, she may as well have been born on a spaceship.

Brianna and Mackenzie were the queen bees, and they presided over the seventh grade. Brianna was the prettiest, Mackenzie the best at sports. Their favorite hobby was having a boyfriend. Jenny wasn't really interested in a boyfriend, but she still liked hanging out with the guys. Mostly she liked to play soccer and basketball with them after school. She liked to wear jeans and T-shirts instead of makeup and miniskirts.

She had barely introduced herself when Brianna and Mackenzie gave her a code name and started calling her Harriet the Hairy Whore. They told everyone Jenny was hooking up with the boys in the woods behind the soccer field. Jenny knew that being called a slut was the worst thing in the world, no matter where you lived. No one was even kissing yet. It was the lowest of the low.

Brianna and Mackenzie started a club called Hate Harriet the Hore Incorporated. They got every girl to join except two who didn't care. All the members had to walk by Jenny in the hallway and say, "Hhiiiiiiiiii. . . ." They made a long sighing noise to make sure she knew they were sounding out the initials of the club: HHHI. Usually two or more girls would say it and then look at each other and laugh. Sometimes they couldn't even say the whole thing, they were laughing so hard.

Then Brianna got the idea to charge into Jenny as she walked the hallways. The other girls followed suit. Wherever Jenny was between classes, a girl would body slam her, knocking Jenny's books, and sometimes Jenny, to the ground. If someone was watching, they'd pretend it was an accident. Even though Jenny was small for her age, only four foot eleven, she decided to start smashing the others first, figuring they'd stop. They didn't. She ended up with a lot of bruises, missing papers, and an uncanny ability to predict when the bells would ring. There was no teacher in the hallway to see.

She tried to shrug it off the first few days, but by the end of the week, Jenny burned with embarrassment and fear. What had she done? It seemed like Mackenzie and Brianna had suddenly made it their goal in life to ruin her. Nothing like this had ever happened before. In San Diego, she had three best friends. She had always been good at everything but not because it was easy. She strove for success in everything she did. In her head she heard her father's voice: "If you try hard enough, you can do anything." This was her first failure.

It was her fault.

She knew she'd never touched a boy, but maybe there was something really wrong with her. There were two other new girls in seventh grade, and they were doing just fine. They worked hard to fit in, and they did. They bought the same clothes and listened to the same music as everyone else.

Jenny closed her eyes. They also let Mackenzie and Brianna and the others determine who they would be. Jenny didn't want that, at any price. She wanted to keep speaking her mind. She liked her California clothes and Mexican embroidered shirts. Maybe she didn't want to try hard in the ways you had to in seventh grade. Her father was right.

Jenny began to weep quietly in her room not long after she realized there would be no end to her torture. She managed to wait until her homework was done, and then she cried, silent always, her sobs muffled by her pillow. There was no *way* she'd tell her mother, and certainly not her father. She felt nauseous just thinking about telling her parents she was such a reject.

Every day was an endless battle. She was exhausted trying not to cry, stiffening her body against the hallway attacks, sitting through lunch after lunch alone. There was no one else to be friends with in the grade because everyone, the few that there were, was against her. Her cousin was a year ahead of her and felt sorry for Jenny. Sometimes she let Jenny hang out with her clique. It was small consolation that they were the popular group of the eighth grade. In fact, it seemed to make Brianna and Mackenzie even angrier.

One night Jenny's sadness left no room for her fear, and she picked up the phone. Jenny called Brianna, Mackenzie, and a few other girls. She asked each of them, "Why do you hate me?" They denied everything. "But why are you doing the Hate Harriet the Hore club?" she pleaded.

Their voices were light and sweet. "We don't have a Hate Harriet the Hore club!" each one assured her, as though they were telling her the earth was round. They were so nice to Jenny that for a second she didn't believe it was really them. Then she could almost feel her heart surging up through her chest. The next morning, she actually looked forward to getting out of bed. It would be different now.

Then she got to school.

"Hhhiiiiiiiii . . . !" *Slam.*

Jenny blinked back tears and locked her jaw. She hated herself for being surprised. She should have known. The strange thing about it was, even though she was used to it, this time her heart felt like it was breaking open. Brianna and Mackenzie had seemed so genuine on the phone. And Jenny, stupid, stupid Jenny, she muttered to herself, had imagined herself at their lunch table in the back of the cafeteria. "Stupid, stupid, stupid," she repeated through gritted teeth, raising her books as a shield as she made her way into homeroom.

One day, months later, searching through desks after seeing the girls pass it around in homeroom, Jenny found the petition. "I, Mackenzie T., promise to Hate Harriet the Hore forever," it said. Every single girl in the class had signed it, and it was appended with a long list of reasons why everyone should hate her. Jenny's eyes bore into the paper until the words blurred. She suddenly felt dizzy. The weight of her anguish was too heavy. She couldn't take it anymore. Jenny felt like her world was crumbling. She went to the principal.

Mr. Williams called Brianna, Mackenzie, and some of the others into his office. They glared at her for weeks but said nothing. HHHI was officially disbanded.

Jenny struggled through seventh grade alone. Because the meanness of her peers was almost invisible, not one teacher had noticed or intervened on her behalf. Because she was a new student, it was difficult to observe changes in her behavior and character. Her parents had known something was wrong, but had they asked her how she was, Jenny told me, "I would have told them, 'Fine.'"

HHHI never resurfaced and Jenny adjusted well over the next several years. She became captain of the softball team and pep club president, but her pain stayed fresh and hidden as she waited patiently for revenge.

Brianna, her chief HHHI tormentor, had begun dating the most popular boy at Cheyenne High School in fifth grade. That was the way things were, Jenny said. "You pretty much picked who you were going to date when you were ten or eleven and that's who you dated until you left Wyoming." Eric was captain of the basketball team and everything else that was important at Cheyenne. Brianna had lost her virginity to him and wanted to marry him.

Jenny's chance came in the fall of her junior year, when she was asked to manage the boys' basketball team. She quickly became friends with Eric. "I made it my goal to steal him from her, and I did," Jenny said. "I know for a fact it had nothing to do with him. It had everything to do with taking what was important to her." Jenny and Eric dated secretly for a month before Jenny made him call Brianna from her bedroom and break up with her. I asked Jenny how it made her feel.

"I just had this feeling of victory. I wanted to rub it in her face. I felt really good that I had hurt her back," she said. "It's vindictive and it's sad, I know, but to this day I hate this girl and I wanted to hurt her." Today Jenny is thirty-two, and she feels neither shame nor remorse, only the anger that still smolders some twenty years later.

relationship and loss

At first glance, the stories of girls not being allowed to eat at the lunch table, attend a party, put their sleeping bag in the middle, or squeeze inside a circle of giggling girls may seem childish. Yet as Carol Gilligan has shown, relationships play an unusually important role in girls' social development. In her work with girls and boys, she found that girls perceive danger in their lives as isolation, especially the fear that by standing out they will be abandoned. Boys, however, describe danger as a fear of entrapment or smothering. This contrast, Gilligan argues, shows that women's development "points toward a different history of human attachment, stressing continuity and change instead of replacement and separation. The primacy of relationship and attachment in the female life also indicates a different experience of and response to loss."[10] The centrality of relationship in girls' lives all but guarantees a different landscape of aggression and bullying, with its own distinctive features worthy of separate study.

To understand girls' conflicts, one must also know girls' intimacy, because intimacy and anger are often inextricable. The intensity of girls' relationships belongs at the center of any analysis of girls' aggression. For long before they love boys, girls love each other, and with great passion.

Girls enjoy unrestricted access to intimacy. Unlike boys, who are encouraged to separate from their mothers and adopt masculine postures of emotional restraint, daughters are urged to identify with the nurturing behavior of their mothers. Girls spend their childhood practicing caretaking and nurturing on each other. It is with best friends that they first discover the joys of intimacy and human connection.

Yet ours is a culture that has ignored the closeness of girlfriends. Many people believe girls should reserve their true emotions for boys, and that girls should channel their caretaking toward husbands and children. Anything up to that life stage is assumed to be practice, if not insignificant.[11]

In fact, it is the deep knowledge girls have of relationship, and the passion they lavish on their closest friends, which characterizes much of their aggression. The most painful attacks are usually fashioned from deep inside a close friendship and are fueled by secrets and once-shared weaknesses.

Moreover, the relationship itself is often the weapon with which girls' battles are fought. Socialized away from aggression, expected to be nice girls who have "perfect relationships," many girls are unprepared to negotiate conflict. As a result, a minor disagreement can call an entire relationship into question.

What do I mean by this? In a normal conflict, two people use language, voice, or fists to settle their dispute. The relationship between them is secondary to the issue being worked out. But when anger cannot be voiced, and when the skills to handle a conflict are absent, the specific matter cannot be addressed. If neither girl wants to be "not nice," the relationship itself may become the problem. And when there are no other tools to use in a conflict, relationship itself may become a weapon.

Since relationship is precisely what good, "perfect" girls are expected to be in, its loss, and the prospect of solitude, can be the most pointed weapons in the hidden culture of girls' aggression.

During her interviews with adults, sociologist Anne Campbell found that where men viewed aggression as a means to control their environment and integrity, women believed it would terminate their relationships.[12] I discovered identical attitudes in my conversations with girls. Expressing fear that even everyday acts of conflict, not to mention severe aggressive outbursts, would result in the loss of the people they most cared about, they refused to engage in even the most basic acts of conflict. Their equation was simple: conflict = loss.

Like clockwork, girl after girl told me twenty variations on the following remark: "I can't tell her how I feel or else she won't want to be my friend anymore." The corollary works like this: "I just don't want to hurt anyone directly, because I want to be friends with everyone."

Fear of solitude is overpowering. In fact, what victims of bullying recalled most to me was their loneliness. Despite the cruel things that happened—the torrents of vulgar e-mail and unsigned notes, the whispered rumors, the slanderous scribblings on desks and walls and lockers, the sneering and name-calling—what crushed girls was being alone. It was as though the absence of bodies nearby with whom to whisper and share triggered in girls a sorrow and fear so profound as to nearly extinguish them.

Girls may try to avoid being alone at all costs, including remaining in an abusive friendship. "You don't want to walk alone at recess," a sixth grader explained when I asked why she wouldn't stay away from a mean friend. "Who are you going to tell your secrets to? Who are you going to help and stuff like that?" An eighth grader, recalling a television documentary, remarked plaintively, "If a female lion is alone, she dies. She has to be part of the group."

As girls mature, the prospect of being seen alone by others becomes just as daunting. They know that "perfect girls" have "perfect relationships." "Walking through a hall and feeling like everyone's looking at you is the worst," a Linden ninth grader told me. "People who are alone are pitied and no one wants to be pitied. They're secluded. Something's wrong with them. Being seen as a loner is one of our biggest fears." Driven by the fear of exclusion, girls cling to their friends like lifeboats on the shifting seas of school life, certain that to be alone is the worst horror imaginable.

Every child, boy or girl, desires acceptance and connection. Most boys would not prefer or even tolerate being alone. Yet as girls grow up, friendship becomes as important as air, and they describe the punishment of loneliness in dramatic terms. "I was so depressed," Sarah explained. "I sat in class with no friends. Everything I cared about completely crumbled." A fifth grader said of her solitude, "It was like my heart was breaking."

it's just a phase

When thirteen-year-old Sherry's friends suddenly stopped speaking to her, her father, worried for his devastated daughter, approached a friend's mother to find out what happened. She was underwhelmed. "Girls will be girls," she said. It's typical girl behavior, nothing to be worried about, a phase girls go through. It will pass. "You are making a mountain out of a molehill," she told him. "What are you getting so upset about?"

Her remarks echo the prevailing wisdom about alternative aggression between girls: girl bullying is a rite of passage, a stage they will outgrow. As one school counselor put it to me, "It's always been this way. It will always be this way. There's nothing we can do about it." Girl bullying, many believe, is a nasty developmental storm we have no choice but to accept. Yet the rite-of-passage argument paralyzes our thinking about how the culture shapes girls' behavior. Most importantly, it stunts the development of anti-bullying strategies.

The rite-of-passage theory suggests several disturbing assumptions about girls. First, it implies that there is nothing we can do to prevent girls from behaving in these ways because it's in their developmental tea leaves to do it. In other words, because so many girls engage in alternative aggressions, they must be naturally predisposed to them. Bullying as a rite of passage also suggests that it is necessary and even positive that girls learn how to relate with each other in these ways. Rites of passage, after all, are rituals that mark the transformation of an individual from one status to another. So the rite of passage means that girls are becoming acquainted with what is in store for them later as adults. Because adult women behave in this way, it means it's acceptable and must be prepared for. (Many despairing mothers I spoke with, as well as those who shrugged off the bullying, confided a sense of consolation that their girls were learn-ing what they'd come to know sooner or later.)

The third assumption emerges directly from the first two: it sug-gests that because it is universal and instructive, meanness among girls is a natural part of their social structure to be tolerated and ex-pected. And there is one final assumption, the most insidious of all: the abuse girls subject each other to is, in fact, not abuse at all.

I have heard schools decline to intervene in girls' conflicts because they do not want to interfere in the "emotional lives" of students. This philosophy makes two value judgments about girls' relation-ships: it suggests that unlike aggressive episodes between the sexes, which are analyzed by lawyers and plastered on evening news pro-grams, problems between girls are insignificant, episodes that will taper off as girls become more involved with boys.

Second, it trivializes the role of peers in children's development, turning into school policy the myth that childhood is "training for life," rather than life itself. A strategy of noninterference resists the truth of girls' friendships, remains aloof from the heart of their interpersonal problems, and devalues the emotional intensity that leaves permanent marks on their self-esteem.

Yet there is an even simpler reason why schools have ignored girls' aggression. They need order in the classroom. On any given day, the typical teacher is racing against the clock to meet a long list of obli-gations. She must complete her lesson plans, fulfill district and state standards requirements, administer tests, and occasionally find time for a birthday party. Like an emergency room doctor, the teacher must perform triage on her discipline problems. Disruptions are caught on the fly and met with swift punishment. Generally, boys are more disorderly. Girls, ever the intuiters of adult stress, know that passing a nasty note or shooting mean looks like rubber bands is un-likely to draw the attention of an exhausted teacher who is intent on completing her lesson plan.

When she sees a perpetrating girl, a teacher has little or no incen-tive to stop the class. Taking the time to address relational discord is not always as easy as yelling at a boy to remove his peer from the trash can. As a sixth grader explained to me, "Teachers separate the boys." Relational problems, however, demand attention to something that is more complex. Invariably, the teacher is far more concerned with the boys flinging balls of paper and distracting the other students.

Schools lack consistent public strategies for dealing with alternative aggressions. In the absence of a shared language to identify and discuss the behavior, student harassment policies are generally vague and favor acts of physical or direct violence. The structure of school days also complicates teacher intervention: in many schools, for instance, lunch aides supervise at recess, when bullying is rampant.

Since alternative aggressions have been largely ignored, their real-life manifestations are often seen through the lens of more "valid" social problems. For example, at many schools, the threat "do this or I won't be your friend anymore" is considered peer pressure, not relational aggression. In academic writings, researchers explain girls' manipulation of relationships as a form of precocity or a way to "establish central position and to dominate the definition of the group's boundaries." Some psychologists classify teasing and nasty jokes as developmentally healthy experiences. They call rumors and gossip spreading "boundary maintenance."[13]

Also common is the assessing of the targets of meanness among girls as having a social skills deficit. According to this school of thought, bullied children are obviously doing something wrong if they are attracting the social abuse of others. This usually puts the onus on the victim, who must toughen up or learn to integrate socially. Perhaps she is responding to social situations inappropriately, failing to "read" the feelings and attitudes of others correctly. Perhaps she needs to pay more attention to clothing trends. Perhaps she is too needy, daring, as one book lamented, to say "Let's be friends" instead of the more subtle "Let's go to the mall this weekend."

Relational aggression in particular is easily mistaken for a social skills problem. When a girl is nice one day and cruel the next, or is

possessive, or overreacts to another child, the behavior can be inter-
preted as a sign of delayed development. This is an especially insidious
problem because the victims may be encouraged to show patience
and respect to their perpetrators. In the course of things, the aggressive aspect of the behavior is lost, and the perpetrator is left alone.

Most disturbingly, what the victim understands to be true about
her own feeling of injury is denied by adults. Since perpetrators are
often friends, girls, ever compassionate, spring easily to the rescue
with their endless understanding shown human mistakes. Annie,
who is profiled in chapter two, remembered Samantha, the girl who
made her cry all night, with whom she was still friends. "Right now
Samantha has a lot of friends and is more socially skilled," Annie explained. "But back then she wasn't really. . . . If she had a friend, and
if they said some slight thing to her, she would think that it was the
most offensive thing that anyone's ever said to her. I don't think I
really ever said [this was wrong]. I think she was trying to keep the
friendship just as she could have it." In order to be a good friend,
Annie showed compassion for Samantha's social limitations while
shelving her own painful feelings.

Misdiagnosing bullying as a social skills problem makes perfect
sense in a culture that demands perfect relationships of its girls at any
cost. Social skills proponents claim that the best interactions are situation appropriate and reinforced by others, reflecting abilities in
which girls are already well schooled. Indeed, the majority of female
bullying incidents occur at the behest of a ringleader whose power
lies in her ability to maintain a facade of girlish tranquillity in the
course of sustained, covert peer abuse. She also directs social consen-
sus among the group. As far as the social skills school is concerned,
then, girl bullies appear from the outside to be doing A-plus work.
At one school trying the social skills solution, for example, the mean
girls were simply urged to be more "discreet."

The trouble with the social skills argument is that it does not
question the existence of meanness, it explains and justifies it. As a
result, it has helped alternative aggressions to persist unquestioned.

As they try fiercely to be nice and stay in perfect relationships,
girls are forced into a game of tug-of-war with their own aggression.
At times girls' anger may break the surface of their niceness, while
at others it may only linger below it, sending confusing messages
to their peers. As a result, friends are often forced to second-guess
themselves and each other. Over time, many grow to mistrust what
others say they are feeling.

The sequestering of anger not only alters the forms in which aggression is expressed, but also how it is perceived. Anger may flash
on and off with lightning speed, making the victim question what
happened—or indeed whether anything happened at all. *Did she just
look at her when I said that? Was she joking? Did she roll her eyes? Not
save the seat on purpose? Lie about her plans? Tell me that she'd invited
me when she hadn't?*

Girls will begin summoning the strength to confront alternative
aggressions when we chart them out in their various shapes and
forms, overt and covert. We need to freeze those fleeting moments
and name them so that girls are no longer besieged by doubt about
what's happening, so that they no longer believe it's their fault when
it does.

CHAPTER *two*

intimate enemies

Ridgewood is a blink-and-you-miss-it working-class town of 2,000 in northern Mississippi. Big enough to have its own Wal-Mart but too small for more than a few traffic lights, Ridgewood is bordered by dusty state roads dotted with service stations and fast-food chains. It is the largest town in a dry county where the mostly Baptist churches outnumber the restaurants. The majority of the town is white, although growing numbers of African American families, mostly poor, are beginning to gather around its edges. Families have long made comfortable livings at local factories here, but threats of an imminent recession have given way to layoffs and a thickening layer of anxiety.

Ridgewood is a fiercely tight-knit community that prides itself in its family-centered values and spirit of care for neighbors. When a tornado cuts a fatal mile-wide swath through town, everyone heads over to rebuild homes and comfort the displaced. Ridgewood is the kind of place where grown children make homes next to their parents and where teenagers safely scatter onto Main Street without looking both ways, drifting in and out of the ice-cream parlor and game room after school. Year-round, going "rolling," toilet papering

an unsuspecting peer or teacher's home, is a favorite pastime, sometimes supervised by parents.

By ten o'clock one October morning in Ridgewood, it was already
eighty-two degrees. The Mississippi sun was blindingly bright, and
the earth was dry, cracked, and dusty. We were having a drought. I
was late getting to school, although the truth is in Ridgewood it
doesn't take longer than a song on the radio to drive anywhere.

I raced through the front door of the elementary school, sunglass
frames in my mouth, spiral notebook in hand. Cassie Smith was waiting. Tall and big-boned, prepubescently round, she had blond hair
that waved gently in strings toward her shoulders, kind green eyes,
glossed pink lips, braces, and a soft, egg-shaped freckled face. She
was missing sixth-grade band class to be with me. Cassie met my eyes
squarely as I nodded to her—I'd been laying low here, trying not to
expose the girls who volunteered to talk to me—and we headed
silently down the long, blue-gray corridor, down the ramp, underneath a still, rusty red fan, and toward the plain, cluttered room I
had been using for interviews. Children were mostly oblivious to us
as they slammed lockers and whirled toward class in single motions,
their teachers standing stiff as flagpoles in the doorways. We passed
class projects in a blur: elaborate trees decorated with sunset-colored
tissue paper to welcome the autumn, which had actually been more
of a summer than anything.

I motioned for Cassie to sit. We made a little small talk. She was
whispering so softly I could barely hear her.

"So," I said gently, leaning back in my chipped metal folding
chair. "Why did you want to come talk with me today?"

Cassie inhaled deeply. "This is happening *right now*, okay?" she
said, as though to admonish me that I was not just some archaeolo-
gist come here to sift through dirt and bones. "My best friend
Becca," she began, staring fiercely at her fingers, which were playing
an absentminded game of itsy-bitsy spider against the lead-smeared
tabletop, "I trusted her and everything. She called me and asked if I
liked Kelly, who is our good friend. Becca said that Kelly talks bad

about me and everything." Cassie sounded nervous. "I really didn't want to say anything back about Kelly because I didn't want to go down to her level." On the phone, Cassie tried to change the subject.

But when Becca called, Kelly had been over at her house. When Becca hung up, she told Kelly that Cassie had called her names. Kelly called back and told Cassie off.

Now, at school, Kelly was teasing Cassie relentlessly—about what she was wearing (she wore that outfit last week) or not (she needs tennis shoes); about how stupid and poor she was. Cassie didn't know what to do.

Cassie and Becca had been best friends since first grade. Last summer, Kelly moved to Ridgewood from Texas, and this fall she'd started hanging around Becca. At first they were all three quite close, with some tension between Cassie and Kelly. And then, Cassie said quietly, over the last few weeks, "Kelly kind of forgot me. They started to get really close and they just forgot me. And then they started ganging up on me and stuff like that."

"How?" I asked.

"They ignored me. They just didn't want to talk with me or anything…" Her voice caught and her eyes filled with tears. I squeezed past some desks to the teacher's table and leaned over to grab a box of tissues.

"Did you try and talk with them about it?" I pulled out a tissue and handed it to her.

"No," she said. "Like, after lunch we have a place where we meet and stuff. We have to line up and go to class. That's when everybody starts talking. We get in a circle and just talk. And they'd put their shoulders together and they wouldn't let me, you know, in the circle or whatever. They would never talk to me, and they would never listen to what I had to say. Stuff like that." She was whispering again.

"I don't think I've ever done anything to them." Her voice shook. "I've always been nice to them."

Lately, it had only gotten worse. Kelly, by now no stranger in the school, had been warning other girls to stay away from Cassie. Becca was saying that Cassie was insulting Kelly behind her back, and Kelly was passing notes that said Cassie lived in a shack and was too poor to buy Sunday clothes.

"So how are you feeling?" I asked.

"Like I don't want to go to school," she whispered, sinking into her red fleece vest.

"Why not?"

"Because I don't know what they'll do every day."

"What have they done so far?" I asked.

"They'll be like, 'Cassie, get back, we're going to talk about you now.'"

"They'll say that?"

"No, they'll just"—she was getting frustrated with me—"*I can tell.* They don't have to say anything. They'll whisper and look at me, and I know they're talking about me."

"Have you talked to your mom?" I asked.

"I talk to my mom but it just...I don't really want to worry her a lot." She began to cry again.

"Does it worry her?"

"It kind of makes her mad because—she says I should ignore them. But I *can't*. They just keep on."

"Why is it hard to ignore them?"

"Because they're like, running over you, you know? And I can't concentrate. They're like—they look at me and stuff like that. They stare at me. I can hear them saying stuff and whispering and they look right at me."

Cassie struggled with the absence of a language to articulate her victimization. As the silent meanness of her friends attracted no teacher's attention, Cassie was filled with a helplessness that was slowly turning into self-blame. Without rules or a public consciousness of this behavior, Cassie's only sense that what was happening was real (or wrong) was her own perspective. For a ten-year-old, that would not be enough.

———

Relational aggression starts in preschool, and so do the first signs of sex differences.[14] The behavior is thought to begin as soon as children become capable of meaningful relationships. By age three, more girls than boys are relationally aggressive, a schism that only widens as children mature. In a series of studies, children cited relational aggression as the "most common angry, hurtful... behavior enacted in girls' peer groups," regardless of the target's sex. By middle childhood, the leading researchers in the field report that "physical aggressors are mostly boys, relational aggressors mostly girls."

Relational aggression harms others "through damage (or the threat of damage) to relationships or feelings of acceptance, friendships, or group inclusion."[15] It includes any act in which relationship is used as a weapon, including manipulation. First identified in 1992, it is the heart of the alternative aggressions, and for many girls an emotionally wrenching experience.

Relational aggression can include indirect aggression, in which the target is not directly confronted (such as the silent treatment), and some social aggression, which targets the victim's self-esteem or social status (such as rumor spreading). Among the most common forms of relational aggression are "do this or I won't be your friend anymore," ganging up against a girl, the silent treatment, and nonverbal gesturing, or body language.[16]

The lifeblood of relational aggression is relationship. As a result, most relational aggression occurs within intimate social or friendship networks. The closer the target to the perpetrator, the more cutting the loss. As one Linden freshman put it, "Your friends know you and how to hurt you. They know what your real weaknesses are. They know exactly what to do to destroy someone's self-worth. They try to destroy you from the inside." Such pointed meanness, an eighth grader explained to me, "can stay with you for your entire life. It can define who you are."

Where relationships are weapons, friendship itself can become a tool of anger. You can, one Ridgewood sixth grader explained, "have a friend, and then go over there and become friends with somebody else, just to make them jealous." Nor must the relationship be withdrawn or even directly threatened: the mere suggestion of loss may be enough. One girl may stand among a group, turn to two friends and sigh, "Wow, I can't *wait* for this weekend!" One girl may pull another away from a group "and tell them secrets, right in front of us," a Mississippi sixth grader said. "When she comes back, people ask her what she said, [and] she's always like, 'Oh, nothing. It's none of your business.'" No rule has been broken here, yet it takes little more than this for a girl to inflict pain on her peers.

A combination of nonphysical, often furtive aggression is extremely dangerous, in large part because it is impossible to detect. Relational aggression has remained invisible because the behavior resists the typical displays that we normally associate with bullying. Two girls playing quietly together in the corner might be two girls playing quietly in the corner—or they might be one girl slowly wearing down the other.

Teachers and parents may not be looking or listening for signs of a problem behind the facade of friendship and play. Who can blame them? Nothing *looks* wrong. It is tempting to interpret signs of trouble as the passing "issues" that afflict all normal childhood relationships, but in some cases, turning the other way can be a terrible mistake.

"Nonverbal gesturing," a fancy word for body language, is a hallmark of relational aggression. Denied the use of their voices by rules against female anger, girls like Becca and Kelly have instead learned to use their bodies. Nonverbal gesturing includes mean looks, certain forms of exclusion, and the silent treatment. It also drives girls to distraction. For one thing, body language is at once infuriatingly empty of detail and bluntly clear. It cuts deep precisely because a girl will know someone is angry at her, but she doesn't get to find out why and sometimes with whom it's happening. In girls' worlds, the worst aggression is the most opaque, creating a sort of emotional poison ivy which makes it hard to concentrate on anything else. Teachers become characters in "Peanuts" cartoons, their lecturing unintelligible. Words swim on the page. The victim of this silent campaign looks around the room and everything—a look exchanged, someone writing a note—has crooked, wildly irrational new signifi-cance, like reflections in a funhouse mirror.

The day after I met Cassie, I spoke with some of her fifth- and sixth-grade classmates about ways girls can be mean without saying a word. Kayla, chubby with sparkling blue eyes, was nearly falling out of her seat hopping and waving and making pleading, wordless noises. I smiled inwardly: This was always my "problem" in class.

"Yes?" I asked.

"Girls can look at you, and you know they're mad!" she ex-claimed. "They don't have to say anything. You look at them and they roll their eyes and they have little slits in them."

Miranda, sitting primly with an arrow-straight arm in the air, added that girls "whisper and you get jealous. They look at you while they're whispering. They might point and start laughing. You see their lips moving."

"So," I said, scanning their faces, "how do you feel when you think you're being whispered about?"

A tiny, tinny voice rose up from a chair in the corner of the room. "It's a funny feeling," Cerise said.

"What do you mean?"

"Like they don't care about you or what you do."

"See, girls don't tease," Tammy explained. "They talk behind [your] backs, they giggle and point at [you]. They start rumors and they totally ignore [you]. Even if they're not teasing, it's still obvious that they don't like you."

As I moved from class to class, from school to school, I learned that the worst kind of silent meanness is the only one with a name: the silent treatment. In this, the most pointed kind of relational ag-gression, one girl ceases speaking to another and, with little or no warning, revokes her friendship. The target, often unaware of why her friend is angry, is consumed by panic and the fear of permanently losing the friendship.

"When you ignore," an Arden eleven-year-old explained, "they"—meaning the target—"get scared over every little thing. They don't understand what's going on."

"Oh, yeah," a classmate chimed in. It's the worst thing you can do. You gain a lot of power and they come crawling back." A twelve-year-old remarked, "Giving someone a look makes [the targets] paranoid. [They] overanalyze it." A Ridgewood eighth grader explained, "You try to find out why they're mad at you and they just kind of laugh at you. They toss their hair and look away." "When someone glares at you," a Linden freshman told me, "it makes you feel lower and deteriorates your insides. Oh God, you think, what are they doing? You ask them why they're mad and they don't say anything. You have no control. It gives them power."

One of the more chilling messages conveyed through silence and staring is that, in eleven-year-old Mary's words, "you're telling them you're not worth my time or me talking to you. It's the worst thing. You're saying, 'I don't want to argue it out.'" Silence throws up an impenetrable wall, shutting down the chance for self-expression and more importantly, the opportunity to play a proactive role in one's conflicts.

Not getting to find out why someone's mad often has the unfortunate effect of making targeted girls believe that whatever's gone wrong is surely their fault—if only they could deduce the unwritten rule they broke. Already prone to self-dissection, girls are only too willing to take up the challenge. Filled with dread, seeking some measure of control, they search for the mistake they're sure they made. In this way, the simple act of silence or a nasty look can take on a life of its own, continuing well beyond the moment it is shared.

To the perpetrator, the silent treatment can be a quick, easy path around a direct confrontation. Putting it simply, a girl at Marymount remarked, "If you don't tell someone why you're mad, you can't get a rebuttal. You win." Girls on the receiving end will usually persist, begging for an explanation. But "when they come around, you just walk away," reported one girl. That's hard, her classmate explained, because if you're on the receiving end "you can try to tell them, try to say you're sorry, and they won't listen or solve the problem."

When confronted, girls often deny that they are angry, even as they project the opposite. Most women remember uncomfortably approaching a friend with the question, "Are you mad at me?" only to get a brusque or even cheery "No!" followed by a quick exit. The supplicant has to take the girl at her word, but she knows the score. As one ninth grader explained, "Last week, I asked my friend why she was mad—I had no idea why—and she said, 'I'm not mad at you.' Right then I knew she was mad at me." To survive in the social jungle, friends learn to doubt what they see and hear and instead search for a second layer of real feeling beneath a false exterior, a quality that comes to dominate girls' interactions.

Mean looks and the silent treatment are the ultimate undercover aggression. The least visible of the alternative aggressions, nonverbal gesturing slips easily beneath teacher radar, allowing girls to remain "good girls." Debbi Canter, a sixth-grade teacher in Ridgewood, said, "I see those looks flying around the room. I call them on it. And they look at me with those big, innocent eyes. 'What are you talking about?'" Indeed, some teachers justify their hands-off attitude toward girls' aggression because they can't confirm it. Middle school assistant principal Pam Bank explained, "If I see a boy tapping his pen, I'll say 'Stop that tapping.' But if I see a girl giving another girl the evil eye, I might say, 'Eyes on me.' I knew the boy was thumping on his pen, but I might not know for sure what the girl was doing."

Girls understand the futility of exposing nonverbal gesturing. Maggie, a Ridgewood sixth grader, said, "Teachers, most of the time, they're like, 'Don't worry, it will be okay, just ignore them.' But it's hard to ignore them. If they do it on purpose and they're right in front of you and they do something to make you really mad, it's hard to ignore them. And it hurts your feelings." Her classmate Emily told me, "If they're whispering, the teacher thinks it's going to be all right because they're not hitting people. She might think they're not hurting her, but if they're punching she might get on them and send them to the office." Kenni added, "Most teachers think, 'Oh, well, she's not hurting you. Don't worry about it.' But really they are hurting you. They're hurting your feelings."

In a social world where anger is not spoken, reading body language becomes an important way for girls to know each others' feelings. Yet the practice can have grave consequences. Bodies at rest are always in motion: no matter how hard a girl tries, it's impossible to be in conscious charge of every move she makes. Misunderstandings happen all the time. A girl passes her friend in the hallway, and her friend doesn't say hello. The girl is certain her friend is angry. Actually, the friend was deep in thought and never even saw the girl. It doesn't matter: a fight begins.

"People look at you and don't mean to, and you think something bad, and it starts something," a Mississippi freshman said. "If girls were more like guys and came out and said what they thought, a lot of stuff wouldn't get started." A Sackler sixth grader remarked, "If you, like, ignore me and don't talk to me so I don't know what's wrong, then maybe I'll turn against you."

Confusing body language can indeed lead to confrontations, albeit bewildering ones. Sixth grader Reena told me, "Last year, in my English class, there was this girl, and I wasn't that good friends with her, but one night she called me up and said, 'You've been mean to me and I want an apology.' And I didn't know what she was talking about because I never really was friends with her so I just said I apologized to her but I never really knew what it was for."

Silence deepens conflict intensity, as each side wonders what the other is thinking. As is often the case when girls avoid confrontations, there may be a long list of possible reasons and past squabbles to plumb. "You each have different ideas about what's going on," a sixth grader at Arden explained. "When you finally do talk, it's worse than when it started."

intimate enemies

Eyes frozen wide in horror, Veronica is gaping at the corpse of her best friend, whom she has handed a now-empty Drano cocktail.

"I just killed my best friend!" gasps the heroine of the film *Heathers.*

"And your worst enemy," purrs her accomplice boyfriend.

"Same difference," she moans.

The word *bully* evokes the image of an enemy, not an intimate, and yet it is often the closest girlfriends who are caught in protracted episodes of emotional abuse. The meanness can unfold secretly under a cover of intimacy and play. Young and ignorant of the signs of relationship abuse, victims struggle to reconcile their circumstances with what they have learned about friendship. Perpetrators tend to be equally unaware that their "possessiveness" or "bossiness" is crossing a line. To the contrary, they are often deeply attached to their victims. In the course of these relationships, both victim and perpetrator often assimilate their behaviors into their concept of friendship. These stories of girl bullying are seldom told. They are a singular alchemy of love and fear, and they defy many of our assumptions about female friendship.

VANESSA'S STORY

Even in the first grade, Vanessa recalled, Stacy was popular and funny. Vanessa was instantly awed by her, and when Stacy asked her to be best friends, she was overjoyed to become part of her clique. Throughout elementary school, Vanessa would relish her status, and especially her power over Nicki and Zoe, who let Vanessa be second-in-command to Stacy. Not long after they became friends, Stacy started asking Vanessa to do things for her. At first, Vanessa felt important when Stacy singled her out, saying she'd like Vanessa if she did whatever it was she wanted at the time. Stacy seemed to leave Nicki and Zoe alone.

"I was very attracted to that," Vanessa, now twenty-seven, told me. Under this arrangement, Vanessa could look tough and still allow herself to be controlled. "I was an insecure kid, but I was confident on the outside," she explained. "And I wanted to be accepted by her, to be her. I wanted to be her second, you know. I wanted to be her right-hand girl."

One night during their frequent sleepovers, when they were nine, Stacy asked Vanessa if they could play dress-up. "I'll be the man, and you'll be the woman," she told Vanessa. That night Stacy kissed Vanessa, and Vanessa enjoyed it. Their sleepovers always included some dress-up for a while after that, and they never told anyone about the game.

In fifth grade, dress-up stopped. The game was never mentioned again, though Vanessa didn't forget about it. The memory became hers instead of theirs; for Vanessa it was strange to have a secret that only she thought about.

That year, Stacy's popularity skyrocketed. Not only was she the first girl in the grade to get MTV, but her parents were cool and let her and her friends eat junk food whenever they wanted. Stacy had the best bike, too. Over at her house, Vanessa told me, "We'd make crank calls. She was always really good and really vicious, and she knew exactly what to do to get the person really upset."

Most of all, though, Stacy was fun, and she had a lot of it by controlling her friends. "She had this way with the other girls," Vanessa recalled. "In a minute, she could make them do anything she wanted. She was the one who always had crushes on boys, and she would tell her friends to go up and tell them something so she didn't have to do anything." She made Vanessa steal candy for her from a local store. "Of course I did it," Vanessa said. "All I wanted to do was make her happy. And of course there was the underlying fear of being rejected by her."

One day, on the bus to school in sixth grade, Vanessa mentioned their old dress-up game. Stacy stared darkly at Vanessa. "What are you talking about?" she snapped. Vanessa stiffened as she watched Stacy turn away.

"Was she afraid?" Vanessa wondered years later. "I think that's when she felt I was a threat. I had this information on her. And that was the beginning of the end."

Stacy began writing songs about Vanessa. "They went something like, 'Vanessa is fat, Vanessa wears a bra.'" Vanessa was the first in the grade to develop breasts, and she had also put on some weight. "There were these limericks. And they would snap my bra all the time," she said. "The boys wouldn't. The girls would."

Nicki and Zoe didn't hesitate to back Stacy up. "They were very creative in the way they would torture me. They would steal my notebooks and they would just write all over [them], 'Vanessa is fat,' 'Vanessa wears a bra,' 'Vanessa sucks,' and all this stuff. In the wintertime they would scratch it into the ice on the bus, and we'd ride around town like that."

The ironic thing, Vanessa recalled, is that Stacy was the only other person developing breasts at the time. "But it was all focused on me," she said. "At the time I thought it was because I was gross and ugly and they didn't want to have anything to do with me. Now I think Stacy saw a lot of things in me that reminded her of herself, and it scared her. I was a bit too close to her. The other girls didn't look at all like her, they didn't act like her, but most of all, they didn't know her secrets."

Vanessa's closeness with Stacy seemed only to inflame Stacy's cruelty. Nevertheless, Vanessa clung to her. "Every day I'm hearing these songs, and every day I'm hanging out with them," she explained. "I'm going to lunch with them. I'm going after school to their houses. It was like I was her best friend, and yet I was her total victim."

The girls promised that it was just a joke. They told Vanessa they needed to write a song and that she was just so easy to write about. Vanessa wanted to believe them, so she did. "I didn't have any other friends," Vanessa said. "I was so wrapped up in these people. There were other people I knew who were really cool, and I just—I was so wrapped up. I was so wrapped up in wanting to be part of this group because it seemed to me to be the center of power." Since Nicki and Zoe were affectionate whenever Stacy wasn't around, it was easier for Vanessa to stay with the group.

It also allowed the bullying to be built around the friendship and vulnerability Stacy sensed in Vanessa. One morning at school, before class started, Stacy somberly announced that her mother had died. Vanessa was devastated for her. She got Stacy lunch, told teachers she wouldn't be able to attend class, and covered for Stacy all day. "I thought, 'She finally needs me,'" Vanessa recalled. "She needs me as emotional support, not just to mess with. I was so excited because I'd take care of her, do anything for her."

At the end of the day, Stacy surrounded Vanessa with a large group of girls and told her she'd lied. You're a sucker, she said. "She had convinced the whole school to be in on this," Vanessa said, anger like gravel in her voice. "She wanted to show everyone that she could manipulate me to such an extent, and everyone else wanted to be involved. They all stood up behind the lie. Everyone. And watched me the whole day feel so sorry for Stacy."

Stacy never lifted a finger against Vanessa. She abused Vanessa quietly, deftly using third parties throughout sixth grade. She sent so many notes and messages through other willing girls that Vanessa, feeling surrounded by hate, stopped wanting to go to school. "Wherever you were," she recalled, "there would be a note waiting for you."

One day, the phone rang at Vanessa's house. It was from a trainer at a local gym, asking if Vanessa was still interested in the weight-loss program that she had signed up for. Her father had answered the phone. Vanessa had never been to the gym. Although this might have been a good opportunity to tell her parents about her peers' abuse, Vanessa pretended the call was a mistake.

When I asked Vanessa why, she replied swiftly.

"I never wanted my parents to think that I was making bad decisions," she explained. "I think deep down inside I knew. I knew this wasn't good for me and that Stacy was mean. But you never want to admit your mistakes to your parents, especially when you're eleven, and you're just starting to feel like you can make your own decisions." It was a comment I would hear often from the adult women I interviewed.

Vanessa's mother, who had begun suspecting her daughter's victimization, didn't help. When Vanessa refused to listen to her mother's warnings about Stacy, her mother countered with sarcasm and anger. Adding to the problem was her increasing pressure on Vanessa to lose weight. Her mother stepped up the encouragement, offering to put coins in a can every time Vanessa lost a pound and buy a new dress with the money.

When Vanessa's mother joined the critical voices of her "friends," Vanessa was left feeling alone, without any allies. That they targeted the area that Vanessa was most sensitive about—her weight— seemed to validate the abuse. As she told me, "There was no way I was going to my mother because I was so sure she'd say, 'Well she's absolutely right, Vanessa.'"

By seventh grade, Vanessa was depressed. She began wearing a black trench coat. Inside the pocket she kept a bottle of pills stolen from her grandfather's medicine cabinet. Vanessa imagined they were sedatives as she walked the hallways in school, sometimes holding them absently in her hand. At night she would stare at them, imagining her funeral. Fortunately, she reported, "I was too much of a wimp to do myself in." In school, her grades nose-dived from A's and B's to straight D's. She started hanging out with kids who smoked pot, and she began smoking cigarettes. Her parents were called in to a conference with her teachers, and that night they confronted Vanessa to ask what was wrong. "I said, you know, all the typical things," Vanessa recalled. "School's boring. I'm not interested anymore. All my teachers suck." Her parents believed her, and Vanessa pulled her grades up to the point where she knew she would be left alone. "At one point, it had gotten so bad," she told me, "that people were ripping my clothes in the hallway. I had a horrible pit in my stomach where I couldn't move and I just wanted to throw up everywhere I went.

"That was when I stopped trusting my parents," she recalled, "because I knew they just didn't get it. And if I had actually broken down and told my parents what was going on at that point, that no one was talking to me, that I was already having suicidal thoughts because I just thought I was totally ugly and fat and disgusting, absolutely uninteresting and so weak, and no one wanted to be friends with me, I don't know what would have happened to me."

———

From the earliest moments of their friendship, Stacy meted out love and acceptance only when Vanessa obeyed her. The purposeful control over the terms of a relationship is a signal aspect of relational aggression. At age six Stacy threatened her friendship over Vanessa's failure to play a game; a few years later, she would use it to make her steal. The style of coercion also evolved. Stacy controlled Vanessa for herself, but she soon graduated to making Vanessa perform acts that affected others. Stacy grew to use Vanessa and others as tools to express her own aggression without suffering the responsibility for it.

Vanessa was a valuable pawn in the collection of followers. "I wasn't a wimp and I wasn't quiet and I wasn't meekish and I wasn't stupid. I was funny, really witty, and I always had these comebacks." Stacy's cruel practical joke, Vanessa concluded, was her way of affirming that "I was just a pawn. I was simply like a representation of her power."

Vanessa's compliance with her bully's demands reveals a distinctive element of girls' bullying. Like most bullied children, Vanessa feared reprisal if she fought Stacy's control. But because she continued to associate with these girls as friends, she chose a damaged relationship over no relationship at all.

More and more, Vanessa's conception of her situation was unrealistic, hankering back to the sunnier days of their friendship. After the faked death of Stacy's mother, Vanessa could hardly contain her excitement and sense of relief that "finally, she needs me. She needs me. . . . She needs me as emotional support. . . ." For Vanessa, fear of being alone was an invisible hand keeping a corroded relationship alive, in spite of her intense pain.

Then, one day, Vanessa was filled with a peculiar sense of certainty about what she had to do. "The bottom dropped out," she recalled. "Either I was going to like kill myself or I was going to have to claim my space back." The next day, she walked straight up to Stacy and ordered her to be outside at lunch. Word got out, and by noon there was a big crowd assembled. Stacy was waiting.

"I said to her, 'I don't fucking care anymore. I have nothing to
lose and I hate you and I hate everything you've done to me, and I
think you're a totally evil person and I don't want to have anything
to do with you. You can make as much fun of me as you want, but
you know what?, like, it doesn't matter anymore.'"

Stacy snarled. She wasn't having any of it. "She pulled out every
single insult. She said, 'Vanessa, you're going to regret this for the
rest of your life, and no one's ever going to forgive you.'"

When Vanessa didn't flinch, Stacy followed up with a reply that
exemplifies the bizarre union of love and cruelty in bullying among
friends. She shouted, "Do you know what you're throwing away?
You know I could have been the best thing for you forever. We could
have been so good together. And yet you just throw it all away."

Vanessa was shocked. She said, "What are you talking about?
There's nothing left." And after that, "I just didn't even look back."
The spell was broken.

Today, Vanessa believes her relationship with Stacy had a major impact on her social and intimate life. After Stacy, she turned away from
girls and became friends with mostly guys. When I asked why, I
heard a response that was echoed repeatedly by women who were
victims of girl bullies. "I think in a way it's because I don't trust
women," Vanessa said. "I don't trust them with my fears." Vanessa
believes that women criticize each other more than men do, and
more frequently than men criticize women. And for Vanessa, as with
countless others, it's not solely a matter of how often women criticize. Vanessa put it succinctly: "When a girl says something, for some
reason, it's like it gets deeper. You take it personally. You can't just
write it off."

Even when she has resolved her problems with other women,
Vanessa can't shake the feeling that "they're going to get you again.
And you've got your defenses up at all times." She added, "I'm so
scared of their underlying motive and the potential breakdown of

[the relationship]. Because the potential breakdown is what, you know, my real fear is. It's like, are they going to hate me? Are they going to make my life miserable? Are they going to just consistently call and write letters and tell me how awful I am and how awful I have been to them? And that my life will never again be happy?"

And yet, Vanessa said, she'll tell a man her deep secrets, even men she doesn't know that well, because she feels safer. Because girls had made her feel so sexually unattractive, she made sure to let me know she has made a point of sleeping with men on the first date, to silence the haunting feeling, instilled by Vanessa, that she would never be "girlfriend material."

ANNIE'S STORY

When meanness and friendship become inextricable, girls lose the ability to distinguish between them. They may come to understand meanness as a component of friendship, learning to explain it away and even justify it. When abuse permeates friendship, some girls lose their ability to defend themselves against it.

Annie Wexler's long legs were flexing off the couch she was sharing with her mother, Petra. At fourteen, she looked every bit the girl athlete in white high-tops, blue mesh shorts, and a long, worn Adidas T-shirt. Her long hair was pulled back in a ponytail, and though her eyes looked tired on this dewy Sunday morning, she smiled cheerfully when I apologized for the hour of my visit. The house was still and large, blending into an affluent suburban bouquet of other still and large homes, the only sound the yellow lab clicking his tail insistently against the dark wood floor.

Annie's story began in the third grade, a time when there were already strict social rules. You were in a group—the nerdy one, the cool kids, the "okay" crowd—but you weren't friends with everyone. Annie was, as she put it, "kind of in between this one group of girls and this other group." She had two best friends, one from each clique. Samantha was a small, scrappy girl on the margins of one group in Annie's math class. "Rapunzel" was Samantha's favorite fairy tale, and she had refused to cut her straight brown hair since she was four. Annie loved to brush and braid it. Samantha sat happily for whole recesses at a time as Annie tried different hairstyles and then went running with Samantha inside to look in the girls' bathroom mirror.

Alison was popular and pretty, the center of her clique's attention. Her friends called her "Glitter Girl." Alison had just gotten her ears pierced, but she had been collecting earrings since she was six. Every day, something different sparkled in her ears. Alison's friends played foursquare in the same corner of the playground every day, and it was a game Annie loved. At recess, Alison brought a maroon ball out of her locker, which she had decorated with glitter and glow-in-the-dark stickers.

Samantha usually asked Annie to play at recess just after they arrived at school, and Annie usually said yes. Once, when she replied, "Well, I was going to play with Alison today," Samantha suddenly shot back, "Then I don't want to be your friend anymore."

Samantha's threats triggered intense arguments between the girls. Annie didn't want to lose Samantha, so she would run over to Alison and tell her that she couldn't play after all. Sometimes Annie insisted on playing with Alison. Samantha would say, "Well, you obviously don't like me, so I guess you don't want to be my friend. You can just go play with her. I don't care." And then, Annie recalled, "she'd go off crying." Afraid, Annie would gingerly approach Alison. The very next day, Samantha would come up to play with Annie as though nothing had happened.

Alison responded competitively to Samantha's behavior. She began to want Annie exclusively, so that if Annie was playing with her, and someone else approached, the request to play was always denied. "It always had to be one on one," Annie said. "Samantha and me. Or Alison and me. And I'd feel flattered that people wanted me."

Alison, powerful and charismatic, disliked Samantha. She and her friends started excluding Annie when she played with Samantha. Eventually, Alison started making the same threats. "If you don't play with me at recess," she warned Annie, "I don't want to be your friend anymore."

On the couch, Annie tucked her legs under her and sat up on her knees. "I always felt in the middle," she said. "Who was I going to play with? I might lose them both." She made the first of a few self-deprecating excuses that would be sprinkled throughout our conversation. "It's kind of hard for you to imagine," she began. "I mean, Samantha is not a big person. It's not like she came up to me and was like 'Grrr! You have to play with me!' She's this big!" Annie thrust two fingers stuck together at her mother, who nodded in agreement. "I'm not kidding. I was bigger than her and a full year older than her."

But, Annie said, "you'd always feel intimidated by her because she was this loudmouthed girl. She wasn't afraid to talk. She was gonna say what she thinks. She was always going to have her way. The right way was her way."

Annie sank down into the couch. "Yet I felt so taken over. If I didn't do this I would lose that friendship, and if I did go I would lose this friendship. They wouldn't allow me to be myself. If I would have just mentioned the slightest thing about getting sick of it, they would drop me. I thought I was kind of like getting smaller and smaller to them, not as a friend but just as a person."

Practically every day, either Samantha or Alison would end her friendship with Annie. In her journal every night, Annie said, "I would always write, 'I broke up with Samantha today,' 'I broke up with Alison today.' I know I used the wrong term for it." She laughed.

Annie was quiet for a moment, eyes fixed on her dog. "It feels really bad when someone says, 'I don't want to be your friend,' because then I would wonder, did I do something wrong? Am I just not a person you want to like, and just stuff like that. It's just so powerful in my mind. So many things go through my mind. Did I do something wrong? Am I just not likable?"

"I know it's kind of weird," she insisted (and of course it wasn't, but I wondered for the first time if Annie was anxious about what I might think of her), "I mean, you want to say, 'Why were you friends with this girl?' But it was hard for me to say 'I won't be your friend if you treat me like this' because I really wanted to keep both friendships."

Petra was shifting on the couch, crossing and uncrossing her legs, and had been for the last twenty minutes. She was eager for her daughter to finish. Above all, Petra told me, she was upset about Samantha. For nearly three years, Samantha smothered Annie. In between her threats she showered Annie with gifts brought to school: bracelets, rings, hair clips, stickers, souvenirs from trips to foreign countries. Samantha would make crafts and draw pictures, even take things from her mother (with permission) for Annie.

"But," Petra said, "if Annie crossed her and said I can't play with you today, or I'm playing with somebody else, then she would give her hate notes. 'You're a bitch.' 'I hate you.' And she'd write long notes asking why Annie wasn't her friend anymore."

At school right before winter vacation, helping Annie clean out her locker, Petra was shocked less by the mess than the contents. "We would haul out—I mean, a bagful of gifts and a bagful of hate notes." Petra threw all the gifts away. "I didn't want them in this house," she said bitterly.

Her voice rose in anger. "Every spare moment of school Samantha was on her—play with me, sit with me, sit with me at lunch, play with me after school. Annie would walk in the house after school at 3:30, and the phone would be ringing. It would be Samantha.

"What I thought was sick," she continued, "was the extreme of the I love you–I hate you thing. And I have to be honest. I saw it as potentially the ingredients for a stalker. I kid you not. I use that word. That's what it felt like. It felt victimizing to me, on Annie's behalf, that this girl was a stalker. Had the situation not faded away, I would have been concerned for her safety. Annie would get in the car upset, Samantha this and Samantha that, and we would no sooner walk in the house and there'd be either a message on the machine or Samantha was calling."

There were times, Petra recalled, when Annie would refuse to answer the phone. Or, Petra said, "when I needed to protect her, and I'd say, you know what Annie, I am not letting you talk on the phone today." Annie would agree happily.

Every day as she pulled into the school car-pool lane to pick Annie up, Petra was filled with anxiety. "I could almost tell by her face. It's like, 'Oh God, what was it today?' She would get in the car and be so upset. And it was frustrating for me because I knew as an adult what was going on. As much as we would say to her, 'Oh just tell her to shut up!' that's not who Annie was. She would say to me, 'I can't, I can't be mean.' That part was so frustrating because I thought, 'Nobody's going to treat my kid like that!'"

Approaching Samantha's mother seemed daunting. She was not a friend of Petra's, and Petra dreaded her response to the so-called problem. Imagining the conversation, Petra grimaced: "Who the hell are you to say this! My daughter is giving your daughter gifts! How can you say that's not a nice thing!"

Annie stepped in. "I don't have a weak personality. I'm very strong and I have good leadership qualities. I'm not just going to be sitting there. But it's so hard for me to say, I don't want you to do this anymore, and I don't like the fact that you're doing this to someone who's my friend."

As she became more isolated, Annie was more vulnerable to Samantha's suffocating attention. Annie was folding into herself in other ways, too. She became fearful of crying or showing emotions in front of her peers.

Finally, at the end of fifth grade, Petra told the school counselor that they needed a break. "I said to [the counselor], she can't be the only one to carry Samantha. It's not fair to Annie." (Petra did not tell Annie about her intervention until our interview.) Petra discovered only then that Annie was not Samantha's only target. Between third and sixth grade, several mothers had asked the counselor to separate their daughters from Samantha.

In sixth grade, Annie had an autograph book that she asked her friends to sign at the end of the year. Most kids wrote in their favorite color or movie, and then they wrote what they liked about Annie. "What I like about Annie is that she's so tall," Petra remembered. "What I like about Annie is that she likes to talk on the phone." And Samantha? "What I like about Annie is that I don't really like her and she's really a bitch. What I like about Annie is that we get in fights all the time but she's still my best friend and I like the fact that she gets over the fights."

Annie was so afraid of isolation that tolerating abuse felt like her only option. She also loved her friends. Like Vanessa, Annie tried to please her friend at any cost, wanting only to save the relationship. Her unremitting focus on staying friends with Samantha allowed abuse to take over the friendship.

With meanness so intermixed with friendship, Annie lost the capacity to tell the difference. Consider Annie's incisive description of Samantha's behavior: "This was her way of saying, 'I am your friend and I like you.' I think she was trying to keep the friendship just as she could have it."

The plight of girls who are victims of relational aggression is usually the hardest to address. When family members know about it, it's often difficult to comprehend a girl's refusal to resist. Annie remembered one night "so clearly. I was crying my head off, going, 'I don't know what to do. I can't do this.'" Annie's brothers were kidding around, and perhaps a little exasperated. They asked, "Why don't you just go over there and beat her up? You're ten times her size."

"They were like, 'Go kick her ass!'" Annie said wistfully. "But I wouldn't do that. I wouldn't just go over and be like, 'Hey! You know what? I don't like the way you're treating me.' I just felt so insecure. I was crying so hard." Annie recalled sitting in the family room, not knowing what to do. "I was nine then—for a nine-year-old girl to be having to go through friendship struggles already, it's ... it wasn't just like, 'I'll see you tomorrow.' It was, 'I don't want to be your friend.' To have that thrown in your face all of a sudden is just so difficult for someone so young, and someone who really thinks that friendship is important."

Our culture's limited understanding of female aggression and intimacy makes it hard for girls to deal with their peer relationships in healthy ways. Most damaging is girls' inability to identify what Carol Gilligan and Lyn Mikel Brown call "relational violations," or dynamics of meanness or abuse.[17] Without an understanding of their unique experience of bullying, girls often end up blaming themselves for their own victimization. Consider Annie, whose interview was dotted with embarrassed explanations of how it was possible that she was bullied by someone half her size and a year younger than she.

That girl bullies are often likely to be the most socially skilled in a group complicates matters further. Like the popular girls profiled by researchers, these girls are mature and worldly. Less often discussed, however, is their intensely charismatic, even seductive aura. Girls like these have almost gravitational pulls on their victims. The friendship is mesmerizing, and often the victim is gripped by dueling desires to be consumed and released by her friend. The victim may rationally understand the relationship's problems, nod in agreement at her parents' entreaties to pull away, and then find herself inexplicably drawn to a bully's side. About a close friend who demeaned her and forced everyone she knew to ignore her, Chastity said, "She's the kind of person that whenever you'd meet her, you'd love her to death. She's the sweetest person. She'd hide her attitude so everybody loved her."

NATALIE'S STORY

In Ridgewood, Dr. Laura Fields, the city superintendent of schools, led me through a multipurpose room teeming with children lining up to leave. She strode confidently between the long brown benches, stopping to chat with students here and there: "How are you! ... Good to hear it! ... Now, don't you think you should close your backpack before you get on the bus? That's a good boy. . . . What a lovely dress!" Some of the kids waved shyly. Others just stared.

Outside at the football field, I marveled at the crowd already gathered. This was the spiritual center of town. Football was just about religion here, and it was common for town residents, even those without school-age children, to drive forty-five minutes on the interstate to fill the stands at away games. Laura led me up through the bleachers, and I could feel people watching me. After we found seats, Laura began chatting with someone while I sat by awkwardly, queasy as I felt the bleachers sway.

The bleachers creaked as a woman plunked down next to me. Short and stocky, with dyed red hair and acid-washed jeans, a cheerful, hearty voice rose up from her belly. "I'm Susan Patterson, how're *you*. I'm real excited for you to speak with my daughter, Natalie." So much for blending in. She turned intense eyes on me and gave me a friendly smack on the shoulder, guy-style. "I think she'd be good for you to talk to."

Natalie seemed less sure. In the days that followed, I said hi to her at school and got little more than a fleeting look before her pageboy hair swung back toward the floor, her locker, anyplace that was not me. I wondered if her mom was forcing her to meet with me.

The day of our interview, I slid into a desk next to her. Natalie was thirteen years old and in the eighth grade. She was wearing blue jeans with a matching jacket and a white T-shirt underneath.

Today Natalie would introduce me to a secret, repeat-offender girl bully in Ridgewood. She was the last one you'd pick in a lineup: picture your typical girl-next-door cheerleader captain. Reese had straight A's, a ponytail that swung like a metronome, and a face that would make Scrooge smile. I was introduced to her mother early on, a charming woman with a quick laugh and a reputation for being at the center of all things off the record in Ridgewood.

Natalie grew up with Reese. Their families had been friends, and the girls started playing in preschool. Natalie felt almost worshipful toward Reese, who always had a new game to pretend. She adored the time spent at Reese's house, which always felt more crowded than it really was.

In third grade, Reese started telling Natalie stories about having a brother who died or a pet that didn't exist. She'd come over to Natalie's house and criticize her outfits and the pictures on her bedroom wall. Natalie was hurt but figured if she changed her clothes and stripped her walls, Reese would stop. She didn't. At school, Reese started pretending Natalie wasn't there when they were around other girls, even though at home they were still best friends.

Reese was the girl version of the stealth bomber: she flew low and she was in and out before anyone knew who did it or what happened. Spectacularly sweet, she was one of the first to spring to mind when teachers ticked off a mental list of girls with good reputations. Which made her the last person most people even thought to look at. "She made good grades and didn't talk out in class," Natalie explained. "The teachers saw, oh, Reese and Natalie are friends, so they'd put us together in groups in class. We were quiet and we'd tell each other things."

But whenever they were grouped or paired together, Natalie clammed up. Reese berated and teased her. "I'd be the quietest girl in the grade because I didn't speak out," Natalie said. Although she had once loved to read aloud from her journal in class, Reese began exchanging looks with other girls, so Natalie stopped. Meanwhile, Reese projected an image to their peers of harmony and affection. "She was all the time trying to be my friend."

I asked Natalie if she'd ever spoken out against Reese. She looked at me quizzically. "I thought she was, you know, like the world. She was my *best friend*." She said this carefully, as if English was not my first language. "I didn't—I was just scared to say something to her because I was afraid she'd get mad at me or dislike me and start talking about me even more." The few moments when Natalie or one of their friends showed signs of resistance, "She tried to make everybody think she was just fine and that it was all me coming up with this stuff in my mind." Reese successfully convinced Natalie that she was not strong enough to fight, even if she'd wanted to. "She took advantage of me and I didn't take up for myself," she told me. "I would let myself believe that she was better than me."

That Natalie hid the problems with Reese from her mother was no surprise. Natalie's downcast eyes were a stark contrast with her mother's easygoing, how-ya-doing personality. Sometimes, when her mother asked if school had been good and Natalie said not really, Susan breezed on to the next subject. She was friends with Reese's mother—looked up to her, in fact—and Natalie never thought her mother would believe her. She was ashamed.

In sixth grade, Reese became close with Drew, who had just moved to town. Reese put Drew through an unusually public torture, and Natalie eventually reached out to her. After watching Drew cry every day at school, Natalie tried to show her that she'd felt the same pain. It wasn't easy. "She was afraid to trust me," Natalie said. "And I was afraid to trust somebody at first, too. I thought I'd never trust anybody again because I put my whole trust in Reese. And she just totally went behind my back and talked about me. She told people everything I had ever told her. So I thought I could never tell anybody anything again. I didn't even tell my mama and my daddy anything."

When I asked Natalie if her friendship with Reese affected her in any way, she was modest. "I think it has affected me just a little," she said. "I used to be loud and funny and everything, but now I barely talk. I used to be the funny person with my friends and everyone would laugh at me. I used to stand out wearing funny clothes but I don't do that anymore because I'm afraid that Reese or somebody would make fun of me or talk about me."

"How does that make you feel?" I asked her.

"When I think about it, it makes me feel like I want to just cry. But I don't because I know that if I cry I'm letting her get to me and I just don't do anything." Natalie had befriended new girls and felt a world of a difference in these new relationships. But fear of new confrontations with Reese lingered.

As she sat before me, Natalie's face was anguished, but the pain was hardly fresh. It seemed stamped there. She had been on the verge of tears the whole time we were talking, reporting the facts with clarity and steadiness.

When we were done, I turned off the tape recorder. I told her how strong and wonderful I thought she was, and how brave. Natalie stood quickly to leave, and I felt intuitively that she would go somewhere else to cry. It was all I could do not to jump out of my chair and hug her, but I knew that was not what she needed. It was what I needed. Listening to her was like looking down into a deep well of sorrow, and the memory of Natalie stayed with me long after I left the building.

CHAPTER *three*

the truth hurts

At 1:15 P.M., my first group of eighth-grade girls at Marymount were looking like they might pass out. It was the right-after-lunch-and-I-need-a-nap class period. On the floor, the girls were drooping against one wall, refusing to make a circle, leaning into one another like reeds. It was March, and outside there was a hint of spring. Though it was no more than sixty-five degrees, many were wearing shorts or tank tops.

I pulled out the Oreos, and as if on cue, they sat up and began to munch. Relieved by these signs of life, I began the discussion by asking them to describe the perfect girl. They looked at me quizzically.

"Like in magazines. Movies. *Dawson's Creek*. Stuff like that."

A few hands went up. Hoping to foster a casual atmosphere, I had asked them to speak without raising their hands. Old habits die hard.

"Skinny!" one says.

"Pretty!"

Okay, I thought. And then: "Nice!"

"What do you mean, nice?" I asked, looking up from my notebook.

"She always has friends."

"She never gets in fights."

"Everybody loves her."

So began my understanding of girls' everyday aggression.

"Okay," I said, stalling to think. "So if one of your friends has done something to bug you or make you mad, or sad, do you tell her about it?"

"No!" came a chorus.

"Why?" I asked.

Silence. I waited.

A girl in the corner took a breath. "Because then it's going to cause a big thing."

"What's 'a big thing'?"

"There's going to be a big fight about it," someone else explained.

"Everyone's going to get involved. It's not worth losing your friendship over something small."

"People make stuff up."

"What if," I asked, "you were just telling someone how you felt, because *you* felt bad? You know, to make yourself—your friendship— feel a little better?"

"Then you might hurt her feelings," one said. Nods. Locking eyes.

"Can you tell someone the truth and not be mean?" I asked.

"The truth hurts," a girl in the corner said quietly. "That's why I lie."

When I set out to write this book, I sought the stories of women and girls who had been victims or perpetrators of severe episodes of bullying. Following the received wisdom of scholars and teachers, I conceived of alternative aggressions as behaviors found outside girls' "normal" social structure. When I met with my first groups of girls, I was broadsided with stories of everyday conflict that bore a striking resemblance to their descriptions of bullying.

Girls don't have to bully, at least as far as we have understood the word, to alienate and injure their peers. In fact, the word *bullying* couldn't be more wrong in describing what some girls do to hurt one another. The day-to-day aggression that persists among girls, a dark underside of their social universe, remains to be charted and explored. We have no real language for it.

Girls describe their social communities as worlds in which unresolved conflicts hang like leaking gas in the air, creating a treacherous emotional terrain in which discord is rarely voiced and yet may explode silently with the slightest spark. For many, if not most, girls, every day can be unpredictable. Alliances shift with whispers under cover of girlish intimacy and play. Many girls will not tell each other why they are sad or angry. Instead, they will employ small armies of mediators, usually willing friends who are uncomfortably caught in the middle or eager for the moments of intimacy that result from lending a hand to someone in trouble.

Alternative aggressions, and the nonassertive behavior they suggest, are as embedded in the daily lives of girls as makeup, boys, and media. A girl learns early on that to voice conflict directly with another girl may result in many others ganging up against her. She learns to channel feelings of hurt and anger to avoid their human instigator, internalizing feelings or sharing them with others. She learns to store away unresolved conflicts with the precision of a bookkeeper, building a stockpile that increasingly crowds her emotional landscape and social choices. She learns to connect with conflict through the discord of others, participating in group acts of aggression where individual ones have been forbidden.

In my conversations with girls, many expressed fear that even everyday acts of conflict would result in the loss of the people they most cared about. They believed speaking a troubled heart was punishable. Isolation, they cautioned, was irreversible, and so too great a price to be paid. As a sixth grader told me, "You don't want to say it to them and if you do, it's like, well, you might as well just walk off because they're not going to want to be your friend." Hannah, an

Arden seventh grader, explained, "If I tell my friends I'm angry at them, I'll have another enemy. It's a vicious cycle." In a world that socializes girls to prize relationships and care above all else, the fear of isolation and loss casts a long shadow over girls' decisions around conflicts, driving them away from direct confrontation. By taking uncomfortable feelings out of everyday relationships, girls come to understand them as dangerous to themselves and others, worthy of being carefully shielded or perhaps not disclosed at all.

Many girls are afraid of not being able to anticipate the response to their anger, so they resolve to maximize what they *can* control. One of the reasons girls like to write letters, an eighth grader told me, is that they "help us to organize our thoughts and get it out perfectly. If I say it to her face, I'm gonna break down, mess up my words, say things I don't mean." Some girls described writing letters that they burned or trashed in order to balance feeling angry and preserving friendship. Letters were preferable, eighth-grader Shelley said, "because if you have a conversation, they can see your face."

A one-on-one conversation is scary, an Arden seventh grader said, because "I don't know what she's going to say next. You don't want to lose the fight. You're scared the friendship's going to end. You don't know what they'll say. And if the discussion goes badly, she might get other people involved. That's why I don't talk." You can't just tell someone that they're being mean, her classmate told me. "You think, 'Oh my God,' [she'll] get mad at me, or [she] won't be my friend anymore. People are afraid she'll spread rumors. You don't know what that person's going to think."

The need to consider others' feelings at the expense of their own was a theme that ran through my interviews. No matter how upset they were, these girls said they would rather not hurt someone else's feelings. Their own needs seemed to them utterly expendable. They described shrinking problems and feelings into "little things," calling them "unimportant," "stupid," "not worth a fight," stowing them somewhere inside, an inner room that would one day be too small to contain them.

boom!

I went to Jennifer's house twice before she agreed to speak to me. The first time, I sat drinking tea with her mom, and the eleven-year-old girl's fuzzy slippers hung slightly over the cracked divide between the kitchen and the den. She was checking me out. The second time I visited, she nodded shyly. On the couch in the den, I was pleasantly surprised to find her animated as a dragonfly, hands streaking the air with energy. Rapid-fire, she said, "My friend and I always ask each other if we're mad at each other. Immediately after we go, 'No,' because you don't want to say, 'I'm mad at you.'"

"Why not?" I asked.

"Because then you make the other person feel bad because you know someone's mad at you."

"Is it important that you feel mad?"

"Yeah, but are you supposed to let it out at the person you're mad at?" she asked, as though she really did not know.

"Some people would say yes because your feelings count," I said.

"What about her feelings?" she asked.

"What about them?" I asked.

"I just...no. We don't talk about this. I don't know if best friends talk about this. This is private." I ceased and desisted.

With twelve-year-old Carmen Peralta, a wry Latina student at a private school in the Northeast, I was asking about what it's like to tell someone you're angry. She said she never did, and I asked why. "Because it sounds weird for one thing! 'Hey, by the way, I'm mad at you!'" she drawled sarcastically. Becoming more serious, she began to stall. "I won't say, 'I'm mad'—it just—I don't know—I don't like that way of dealing with things because it's weird—just to say, 'I'm

mad at you.'...It's kind of like *boom!*"—Carmen made a huge, sat-
isfying noise—"to them. They're just like, 'What did I do?' And if
you say, 'Hey, I need you to know I'm mad at you,' it's just like
boom! I think they'll end up thinking less of you." For Carmen, conflict falls like a bomb inside friendship, apparently blowing it to
smithereens. Conflict for Carmen is outside words, outside relationship, indeed seems to have no comfortable place anywhere in her life.

Some girls face conflict by appealing to lifelong lessons in being
nice. In Mississippi, ten-year-old Melanie was explaining to her classmates why she couldn't tell Kaya she was mad.

"You can't do that!" she cried.

"Why not?"

"Because some people are really sensitive in our school, and if you
said something like that, they'd bust out crying."

"But you'd be saying how you felt, right?" I was pushing for a
reason.

"But then you'd be hurting some people's feelings."

"But what if you're *reeeeeeallllly* upset?" I asked, and some girls
giggled.

"Sometimes you tell your friends but [sometimes you don't] tell
anybody," she decided. Anyway, she said, you'll probably get a
chance later to be mad at them. "You'll go up to somebody and say,
'Oh you know, Kaya gets on my nerves. She told me that so and so,
and so and so.'"

"But why don't you go up to Kaya and just say, 'Hey, you made
me mad!'"

"Because," she said simply, looking at me with cautious eyes,
"you want to get back at them."

For most girls, anger and hurt become the elephant in the room.
As the feelings grow in size and intensity, so does the challenge of
restraint.

Her best efforts notwithstanding, Meredith at Arden thinks it's
useless to hold in her anger. "When you don't let one of your friends

know, it builds up inside you. There's bitterness inside you. It's hard for them and for you." Charlotte agreed. "You can't make the feel- ings go away. If it's hidden it gets stronger and it gets harder and harder to hold in."

One student told me when she felt angry she kicked her dog. Plenty more said they hit their siblings. Some students I interviewed described feeling depressed as they tried to sequester their anger. Others told stories of escalating fury. "You get angrier and angrier when you can't hold it in. Then you explode," said Emily at Mary- mount. "It gets bigger and you find even more stuff to dislike about that girl." Disturbingly, the more intense the problem, the more likely a girl may pretend that everything's cool. Said Nancy at Mary- mount, "I was so angry I couldn't tell her about it. It was easier not to say anything and for her not to know I was so angry."

Fear of speaking face to face usually ends up worsening girls' con- flicts by forcing them to involve third parties. When Shelley couldn't get Sarah to talk directly about the problem between them, Shelley began asking others what was wrong with Sarah. But to the ignorant observer—say, Sarah—Shelley looked like she was going behind her back. Sarah was enraged. "But I'm getting advice!" Shelley ex- claimed, echoing innumerable girls I spoke with. A Mississippi fifth grader saw it as damage control: "If you tell the person you're angry at yourself, they're going to be madder quicker than if you tell some- one else. And then later you have time to think what you're going to say and what you're going to do." A sixth grader from the same school described it this way: "You're scared the person will take it the wrong way, so you try out different versions and opinions. Other- wise, you might get it wrong and make it worse." Unwittingly, they are doing just that.

Other girls believe anything is preferable to the loss of a relation- ship. In their minds, they are merely choosing a lesser evil. "Girls can break each other," Hannah said simply. "Instead, they cool off by gossiping behind their backs. Otherwise you could end the friend- ship." Some girls reported trying to circumvent the conflict process by expecting their friends simply to know, like mind-readers or super-heroes with X-ray vision, that they were upset. Linden sophomore Lily Carter, whose quiet thoughtfulness gave the impression of her being far older than she really was, laughed shyly as she handed me a tiny pink journal that she promised would detail the social chaos of her middle-school years. She had already flagged the pages with yellow post-it notes, and in the very first entry of seventh grade she wrote, "It's hard having my feelings bottled up inside. I'm a sensor. I sense things and give people hints to how I'm feeling." She later noted:

> It's strange kinda feeling that the people you've been friends with so long can't get the hints I give. You'd think they'd know. When I'm not with them, they NEVER ask if I'm mad at them or try to talk to me. They just ignore me, as if I don't exist or like "thank heavens she's gone." I'm MISIRABLE [sic]!

Like a boat adrift at sea, Lily was sending distress messages no one could hear. The more she used indecipherable speech and gesturing to communicate, the more alone and abandoned she felt.

When silent pleas are ignored, a girl's despair can turn swiftly to anger. Many girls reported feeling indignant because their friends didn't know how they felt. These girls felt it should be obvious from the clipped tone of their voices, the terseness of their notes, the nights they didn't call. Yet their friends never responded. And as the girls silently willed their friends to know their inner feelings, their rage doubled when their friends didn't.

not my fault

Why not just take the girl aside and tell her calmly, in a nice way, what's bothering you? It's a question countless parents, guidance counselors, and bullying experts have asked. So did I.

"I try that," a Linden ninth grader told me anxiously, "but she tells me something I did wrong and then it's my fault." It was a comment I would hear over and over again, from girls of all ages. "She'll turn it around," "she'll make it about me," or "she'll get everyone on her side." Because so many girls lack facility with everyday conflict, expressions of anger make listeners skittish and defensive. The sound of someone upset feels like the first sign of impending isolation, a kind of social thunder rumbling in the distance.

For these girls, absorbing anger is just as frightful as voicing it. The idea that they may be "at fault" or "wrong" makes them uneasy, and it can breed panic and impulsive decision making. In many cases, they grasp for whatever will move the harsh spotlight away from them and onto someone else; sometimes, using alliance building (explored later in the chapter), they grasp for the girl who will stand with them and assure them of continuous, unconditional friendship. Raised in a culture that prizes sweetness, what feels right to these girls is an anxious scramble to remain the "good" girl; to hold up a mirror to their friend and, instead of listening, point out a past infraction. Needless to say, such conflicts escalate swiftly, often leaving both girls filled with regret and fear.

i'm sorry

The surface of a girl fight can be silent and smooth as a marble. You know that if you've ever been the last person to find out someone's mad at you. Many girls use double doses of distance and silence to announce their anger, leaving defendants clueless about what they've done. Beneath the surface, of course, is another story.

Girls approach the rituals of fighting and peacemaking with an eerie rigidity. For many, the shared knowledge that they are "*in* a fight" is much easier than actually going to the trouble of having one. Freyda and Lissa's "fight" may entail passing each other in the hallway silently for days before anyone speaks. No matter that the source of their conflict is utterly trivial and that in the silence between them the conflict will swell, taking on a life of its own. As one girl waits for the other to give in and say she's sorry, both girls may lose track of why they are fighting at all. "When [girls are] angry, they won't listen, and if you don't talk, [girls will] build up with anger and then you won't remember why you're in a fight," explained a

Sackler sixth grader. "Sometimes it's over, but you have to keep going," an Arden sixth grader remarked. "You don't want to give up. You don't want to drop it. You don't want to be the loser."

When the fight is concluded, one girl has usually surrendered and apologized—via note, messenger, e-mail, instant message, or in person—while the other has "won." It is not uncommon for girls, especially preadolescents, to avoid processing what happened beyond the immediate apology and relief. Many sit on the sidelines of their own discord, skirting the substance of conflict and instead clinging to process—to the rituals of a fight's beginning, middle, and end. Lyn Mikel Brown and Carol Gilligan observed in girls an uncanny ability to say "I'm sorry" and give conflicts "almost fairy-tale-like happy endings, so that strong feelings of pain and indignation end abruptly with this final act of attrition."[18]

So the denouement is often as troubled as the fight itself. The prime directive for girls is to maintain the relationship at any cost; this, along with the accompanying fear of a lost relationship, is what drives almost every step of a fight. *Sorry* may be a universal code word for a truce, but it is often perfunctory and swift, casual and automatic, like saying "bless you" when someone sneezes. However it is delivered, via written, cyber, or human medium, sorry is a razor-sharp, clean slice through a fight, shutting it down as abruptly as pulling the plug on a blaring stereo. And because this perfunctory apology often comes when a fight has not yet played itself out, because it is driven more by the fear of a lost relationship than the need to clear the air, sorry is often a purely procedural event, calling for peace while the source of the conflict still festers, tucked away like a genie stuffed into a bottle, stewing unresolved until the next trigger comes.

One girl recalled her usual "make-up" line: "Let's just be friends. I can't understand why we got in such a stupid fight." Steering clear of the details, a sixth grader told me, avoids being brought too close to the precipice of her own anger. "Someone might say the wrong thing again," she explained. Others simply can no longer endure the isolation. "I didn't want her to stay mad at me," her classmate explained, "so I'd just say sorry." Anyway, another girl offered, if you wait it out, "your anger just melts away." A Ridgewood eighth grader said, "You forget about what you're mad about because you don't want to lose the friendship." Still another recalled an erstwhile friend who bullied her mercilessly, then approached her at school and inexplicably apologized. "It just happened," she said. "Sorry."

Carmen Peralta said being direct with friends doesn't work for her, since everyone she knows gives knee-jerk apologies instead of really talking about their feelings. "When a person tells you [she's angry], it makes you feel like you're going to say sorry automatically—automatically, not thinking. But if you don't say, 'I'm mad at you,'" she said, and instead speak without words, forcing the person to wonder why you are acting strangely around her, "the person will actually think about what [she's] doing wrong."

Sometimes Carmen does apologize, but she can't stand it that she's always the one to say it first. "Sometimes when I say, 'I'm sorry,' [it's because] I just feel more guilty [not because I] understand what the person's saying. I just figure, 'What the hell, I'll say I'm sorry and make it all better.' I don't think that does make it all better," she added, shrugging, "because I'll probably still act the way that's annoying the person."

Under these social conditions, a cycle gets put into motion. Old conflicts are printed indelibly into memories and, unresolved, are summoned for use in the next conflict. One of the most common grievances I heard from girls was: "We remember everything. We never forget." One girl explained why: "Boys duke it out. Girls, they don't finish [the fight]. It grows bigger. And there's another fight and the next one's huge. That's what leads to people not being friends anymore." A Sackler sixth grader said, "You go back to these teeny tiny things that you didn't talk about before. Then it gets bigger." Lisa, at Arden, said, "Girls always look back at what you did the last time."

just kidding

Girls who want to bypass conflict entirely may turn to other behavioral pathways. Humor is an especially popular way to injure a peer indirectly. Joking weaves a membrane of protection around the perpetrator as she jabs at a target. A sixth grader described a classmate who easily got away with teasing. "She'd say something, the teacher would kind of look, and she's like, 'I was just kidding!'" At Linden, students talked about the moment in which teasing crosses over into insult. "Slut is the worst insult," said Erica. "Ho is said easily. Like, 'That's such a ho outfit.'" When the jostling goes into shaky territory, someone quickly exclaims, "We were just kidding!"

Rarely, if ever, does the targeted girl disagree. The fear of being called hypersensitive—*Can't you take a joke?*—is enormous. Nobody wants to hang out with someone like that, and everyone knows it. "What's the big deal?" can sting when you're trying to act cool. "When a girl is the butt of all jokes, she wants to tell her friends it hurts her," sixteen-year-old Ellie said. "She thinks, 'I know they're not doing it to hurt me.' And they deny it. But it beats at your self-esteem."

The feeling of being crazy plagues the target of these "jokes," as she must choose between the sting of her own feelings and what she wants to believe about her friends. Believing a friend while ignoring the hum of her own instinct is an important example of how a girl can "give up or give over [her] version of reality to those who have the power to name or reconfigure [her] experience," a major symptom of girls' loss of self-esteem observed by Brown and Gilligan.[19]

Fear of reprisal is not the only deterrent to speaking up. Tasha Keller had just gotten her learner's permit, and she was scarfing down a bagel at a deli as we talked about how she responds when girls use jokes to cover their true feelings.

"In the end you see how foolish it is to get upset," she said, her words muffled with chewing.

"Even though someone's being nasty?" I asked.

"If someone's joking around, you're not supposed to think it's such a big thing."

"Even if someone hurts your feelings?"

"If someone told you something that hurt your feelings, would you think that's worse than being beaten up? The bigger thing would have been if someone's beating you up at school. That's what you think of a bully as." She was practically lecturing me now. "You don't think of it as someone who's..." She paused, searching to describe the phenomenon that has for so long remained unnamed— "*nicely abusing* you also."

Some mainstream psychologists view the ritual of comic or casual peer insults as formative to child development. University of California at Berkeley professor Dacher Keltner argues that "teasers convey that they are joking through laughter, knowing looks and nudges, and tone of voice."[20] Here girls' social world is again seen through a male lens. With access to a much wider range of opportunities for direct aggression, boys' use of humorous one-upping can be clearly distinguished from "real" or serious moments of anger. For girls, whose aggressions are frequently conveyed in body language, and who mostly share in common the need to sequester anger, the use of humor serves a different purpose. "A lot of times," thirteen-year-old Jasmine told me, "what you say when you're joking is really what you mean but you're too afraid to say it." And, she added, "humor doesn't work unless both people know it's true."

ganging up

"It's weird how time erases things," muses the once-popular, now-outcast Julie in the film *Jawbreaker*.

"Time doesn't erase things," replies the once-outcast, now-popular Fern. "People erase things."

"People erase people." Julie sighs.

Nothing launches a girl faster, or takes her down harder, than alliance building, or "ganging up." The ultimate relational aggression, alliance building forces the victim to face not only the potential loss of the relationship with her opponent, but with many of her friends. It goes like this: Spotting a conflict on the horizon, a girl will begin a scrupulous underground campaign to best her opponent. Like a skilled politician, she will methodically build a coalition of other girls willing to throw their support behind her. Friends who have "endorsed" her will ignore the target, lobby others for support, or confront the target directly until she is partly or completely isolated. "You kind of declare war in your own way," explained Daniella, a sixth grader.

Ganging up is the product of a secret relational ecosystem that flourishes in an atmosphere where direct conflict between individuals is forbidden. By engaging in conflict as a group, no one girl is ever directly responsible for her aggression. Anger is often conveyed wordlessly, and the facade of the group functions as an eave under which a girl can preserve her "nice girl" image. The loser usually ends up isolated from others, giving her exactly what she fears conflict begets: relational loss. The specter of isolation is often enough to make most people "forget" their angry feelings.

Girls use alliance building to short-circuit the link expected between anger and the loss of relationship. Victoria, interviewed by Brown and Gilligan, explains that when people get mad it helps to "pass [their feelings] on to someone else and it will keep on going around so everyone can pick corners." Kenya, a Ridgewood sixth grader, explained, "They are mad at their friend, and their friend's mad at them, and they need to go find another friend and get to know them better and tell them about their problem, and maybe that will help another friendship to start." In this way, alliance building becomes an event of friendship. It provides a way for girls to displace their aggression while remaining connected to others. No matter how intense the fight, a girl is assured of a friendship that will outlast it; the girls who rally to her side promise her that with their presence. In this way, the trials of conflict are transformed into a series of relationships to be negotiated, a skill at which girls excel.

Nikki, an eighth grader from Marymount, described how it works: "If I'm mad at someone, it's just a lot easier to tell everyone else and turn them against the person because then I'm the one who's right. If you just tell the person, one-on-one, then the two of you are out there to be judged by the whole grade, and you can't know if you are going to be the one who's considered right by the others."

During alliance building, discussions spread like wildfire through circles of friends, growing in intensity until they dominate the day. "First people tell each other; then they use the phone, then the Internet; it gets bigger and bigger; they cut and paste conversations [from instant messages]," recalled thirteen-year-old Rebecca at Marymount. One girl wins, her classmate Maria noted, when she "gets people not to like the other one."

Another girl described it this way: "I think it was mostly just like, nobody can get mad at me for something. I was the good friend. I wasn't the problem. I am like best friends with all of these people now that I didn't used to be friends with. I have everything that she thought she had. It was just like a sense of empowerment."

Alliance building also conforms to girls' tendency to stockpile old conflicts. The perpetrator's strategy is to appeal to those who have a history with the target. Particularly where girls have known each other for many years, the perpetrator can plumb a rich history of relational trouble.

Alliance building was in full swing among the Mississippi fifth graders. Danika explained, "Girls try to get information from you about your other friend, [who] is their enemy. Such as, do you like so and so?" I asked how it works.

"They take [the information] from you and say, 'Thank you.' Then you say you have to be right back, that you're going to see somebody, and you go tell [your friend]. It's just like collecting information from the enemy." The potential foot soldiers have usually been waiting for the right opportunity. Beccy explained, "One person can have a problem, talk to one person, and she's got something she remembers from last week."

This is classic indirection, since it allows girls to hold the conflict at arm's length as they watch others fight it. Girls have multiple incentives to become embroiled in each others' conflicts. First, alliance building offers a chance for girls to belong, even briefly, to an ad hoc clique. Jumping on another girl's bandwagon to show support in her time of conflict affords a rare moment of inclusion and comfort. Nikki remarked, "People don't know what we're fighting about, but they want to be in it. They want to be part of the gossip." Said her classmate Mallory, "It gives you something to belong to, and inclusion is such a big deal." Since the girl coordinating the alliance is usually vulnerable, stepping in with support is an opportunity to be a friend while racking up a future favor for when your turn inevitably rolls around. Needless to say, effective foot soldiers can take leaps up the social ladder. "If you take sides," Rachel explained, "you can become popular through them and be their friend."

Indeed, popularity itself is in large part defined by the ability of one girl to turn her friends against someone else. If isolation is trauma for girls, there is power to be found in relationships. Having girls on her side offers a girl a sense of personal strength. "It makes you feel more popular and like you have more power. You're in the right," explained Lauren at Marymount. Said eleven-year-old Mary at Arden, "It gives you a feeling of security. If you know people are gathering on your side, you think, 'Wow I am powerful. I have a feeling of power.'"

Alliance building is a sign of peer affirmation, an unspoken contract that means, for the moment anyway, that a girl will not be abandoned. If she can turn everyone against a target, it is impossible for them to turn against her. "It's a way of getting people to say you're cool and strong," Dana noted.

So ingrained is alliance building in girls' lives that many I spoke with struggled to imagine life without it. "You don't do it on purpose," said Lauren, shrugging. "It's your natural instinct. I tell other people and try to make myself look good."

"When you can't tell anyone, you feel helpless," explained Dana. "You don't know who to go to. It builds up."

Of course, there are troubling social and individual costs to this activity. Lauren described how to attract more supporters when the marrow of a conflict thins: "You bring other stuff into it. 'Oh, do you see what she's wearing.'" And sometimes, invariably, "you exaggerate and don't tell the whole truth." She explained, "When more people get involved, there's a lot more pressure to win." In this way, alliance building encourages other alternative aggressions, including rumor spreading and secret telling. Alliance building can distort the conflicts, and it makes fights last longer than they would have if they had been played out directly.

For the victim, the mass shutting down of one by many has consequences that reach far beyond the moment. "It's like your life is a pond," a seventh grader told me, "and a girl throws a stone inside it, and the ripples mess up your life." If fights are ultimately a contest of relationships, the facts of the conflict are easily dwarfed by the alliances forming around them. As a result, girls are often forced to question their own version of events, feeling crazy once again. "When I'm in fights with people, they turn it against me," said Cari at Marymount. "They say it's my fault. Everyone will say you have no right to be angry. They make you think you're crazy." By lobbing the conflict out to others to judge and decide, said her classmate Courtney, "You can never win. The entire grade takes sides."

When fights cannot be enacted and concluded directly, girls learn it may be easier to stay silent. Noura, interviewed by Brown and Gilligan, described a typical episode of gossip, explaining that if she disagreed with someone's perception, "that person would get mad . . . and so sometimes I just don't know what to say, and it's hard to say something." Gradually, like a circus leaving town, the lights go out of the voices, opinions, and feelings of these girls.

Most fascinating about the ritual of alliance building is how it validates the experience of aggression for girls. Girls understand that face-to-face, one-on-one aggression with another girl is unacceptable. "If you have no sympathizers, you're the bad one. You're randomly mean," says Courtney. Megan, who lost the support of her peers in a campaign against Melissa, concluded that she "felt foolish being mean to someone without my friends."

Together, however, it's another story. A plurality creates a safe space for girls to be mean in a culture that refuses to allow girls individual acts of aggression, making alliance building a rare intersection of peer approval with aggression. Alliances create underground networks in which girls can be in charge of their own social norms, deciding together when the use of aggression is deserved.

A Sackler sixth grader explained alliance building as a way to circumvent punishment. "You don't want to be blamed for it, and so you blame it on other people, saying 'Pass it on.'" Aggressive boys may be just as likely to seek refuge from punishment or guilt in a gang. The different rules of the aggression game, however, make it likely that angry girls will seek and need company. A study confirmed that the guilt girls experience during aggressive acts decreases significantly when responsibility can be shared with other people.[21]

middlegirls

Even if a girl manages to avoid being on either end of a conflict, she may end up stuck in the middle of it, a position just as perilous. When it's clear girls have no choice but to be drawn into conflict, many adapt by resorting to a skill they know well, one they have long observed in the adult women around them. Over the treachery of taking a side, they choose to be mediators, or what I call "middlegirls."

When a girl's friends are the two people fighting, being in the middle is often the riskiest place. With both girls lobbying for a friend's support, both friendships can become endangered, or destroyed. Julia from Arden explained, "If you have two best friends, you feel you have to pick sides. [But] if you pick one side, the other girl starts whispering. You feel defeated and you want to give up. You become the one at fault." What's more, suballiances can develop, increasing pressure on a girl in the middle to act. "Then there are so many people against you," Stacy said, "and you just get defeated and stop."

Since girls often refuse to talk to one another when they're mad, middlegirls are critical players in the conflict process. By the time a middlegirl enters the lives of girls in conflict, the foes are usually running scared. The middlegirl's prime directive is to broker a compro-

mise between the rival parties. By acting as an affectionate diplomat
of sorts, she effectively rescues both girls from their isolation.

But the consequences for the middlegirl can be mixed. For instance, in the course of her diplomacy, the middlegirl learns she will
be valued when she maintains the health of others' relationships, a
skill prized in the feminine character. "I feel really good about myself
when I can get my friends to sit down and talk," an eleven-year-old
told me.

The warring girls face equally uncertain outcomes. A middlegirl holds their social future in her hands, and she knows it. She can
just as soon gut a friendship as she can stitch it back together. A
middlegirl may have her own agenda with one of the girls. Perhaps,
as one sixth grader told me, she will lie to avoid being caught in
a crossfire that is getting dangerously close. In that case, she said,
"[you] would be afraid that the person would start telling rumors
about you and then telling lies and then they won't be your friend
anymore."

In Mississippi, I was sitting with seventh graders talking about alliance building.

"Why do lots of girls get involved in a person's fight?" I asked.

"She gets to watch it," Beth said.

"They'll be able to go tell other people what happened. 'Oh I
know what happened!'" Andra sneered.

"You might want to be somebody's best friend so you make the
fight worse than it is," Angela added.

"Sometimes people change things and make someone even madder," Beth said.

"Why," I asked, "would someone want to do that?"

"Because they don't really like that person or anything."

"—because you want to make them fight."

"And the person in the middle can add to the rumors."

"What does she stand to gain?" I asked.

"The messenger might have added or changed the story because
one of the girls had made her mad before," Beth continued. "She

had done something to her but she was waiting for a chance to get her back."

Forced to prioritize others' relationships at the expense of their own, middlegirls can quickly become part of the conflict itself. A sixth grader at Arden described her often futile attempts to bring girls together. "No matter how much I try to help, they ended up getting mad at me anyway. The way they made peace is over being mad at me." A classmate of hers got burned by choosing not to take sides. "They both got mad when I was with the other one." A fifth grader at a private religious school wrote simply, "I got into a fight talking about a fight." The words of a classmate were telling in describing her social problems that year: "I had a fight *between* Adelia and Marina" (my italics).

Rebecca, a sixth grader at the religious school, explained it this way: "I think of it as a Ping-Pong game. A championship. And like, you're gonna win. And the middlegirl is the ball, and one friend's on one side and one friend's on the other. And you want to keep on bouncing back and forth because you don't want to stop on one side or the other but eventually you have to land somewhere."

The increasing importance of the middlegirl is a result of a social community in which open conflict is feared and forbidden. The middlegirl helps filter and tamp down the anger that would otherwise flow freely between girls. She is a human tool girls use to avoid the possibility that they will say something the wrong way, or speak words they don't mean. As an Arden seventh grader put it, "When two of my friends were in a huge fight, it had become necessary that I was there. It was about me, too. They needed me to control themselves." Girls in conflict use middlegirls to fence in their own anger, helping them to stay "nice" at the moments that most challenge their feminine identities.

The middlegirl role has built itself not only into the structure of girls' conflicts but into their friendships. One researcher found that the failure of a girl to mediate conflict among her friends was actually perceived by her peers as overtly aggressive behavior.[22] Like girls who take sides, middlegirls who step in to help someone out in their time of need are met with the sort of gratitude and affection that thrives in situations where one person has a disproportionate amount of power. "Sometimes," a Sackler sixth grader told me, "there could be a fight with a popular girl. And the only reason you're helping her is because she's using you and you think that's so cool. The middlegirl is really thinking it's good for her."

The phenomenon of alliance building evokes the image of a daily relational minefield for girls. Each and every day presents the possibility of a relationship's endangerment. Friendships must be consistently charted, tallied, and negotiated. In waging these underground campaigns, the features of friendship become corrupted.

In 2000, UCLA researchers identified sex differences in the human response to immediate danger. Where males opted for "fight or flight," females would "tend and befriend," often nurturing or seeking the support of others rather than attempting to aggress or escape. The study, which exposed the troubling bias of research toward male subjects and the "fight or flight" response, showed that in stressful situations, females often seek company.[23] The findings suggest that girls' tendency to seek group comfort when threatened is a historic phenomenon, the study of which may yield more information on female aggression.

cliques

In 2000, the television show *Survivor* gripped America with a contest of sixteen "real" people vying to be the last one standing on a precarious deserted island. At the end of each weekly episode, viewers watched the disturbing spectacle of once-chummy Survivors coldly voting one of their own off the island. Every week, fans waited eagerly to see who would be next.

With just three contestants remaining, Kelly, long predicted the winner, was voted off. But it wasn't her surprise loss that made headlines that week. It was a breathtakingly cruel farewell from her fellow player, Sue. Calmly, before a spellbound audience of 55 million, Sue warned, "If I was ever to pass you along in life again and you were laying there dying of thirst, I would not give you a drink of water. I would let the vultures take you and do whatever they want with you, with no ill regrets." Mouths fell open across the nation.

Survivor's rite of expulsion resembles a disturbing ritual in cliques of girls. With little or no warning a clique will rise up and cut down one of its own. For the targeted girl, the sheer force of this unexpected expulsion can be startling, unpredictable, and even devastating.

In clique expulsions, punishments range from pretending the girl never existed to embarking on campaigns of scorching cruelty. These expulsions may seem sudden, arbitrary, and just plain mean. Bystanders may well wonder how a group could turn against one of their own with such intensity. Yet if we listen to the voices of girls, it does not take long to understand the intensity. Their anger is explained not by a root evil churning deep in their hearts, a pathetically common explanation, but rather by the imperative to above all be nice. Because these girls lack the tools to deal with everyday feelings of anger, hurt, betrayal, and jealousy, their feelings stew and fester before boiling to the surface and unleashing torrents of rage.

ERIN AND MICHELLE:
TWO FACES IN THE MIRROR?

Dr. Diane Harrigan remembers the day she ran into a teacher at her daughter's school. As she escorted Erin to class late in the day—it was a victory when her daughter could muster the strength to come to school at all—the unfamiliar woman stopped and touched her hand lightly to Diane's shoulder. "I just want you to know," she said quietly, "I know what you're going through." The teacher's own daughter, now thirty, was so shaken by being suddenly abandoned by her best friends as a teen that when she unexpectedly spied the ringleader at a bookstore recently, she'd had to leave. "It's still hard," the woman said. Diane felt tears start. "I know," she replied.

"She was the only person that really got it in the whole school," Diane told me. A clinical psychologist, Diane was the first parent to call me after the letters about my research went out to her daughter's class. Her daughter Erin had been the target of a clique expulsion and was still suffering the consequences.

Michelle was angry. She'd been assigned to buddy the new girl, Erin Harrigan, the summer before fifth grade. After talking on the phone and instant messaging, Michelle thought that Erin seemed really nice. But the first week of class, Erin sailed around like she was the most popular girl in the grade, like she always had been. She marched right up to the cool clique at lunch, sparkling with self-assurance and grace. Michelle said hi to her in the hallway, and she was pretty sure Erin didn't say hi back. Now they were going to be in a fight.

As groups became more defined in fifth and sixth grade, Michelle wasn't sure where she fit in. Sometimes the social tide brought her closer to the cool girls, and other times she drifted into the faceless sea of regular kids. She watched Erin beat out Kelly as most popular girl in sixth grade, become best friends with Nicole and exclude Kelly, and attract the hottest guys. She felt the constant rub of anger. Erin was confident and boy crazy, and she knew it.

When Nicole moved away the summer after sixth grade, Erin sent Michelle an instant message. It was good timing. Michelle had been getting annoyed with her friends, and Erin was a welcome change. Michelle's bitterness was quickly swallowed as her new friendship swept her into the popular group. Erin's friendship was intoxicating, the transformation quick and clean. Suddenly, Michelle was cool.

Three years later, fifteen-year-old Michelle and I were talking over cups of tea at a café near her school. "Erin's the kind of person so that when you're first friends with her, it's like a drug almost," she said. "She just seems like such a good friend. She's so nice and fun, not to mention the fact that she's really popular, and you're like, why is she friends with me? She says everything that you want her to say and she acts like she's such a good friend and acts like you're the best thing ever to happen to her, and you're kind of excited because you're like insecure and you're her everything. That's what people generally want to be. They want to be important to somebody else." Reveling in her proximity to Erin, Michelle enjoyed the rush she felt at being at the center of everything exciting.

The girls' friendship soon seemed fated: they had all their seventh-grade classes together. Michelle spent less and less time with her other friends. Then, after the first science quiz came back, Michelle felt an unfamiliar pang of something—was it panic?—when Erin scored six points higher. She noticed Erin's frustration when the tables turned in class, and soon, secret over-the-shoulder glances exploded into full-blown competition. "She'd do well on a test, and I'd get really mad, or if I did better than she did, she'd get really mad," Michelle explained. Michelle worked so hard to beat Erin that she got straight A's, and "Every time she got a bad grade I was *so* happy," she said.

The girls remained best friends, even as Michelle felt unease watching her old friends drift out toward the periphery of their crowd. That spring, on the bus, Michelle told Erin she secretly liked Luke, a guy in their grade. The next day at lunch, Erin announced, "Well, you know, I like Luke, too." Michelle was surprised, then angry, but she found herself unable to say anything to her friend.

The next night, Erin asked Luke out.

"Once she found out [that I liked him], she decided that *she* did. And she could have him because he had always kind of liked her. She asked him out," Michelle said, still incredulous, "and he said yes. I was like, 'Whatever, I don't really care, I'm not going to get in the middle of this.' But," she added, "obviously it bothered me."

Still, Michelle held her tongue. The next day, simmering, Michelle made Erin give her back a bracelet she had borrowed, just as Erin was putting it on. Erin was silent. She glared. Michelle felt a cold shock of fear ricochet through her. "She was the scariest person to have mad at you," Michelle explained. "I really didn't want her to be mad at me." To smooth things over, she asked what was wrong, and

Erin snapped that she was sick of Michelle's bad attitude. Michelle told her softly, "I'm sorry. I don't want to be in a fight."

The girls' later conflicts would resemble this first one, and as Michelle pushed down with all her might on her own anger, the girls fought more and more. As before, Michelle explained, "If you were mad at her about something, she would turn it around so that it was your fault. It would always be my fault, my fault, my fault."

"I always thought of it as like a dictatorship," she continued. "Kind of like where she has total control. If you say anything different, then you're wrong and she's right. *She* doesn't do anything wrong—it's all you."

Michelle refused to tell Erin how she felt. "No!" she exclaimed. "Because I couldn't say it. I was afraid to say anything." She told Erin she thought they shouldn't be exclusive with each other, which allowed her some distance without as many fights. As Michelle grew closer with girls in another group, the one Erin didn't rule, Erin became fast friends with Jessica, another eighth grader. It made Michelle angry, despite her relief that she was finally away from Erin.

Hanging out with new girls in eighth grade, away from the hypnotic pull of Erin, Michelle quickly discovered many of them thought Erin was a bitch. Kelly was angry because her ex-boyfriend Denis broke up with her for Erin; she had also not forgotten losing the popularity contest three years earlier. Mira was stewing, too. She had been best friends with Jessica when Erin had cast her spell. Now, watching Jessica and Erin at lunch, she was alone.

As Michelle grew even closer with the other girls, she realized that she just didn't need Erin anymore. The girl was always thinking about herself. "She'll just be sitting here and everybody'll be getting ready and she'll be like, 'How do I look, you guys? Does this look okay?' Everything's about herself." If Michelle got a new purse, Erin would show off hers. "She has this egotistical thing," Michelle explained.

So one day, when Erin called to borrow history notes, Michelle found it almost easy to refuse and hang up abruptly. Erin called back "thirty times," but Michelle let the calls go. Although she didn't need Erin, she was still unwilling to fight her. The specter of their past conflicts still haunted Michelle. "She would have turned it on me. She would have made me upset!" she predicted. "She would have told me I was a bad friend. Everything would be my fault and I didn't want to give up because it wasn't my fault!"

In the meantime, Ashley had begun dating Luke, who still pined for Erin. One day, when Erin was over at his house, Luke kissed her. Erin says she stopped it, but a week later it happened again. Luke told Kelly. Erin told Jessica. As it turned out, Jessica had been nursing a long crush on Luke, and her adoration for Erin began to falter. But like Michelle, Jessica feared saying anything to upset her status as "Erin's everything."

The next weekend, after Erin scored the winning goal in the field hockey finals, Kelly watched Ashley hug her and noted their increasing closeness. That night, Kelly slept over at Ashley's house with Michelle, and everything changed forever.

"Ashley," Kelly said somberly. "I just have to tell you."

"What?" Ashley asked, leaning forward.

"Erin hooked up with Luke twice while you were going out."

Ashley's face twitched in shock and she began to cry. Then she started throwing things. "That bitch!" she yelled.

"This is *so* it," Kelly said quickly. "We're not talking to her anymore."

"This is *such* bullshit!" screamed Ashley.

"Forget it," Kelly said. "Let me handle this." She picked up the phone and called Erin. "Hi," she said. "You know what? Luke told me about you guys, and Ashley saw the e-mail. She knows everything. Okay? Sorry. I have to go. 'Kay . . . bye." She hung up and smiled. "She's *really* upset," she said. The phone rang, piercing the silence.

"Don't get it!" Ashley snapped.

"Don't worry," replied Kelly.

Finally, a reason to be angry. It was, Michelle added, "a reason Erin couldn't defend." And, she said, "Once one person got mad, it was kind of like everybody did." The next day, Erin called Michelle, who said she couldn't talk and hastily hung up the phone. Then Michelle called Jessica.

Jessica was just leaving. "And I said, 'Jessica, how do you feel that Erin did that to you?'" Jessica said she didn't know. "I said, 'Jessica, I'm not going to tell anybody anything you say, I just want you to tell me, do you ever feel like you're afraid to get mad at her and you're afraid to talk to her?'" Michelle described her own feelings of fear.

"That's *exactly* how I feel!" Jessica cried. She had, Michelle believed, "come to some sort of realization on the phone." Then Jessica stopped taking Erin's calls.

From then on, Michelle explained, "it was kind of like we had to go around convincing people, saying you don't have to be afraid of her, you know? You don't." When the girls arrived at school on Monday, everyone ignored Erin.

"We're all sitting together—*beaming!*—because we're so happy we don't have to have that kind of relationship [with Erin] anymore." Then Erin walked into class, wiping away tears as she sat next to a girl, Michelle recalled, "who she may have talked to once, who was kind of insecure, who was kind of overweight, and all of a sudden she became her friend, because she needed to have someone to sit with." The girls watched Erin spend lunch with people who had always wanted to be her friend, but whom Erin had talked about behind their backs. The sight of Erin eluding the isolation they had used to punish her enraged them. That, Michelle said, "is when it really started."

Kelly would just laugh at Erin when she walked by. "It was because of Denis," Michelle explained, "because of when Erin and Nicole had excluded [Kelly], and I mean—we were like sticking together." The group became especially tight in Erin's absence. "We got so close and would always be like standing together in the hall, sharing our Erin stories. 'She asked me for this, and I was just like *no!*' and it felt soooo good because we could finally—like—be—people."

The girls flooded Erin's e-mail account with angry messages. It seemed that everyone was in on it; even students who had no connection to the incident were volunteering reasons for shunning Erin.

Some called her a bitch. Ashley wrote that it made her sick to look at Erin.

At what point, I asked Michelle, were people planning on talking with Erin, even forgiving her and moving on?

"Oh, *no!*" Michelle said, surprised. "Nobody wanted to be friends with her anymore. They just wanted to see her suffer like she had done to everyone else."

But let's assume, I said, that Erin would do anything to be forgiven, that she'd promise to be a better friend.

"We *knew* her. We knew that she wasn't going to be. We were all sick of it and we just wanted to get away from it."

"What would you have rather happened?" I asked.

"Well, she was suffering, but she was getting friends. We wanted her to see what it was like. I mean, subconsciously, we wanted her to see what it was like to not have anybody there, because she needed to."

Every day the girls tallied their sightings of Erin's anguish. They shot her dirty looks when she passed by. "We were like, 'This is brilliant.' We'd just be so happy. Everyone was so happy that it was finally being taken care of."

"That was the end of it," Erin said, "and they were my world! They were my everything! I didn't care about my family; I didn't care about anyone else but that one group of people. Oh my God."

We were sitting on Erin's bed talking, and I had promised we would be done in time to watch *Dawson's Creek.*

"They *loved* to see me cry," she recalled. The girls would stand in a circle a few feet from Erin's locker. "Today is going to be *so* much fun!" they'd crow, casting sidelong glances at Erin. "They would just talk to each other right in front of my face and they wouldn't look at me. They'd be like, 'Come to the bathroom with me?' and I'd walk by in tears."

When Erin went home, her parents didn't understand. "I would

come home and scream, *'Get away!'* I was like, my life is over. My life
is over."

Erin had no idea what was going on. She knew she had screwed
up, but she didn't understand why everyone was involved. The confusion spun her downward as her grades went from straight A's to
straight C's. She'd never needed help with homework, and now her
mother had to sit with her every night and pull the essays out of her.
"I could not do anything," Erin said. "I lost all my confidence. They
totally ripped me down to nothing. They told me how horrible a
person I was. So I was just nothing anymore. I just remember telling
myself, 'A month ago you were so happy.'"

Bewildered at the sheer intensity of her friends' anger, Erin became despondent. The light went out of her. "I wasn't anything anymore because they had made me who I was, so I didn't even know
who I was. I was always depressed."

The hardest moments for Erin were when she saw all of them together, without her. It felt as though she had died and was now a
ghost. "I wasn't there. There was no Erin anymore."

The girls broke into her e-mail account and changed her password
to "Slut." Luke broke in and deleted his love letters so he wouldn't
look responsible for their kiss. Not that anyone had blamed him to
begin with.

Erin's mother was frantic. The more Erin stayed out of school, "the
more she fell apart." Erin was lethargic and depressed. Like a top
ceasing to spin, Erin simply stopped doing everything. "She seemed
very childlike again. She sort of crumbled in our arms." Diane remembers pleading with her to come to school, coaxing her with anything that came to mind to get her to school before noon.

By the time they got there, even Diane was filled with dread. "Here
were these kids who had spent the night at our house, who had eaten
at our house—whatever—and they would act like I wasn't there. It
was just so"—she inhaled sharply—"so aggressive! I couldn't understand how they could be so rude to another adult. They were so

defiant, so hostile, the look in their eyes was just—I was really—" Her voice broke. "We were devastated for her."

Diane watched as her daughter wept uncontrollably every night. The days Diane couldn't arrive early to be in the car-pool lane when the last bell rang, she'd find Erin alone on the curb, her shadow almost touching her friends', who stood chatting close by. In the car, Erin would dissolve into tears. Embarrassed, she refused to tell her mother what happened with Luke. Diane found a psychotherapist she prayed Erin would confide in and began sending Erin every week.

"Erin tried to talk to us," Michelle said. "She's the kind of person that no matter how upset she is, she loves herself too much to hurt herself. Everybody knows that about her. She wrote Jessica these e-mails that were like little poems: 'I have no one. I have no life anymore. I lost you.'" Michelle sounded confused. "Like all these random, random things so you're like *what* is she doing? And we'd see them and we'd be like, that is *so* funny and we'd like forward them to each other."

When Erin told a male friend that she wanted to kill herself, he became alarmed and told the other girls. They laughed it off. "She was like, 'I don't want to live anymore!'" Michelle said. "She was doing it all for attention. We knew she wasn't going to."

One day, as Michelle and Ashley were shelving their trays in the cafeteria, Erin approached. She took a deep breath.

"I am really, really sorry about what happened with Luke. Please forgive me."

Michelle shrugged. "That's not what it was about. It was about the kind of friend you were to everybody." They walked off.

By then, there was no going back. "She was such a bad friend, but I didn't know it," Michelle told me, then paused. "She's like *evil*!"

Diane went to the guidance counselor almost every day. "They kept telling me, 'It's going to pass, it's going to pass, believe us, it's going to pass.'" It was only when a boy sent Erin an e-mail that began with "You disgusting whore" that the school called a meeting to set limits on student e-mail. Diane watched helplessly as her daughter took to bed, claiming headaches, crying at night that she wanted to die.

In May, at eighth-grade graduation, Erin stood alone with her family. Her friends linked arms and skipped away, mortarboards and gowns trailing like streamers, to parties that would last all night. "We left," Diane said. "I was crying. I had tears streaming down my face. It was so painful." In the parking lot, a mother approached Diane. The woman had commented to Ashley's mother about how hard this must be for Erin. "That girl got everything she deserved," Ashley's mother had replied.

Diane knew she was missing a huge piece of what had happened, but despite her tearful entreaties, Erin stayed quiet. That summer, Diane sent Erin to visit her family in California. On sleepaway camp buses, at friends' houses, even in kindergarten, Erin had been the intrepid girl who never looked back, not even to wave good-bye. In Santa Monica she disintegrated, calling her parents sobbing in the middle of the night, unable to sleep, hyperventilating with anxiety.

At some point over the summer, Michelle relented. "Part of me missed her, part of me felt bad, and part of me just like wanted to be a good person and talk to her." At Ashley's house one day, Michelle called Erin to ask for some money Erin had owed her for a long time. Michelle knew she was looking for a reason to call her, plus Ashley had wanted some shorts she had lent her, and Jessica wanted to say hi, too. The conversation was "nice." But there wasn't much to say.

Right before school started, Michelle was ready to start over, though she feared breaking the group's official silence. "I was like, 'Okay, it's a new year. I can let myself do this. I don't have to be worried about what my friends are going to say.'" Besides, she'd been having trouble with some of the other girls, and as it had been in seventh grade, Erin offered a willing ear.

Together, the two girls felt at once new and old, comfortable and tense. But by then Erin had made other friends, making Michelle's friendship with her too difficult to sustain. Michelle feared "getting sucked in" to the old dynamics that irked her before. Nowadays, Erin is "just another person we walk by in the hall." Reflecting about what happened at the end of eighth grade, Michelle said, "I was feeling kind of bad, like maybe we should have gone about it a different way. . . . It was just a big part of all of our lives. It was probably something that needed to happen." Anyway, Michelle told me, Erin hadn't really changed. Everyone agreed about that. Which made Michelle feel okay about where things were in the end.

In her mind, Erin felt she'd changed completely. "I'm such a scared person now," she told me. "I'm always worried about what people think about me. I'm always worried about what people are going to say about me behind my back. I never used to care! Because people talked about me all the time, and I just didn't care. I'm always worried about why people hate me," she said. "They made me like this now."

Trusting her new friends is daily work. "I'm better about it, but I still become a wreck just because I'm scared that it will happen again, or I'll be a bad friend."

Erin spent ninth grade narrowly avoiding being asked to leave her school. Her academic performance continued to falter, and she was tortured by anxiety, finding normally easy assignments overwhelming. She remained in intensive therapy and was diagnosed with anxiety and depression. Fearing a recurrence of her peers' anger, she refused to let them see her appear weak. "I was trying to prove to them I could be okay. I was like, no, I'm going to have just as much fun." So she hung out with seniors, got invited to parties, and managed to appear as cool as she had been. Unfortunately, school administrators found it hard to believe she was as depressed and anxious as her parents claimed.

Erin grew close with Kim again, and she began to feel confused
as the friendship offered her a second glimpse inside her old clique.
She missed them, and apparently, they'd missed her. "How come I
still get upset and miss stuff from before?" she asked me. "It's bad
because I should know. I'm like, 'Why am I still friends with you?
After everything you've done,'" she said. "I'm a completely different
person."

The most marked change in her, she told me, is the way she approaches her friends. Before, when she was popular, she'd felt the
need to be perfect, to perform in a particular way for others. Now,
she can see how the strategy backfired.

"I think that being perfect was [my] way. You have to go up [in
status]. You don't even look. Your peripheral vision is—you don't
even care about the people next to you because you have to be better than them. . . . In some ways you know people are looking at you.
And you're kind of like a show for people to see. You know when
you walk down the hall that people are like, 'Oh, she's cool.' But
you don't realize that they're like, 'Oh, and she's a bitch, too.' You
don't know you're a bitch. You deny things; you avoid things. You
should know it, but you don't know it because it's a normal thing to
do and if you don't do it you're out of there."

She is chagrined about the person she was, about the mistakes
popularity led her to make, yet she struggles to understand the force
of her friends' anger.

So does Diane. Watching Erin in the days after her friends retali-
ated, she could never have predicted the crushing impact their anger
would have on her child. Today, she shares with me an abiding regret
that she did not try harder to force the school into action. Even this
year, as the school has questioned whether it is appropriate for Erin to
continue at Linden, Diane has been awed at the school's willful ignorance of the incident that so clearly marred her daughter's confidence.

During her sophomore year, Erin finally righted herself academically, bringing home all B's and one A. It's an "amazing feat!" she

crowed in a recent e-mail to me. And, she reported, she'd fallen in love.

Erin's story illustrates with terrible clarity the consequences of girls' repression of their true feelings. Over three long years, each of Erin's friends buried everyday bursts of jealousy, anger, competition, and betrayal deep inside her. The point at which their anger finally broke the surface of their silence is extremely significant. Of all the incidents that upset the girls, the only one that incited them into response had two important features: it was an event they could experience and act upon together, and it was a socially acceptable reason for female anger.

At home in a culture obsessed with romantic love, where talk shows feature women sparring in you-took-my-man catfights, the girls knew instantly that kissing Luke was a valid cause for anger. This was not like the awkward feelings of jealousy for not being popular or not having the guy you want like you; it was not the discomfort of secret competition over grades or the sadness of having been abandoned by a friend. This was clearly wrong, a misstep no one could deny.

The trouble was, once the girls got going, their anger got out of control. Every past grievance shot to the surface and crashed down on Erin. Because the girls had sequestered their feelings, hurt and jealousy were transformed into a dangerous well of rage. Michelle celebrated that no one would have to be afraid of Erin any longer. She might have added that no one would have to be afraid of conflict and anger, either.

Yet at the peak of their fury, what these girls wanted was nothing more than to isolate Erin. They didn't want to strike her, spread rumors about her, or confront her. They wanted her alone. When Erin tried to hang out with less popular girls, her friends were even angrier. "She was getting friends," Michelle said. "We wanted her to see what it was like to not have anybody there."

Michelle's willingness to speak with me about her feelings toward Erin was extraordinary. She is an example to all of us who struggle to express our own anger. Yet she's very much an ordinary girl: fun-loving, sensitive, kind, and smart. She is the very opposite of cruel. What she struggled with was how to negotiate her anger and still maximize her intimacy with the friend she loved most.

The salience of relationship in girls' lives makes their practice of imposing isolation worthy of our attention. As we have seen, girls experience isolation as especially terrifying. Since girls earn social capital by their relationships with others, isolation cuts to the core of their identities. For most girls there is little more painful than to stand alone at recess or lunch.

Erin's fear of her new friends' anger is echoed in different degrees by many survivors of bullying. These girls described feeling unfamiliar with the most basic rules of relationship, things taken for granted by any socially adjusted person. They no longer feel certain of what makes people angry or upset, not to mention how to tell when someone is feeling that way. Their emotional radar is incapacitated. This can turn a girl into a cautious ghost of her former self, stifled and silenced by fear.

The fear is felt by degrees among girls who struggle with everyday conflict. One of the chief symptoms of girls' loss of self-esteem is the sense of being crazy, of not being able to trust one's own interpretation of people's actions or events. *Did she just look at her when I said that? Was she joking? Did she roll her eyes? Not save the seat on purpose? Lie about her plans? Tell me that she'd invited me when she hadn't?* The girls I interviewed confirmed a similar unrest, the disturbing belief that what they were sure they knew or saw wasn't that at all, but was in fact something quite different. In discord between girls, gestures of conflict often contradict speech, confounding their intended targets. In such a universe, for a girl to trust her own truths, her own version of events, can be excruciatingly difficult. At the cusp of their most tumultuous years of development, girls cling tightly to one another to know, as one told me, "that we're not crazy." Yet it is their close peer relationships, and the rules against truth telling, that often trigger these feelings.

CHAPTER *four*

she's all that

From the outside looking in, Erin seems an unlikely candidate for bullying. Beautiful and popular, she is the kind of girl I might have worshiped in junior high. Yet Erin was punished in part because girls resented her social success. As I asked around after girls like Erin, I learned she was probably always a vulnerable target. Erin was a girl who "thinks she's all that."

At 8:00 A.M. in Mississippi, nineteen seventh-grade girls were slumped in their chairs, limbs dangling listlessly over metal and plastic and wood, cheeks pressing into the cool desktops. I felt like Atlas holding up the conversation, until I asked, "So, what is the big deal about a girl who thinks she's all that?"

The bodies rustled and looks slung around the room like arrows.

For once Amber didn't bother raising her hand. "They think they're better than all of us."

Christina added, "They put everyone else down."

"Sometimes they just push the girl out of the way and go after the boys. And they don't act like that to the boys."

"Mostly what they do is they try to flirt with all of their friends' boyfriends, and they think they can get anybody."

"They act like they're stuck up," Lacey said.

The next day, with the fifth graders, I asked, "Why don't we like the girl who thinks she's all that?"

"She thinks she's pretty!" one said indignantly.

"What's wrong with that?"

"She brags about it," Dee Dee said. "Most girls walk around like they're everything, prancing around, walking down halls saying 'I'm better than you are.'"

"What does she do when she brags?" I asked.

"My hair's so pretty," she sneered, imitating.

"Is that how she says it?"

"I'm prettier than you are. I'm just way better than you!" she replied in a sultry voice, then choked into giggles.

"Okay," I said. "Act it out. Let me see."

"They fix their hair during class. They prance around!"

"So let's see it," I urged. Raneesha jumped out of her chair and sauntered down the middle of the circle, swinging her behind dramatically.

"She's shaking her booty, right?" I asked. The girls roared. "So why don't we like that?"

The laughter settled gently like a sheet laid on grass. Silence.

"We may go somewhere, and she may be getting [the boys'] attention. And they may start liking her and not me," Dee Dee said.

"What's the right way to act, then?" I pushed.

"You just don't say it all the time," Lizzie said.

"Keep it to yourself."

"Act regular!"

"Act normal!"

"What's normal?" I asked.

"Just walk around not shaking your booty!" Lana said, frustrated.

"Act like everybody else."

"Act quiet," Raneesha said firmly.

"You can be friendly and happy and just . . . do things that everyone else does and don't hurt other people!" Lizzie exclaimed.

Two periods later, I asked the ninth graders to define a girl who thinks she's all that. Katie explained. "Say like you don't have as much money as them. They always get all the nice clothes and everything. They hang around the big groups and stuff. They think they're all that. They're like, well, you *wish* you could be in our group."

Lauren took up the slack. "Somebody's popular and they think they can get any boy in the school that they want, a lot of money and fancy clothes and stuff like that. She thinks she's so perfect."

"Yeah," Tanya said, "she's stuck up and she don't want to talk to nobody, but she might not be—you never gave her the chance to find out how she is."

"So why not?" I asked. "Why do we make those judgments?"

Heather again: "I was going to say she got it in her head that she thinks she's all that. She's snobby and stuff. She's got on Tommy Hilfiger and the other girls got on Jordache, and she goes up and says, look at my watch, I got it at such and such and it was $180."

"It's all about their attitude," Tanya said.

"You should be noticed," Kelly said, "but not calling attention to yourself. Have good posture and be confident and stand out but without saying anything."

"What's the biggest thing girls fight over?" I asked my first group of Ridgewood ninth graders. Toya raised her hand.

"If you go into a new school or something, and you come in decked out and got your hair down and stuff, other girls are going to be hating on you. They'll be like, she thinks she's all that. She too cute."

Tiffany added, "If you're at a new school they'll come up to you and be like, um, what's your name, why you tryin' to talk to my man, and all this stuff?"

"Why would girls do that?" I asked.

"They want to take you out!" Keisha crowed, and all the girls jumped in, their voices clotting indecipherably.

Today's girls come of age in a world that has replaced the glass ceiling with a space station. The twenty-first-century girl is a pro ballplayer, a CEO-in-training, a fighter pilot. She is anything she wants to be. Today, girl power is a cultural juggernaut.

And yet. The message that modesty and restraint are the essence of femininity persists. Contemporary feminist research shows that our culture continues to pressure girls to be chaste, quiet, thin, and giving, denying the desire for sexual pleasure, voice, food, and self-interest.[24]

In schools, the American Association of University Women found "the lessons of the hidden curriculum teach girls to value silence and compliance, to view those qualities as a virtue." Journalist Peggy Orenstein found that girls value in each other social characteristics of "sweet" and "cute," a term she found interchangeable with "deferential," "polite," or "passive." The good girl, Orenstein concluded, "is nice before she is anything else—before she is vigorous, bright, even before she is honest."[25]

Small wonder that singer Ani DiFranco is telling her legions of young female fans that everyone secretly hates the prettiest girl in the room. Or, she might have added, the most popular, the smartest, the thinnest, the sexiest, or the best dressed. Because, girl power or not, most girls know deep down that standing out can get you in big trouble. In *USA Today*,[26] a Virginia high school teacher warned of a dangerous trip wire for girls at his school. Although a new student is usually ignored, he wrote, "as soon as she becomes a threat, especially if guys like her, she'll get ripped apart."

When I first started interviewing girls, I'd planned to organize their stories according to the qualities I assumed girls got punished for: the differently abled, the overweight, the poor, the haplessly uncool. I had not expected to find that girls became angry with each other for quite the opposite reason.

As most any girl knows, one of the worst insults is to be called a girl who "thinks she's all that." This girl, loosely defined as conceited, is considered a show-off, obnoxious, or full of herself. By fifth grade, girls are intimately familiar with "all that," an epithet that grows with them into adulthood, gradually evolving into the more genteel belief that "she thinks she's better than me."

How can you tell a girl who thinks she's all that? Well, it all depends.

The first people Stephanie met after switching schools were Marissa and Lori. Best friends since preschool, the girls made an odd couple: Marissa was the bubbly, magazine-cutout-cute cheerleader. Lori was stick thin and scrappy. Alphabetized seats in freshman homeroom fated Marissa and Stephanie to friendship.

Stephanie was pretty. She was no cover girl, but she had majestic height and a head of perfectly blow-dried, blond-streaked hair that made her, she said wryly, the "preppiest girl in school." She was also smart and a talented actor. Coming from the tiny, bland Catholic school where she'd been cooling her heels for the last eight years, Stephanie still felt queasy about starting at a much bigger place. Finding Marissa and Lori was a huge relief. When Stephanie got a crush on Josh after he headed a soccer ball into her locker, she sensed that things might just end up right.

On a Saturday night in late fall, Stephanie was invited for her first sleepover at Lori's. The three girls holed up in a makeshift mountain of pillows, sleeping bags, and junk food. While they were watching a movie and doing their nails, Lori's brother Steve came into the den with his friend Jeremy. Steve sat next to Stephanie on the floor. Everyone talked and joked for a while, the boys threw handfuls of popcorn at the girls, Lori got angry at Steve, and the boys left. The girls finished their movie and fell asleep on the TV-room floor.

On Monday, after study hall, Stephanie stood very still before her locker sensing something might have changed in a way she didn't understand. She felt dread. She opened her locker door. No notes from Marissa and Lori. She went to the bathroom. No one waiting for her there as usual. Stephanie drifted through the afternoon classes obsessing silently over what could be wrong, and why.

She decided to sleep on it. The next day, Marissa and Lori ignored her during homeroom, and her eyes nearly burned out of her head trying to hold their gaze. Later that morning, two girls informed Stephanie that people had been talking. Something was going on behind her back. Still, no one had spoken to her. Marissa and Lori were nowhere to be found. Yet everyone seemed in the know. Stephanie was out, gone from the group. No one would acknowledge her. She was invisible.

By fifth period, Stephanie was reeling. She didn't understand what had happened or why, only that she had no control over it. No friends. She slouched, sobbing and gasping, on the linty rug by her locker, hiding her face in her coat sleeves. What was going on? Was it because a geeky senior had asked her to the prom and she was only a freshman? (*She'd said no!*) Was it that she tried out for the play? Had Marissa not been joking when she'd called her a copycat for buying the same Gap pants? Maybe she'd been trying too hard. Maybe she needed to back away from people so they didn't get mad at her so quickly.

Soon Stephanie learned the truth. The whispers found her in the cafeteria as she sat alone behind a crowded table: At Lori's house she had flirted with Steve. Marissa had a crush on him and was furious. Stephanie was too stunned to move.

She had not flirted with Steve. She'd never *meant* to, anyway. It was Josh she thought constantly about. They knew it! What did it mean that she had flirted? What had she done, and when? And if she didn't know the answer, how would she ever know if she was doing it again?

No one would tell her. For the rest of the year, Marissa and Lori pummeled Stephanie with cruel, invisible abuse. On Valentine's Day, they sent her flowers from Josh. When Stephanie called to thank him, he was clueless and she died of embarrassment. The girls threatened to tell Stephanie's parents she smoked if she ever spoke to Steve again. When Stephanie did well on a test, they told people she cheated. They quietly advised the teacher to keep an eye on her. Lori wrote a letter to an enemy of Stephanie's, telling her Stephanie had called her ugly names, and the girl threw Stephanie against the wall, stuck her face up close, and threatened to kill her. Lori wrote a sexually explicit letter to Josh and signed Stephanie's name.

Now twenty-nine, Stephanie was sitting on a couch in her Washington, D.C. apartment, her mitt-sized mutt, Buddy, next to her. Sensing as only dogs can that I was there to ask tough questions, Buddy had indicated we were not going to be friends. Perched on a barstool, my feet tucked as high as I could get them, I asked Stephanie how her parents had handled it. She sighed.

"Do people get upset when they talk to you about this?" she asked.

"Sometimes."

"Okay. Because I'm getting upset." I offered her a tissue, which I had learned to carry with me. The dog growled. I curled my feet tighter around the stool as I told Stephanie that my closest friends waited years to confide their most painful stories. She continued.

Stephanie told me that she waited until after college to tell anyone about her experience. I was only the second person to know, but if it would help another girl, she'd do it. "I wouldn't take any amount of money to be fifteen again. Ever," she said, settling cross-legged on her couch. "I'm ready. I'm totally ready." She continued her story.

Over the next weeks and months, Stephanie refused to tell her parents. She didn't want them to worry or to see the punishment she was being forced through. Plus, she had friends from a nearby public school, so she never seemed as alone as she felt. Instead, she started dieting and exercising obsessively. "I thought if I lost twenty pounds it would all get better, you know?" It also seemed to Stephanie that if she could hide what was going on, it would all be less real. "If you handle this enough and if you just keep it inside, if you don't actually say out loud that everybody hates me, it's not true. You know what I mean? You build the armor around yourself."

But slowly, Stephanie turned inward as her confidence and self-esteem withered. Since she didn't understand what she'd done, since there had been no fight, no moment of confrontation, she decided it could only be her fault, that her habit of saying anything on her mind was a mistake. She talked too much; she was a flirt. The answer, she decided, was to disappear.

"I blamed myself for speaking. For confiding so much in them. For letting them know so much about me," she said. Stephanie no longer trusted people. "I saw the negative in everything people said to me." She stopped sleeping. She quit the swim team after she had an anxiety attack during a relay race. She left the house wearing her new team jacket and then tried to lose it at school. She didn't look anyone in the eye, a habit that would take years to unlearn. Fearing she'd be dissected by the other girls for wearing loafers, or a cheaper brand of sweater, or unmatched colors, it was all she could do to get dressed in the morning. When her mother bought sweaters for her uniform and Stephanie feared they were too loud, she wore them out the door and removed them in the school bathroom, shivering through the day.

"I did anything and everything to just try to be [unobtrusive]," she told me. "I didn't want to have anything. I didn't want anything to draw attention to myself at all."

If she found herself having feelings for a guy, Stephanie was terrified that someone would find out. "I didn't look twice at them," she told me. All she could think about was what people would say if they saw her. "I just closed down from people."

During this period, Stephanie began remembering the month before her life changed. She had never thought twice when Marissa and Lori were being rude to her. One time, the two girls had given each other the names of girls in a popular band, but Stephanie didn't get one. The week before the sleepover, they'd chalked all over the homeroom blackboard that she loved Josh, humiliating her. "We're just playing with you," they'd said. "It was always, 'We're just playing with you,'" Stephanie told me. "'Don't be so uptight.' 'Don't be such a tight ass.'"

She recalled how some weeks before, at a school dance, a hot guy from the boys' school had come up to her and asked if she wanted to dance. "All right," Stephanie had said. "Well, I don't," he sneered, laughing as he walked away. Earlier that week at a softball game, Stephanie had told Marissa and Lori she thought the guy was cute. She'd been so sure that letting it all slide would be easier than confronting them. She had forgiven them immediately. "I just never saw the signals," she explained.

Marissa and Lori played down the prank at the dance, making light of it. "They were like, 'Oh, Stephanie, we just thought you'd laugh.'" Fifteen years later, Stephanie told me, "I remember what I was wearing. I remember what it smelled like. I remember what song was playing. I remember everything about that moment. I remember every single time I saw him after that I could not speak."

Stephanie coped by creating what she calls an "alter personality." Monday through Friday she was tortured and afraid. Friday nights she went out with friends from another school and appeared to be having a blast. But the stress at school literally consumed her from within. At fifteen, she was diagnosed with an ulcer. Her parents were astonished. "So my mother's saying 'What, doctor, why does she have an ulcer? She's fifteen years old,'" Stephanie recalled. "'Why is she puking and why is she throwing up food, and why [are] burps . . . coming out of her body that smell like ninety-year-old eggs that have been cracked open?'"

Someone suggested Stephanie see a psychologist. For twelve weeks, at the end of each forty-five-minute session, her mother thrust a wad of bills at the doctor as Stephanie watched. "She said she didn't want to write a check to a therapist, because she told me she didn't want it to come back and haunt me that I had seen someone." The weekly ritual did little to encourage Stephanie to talk about what was haunting her. Nor did it assure her that it was not her fault to begin with.

It all ended as quickly as it began. One day, the girls simply lost interest. But in the eerie silence that lingered in their absence, Stephanie only intensified picking apart everything she'd ever done in an effort to understand what triggered the nightmare.

Alone, Stephanie wandered through the halls at the beginning of sophomore year. The lockers and the rug were the same, but she knew she'd changed. "I didn't trust people at all...if they were nice to me, I didn't trust them at all. If one of the popular girls said 'Stephanie, I like your hair,' I thought they were being, like taking pity on me, like 'Oh, she's the big loser,' and rather than just being, 'Yeah, you have cool pants on and they're nice and everybody likes them.'...I didn't trust anybody with any of my secrets. No one. No one knew anything that I thought, [it] like had to be kept close....I remember kissing someone at a dance at the end of that year, like the last dance of the school year, and being literally petrified to the point where it wasn't even healthy, because like what are people going to say if they saw me kissing, and I don't even remember who it was. I closed down from people....Even when you think it's over...."

By the end of sophomore year, Stephanie convinced her parents that the school didn't challenge her academically. She asked to transfer to the other public school, and they agreed.

At the new school, Stephanie became popular so swiftly that when she told me about it, she averted her eyes as though she thought I wouldn't believe her. By the end of October, she had half the junior class partying at her house on her birthday. The change was as instant as it was unbelievable. "I didn't understand it; I didn't try. I didn't know where it came from, and I was really, you know, becoming friends with people." Still guarded, she deflected her new friends' questions about transferring from her old school with the same answer: the classes had been a disappointment.

When Stephanie was invited to a ten-year reunion at the school she'd left, she mulled it over. "There was a part of me that hoped...

I could show up and be like, yeah, I'm a consultant and I live on my own and I have a great life and I feel fantastic, and I love every part of my body, I love every part of my skin, I love everything I do. And you know not because I'm faking it, not because I'm pretending, but because I'm genuinely, I'm like okay, everything's not perfect, but it ain't that bad. And that's how I feel right now. And I would love to, kind of like, show it to them, and that I can't believe it's still there. That the wounds were so deep fifteen years ago...I still wanted to kind of like say, you know, fuck you, look how cool I am now. You were totally wrong. And you have no idea how deep the wounds were. I didn't."

Despite what happened, Stephanie told me she is most grateful for the women in her life. "Women," she said, "are the strongest people in the world. Everything we do is harder and I really believe that. I think women are incredible creatures." Stephanie credits the women in her childhood for teaching her to hold fast to her own self-worth, no matter the obstacles. Thinking often of what she "owe[s] to the girls coming after me," she volunteers frequently with children. "I feel," she said, "like I have to always work with some connection to children for the rest of my life, simply because I think it's so important to tell them our stories and to witness what they're talking about and really make them feel comfortable talking about whatever they think is important." And it's women, she reminded me, who gave her back the strength to trust again. About her best friends, she said, "I know that I could give them my wallet and car keys and my dog and my boyfriend and I would get everything back."

As I discovered with the girls I interviewed, every clique can draw its own invisible lines. Not surprisingly, it is often the new girl in class who unwittingly crosses them, triggering resentment in her peers. Listen to Megan and Taylor, two ninth-grade classmates talking about their best friend Jenny when she first switched schools.

"Remember," Megan said, "when Jenny first came from [the school] where she was, like, the shit? And she came and before she made any other friends she had already gotten this cocky attitude. People didn't even know her. We were just talking about this—remember what a bitch she was?"

"Yeah." Taylor nodded. "She had so much confidence, too. And you come to a new situation, it's just like, why is she doing that? She has *no* place—"

"No right!" Megan interjected.

"—to be doing that. I remember before Jenny came she was telling me that she knew *so* many people. She acted like she knew everything. I don't know. That made me feel like, gosh, I don't know anybody. I don't have any friends. It's like, excuse me, what do you think you're doing?"

Or listen to a group of ninth graders in Mississippi, where I asked, "How do we feel about a girl who walks into the room who we don't know and who's pretty?"

"We automatically feel a hate towards her," Keisha said immediately.

"We feel offended," Toya offered.

"She's the most attractive person—," said Melissa.

"And she's new and she's going to be getting all the attention," Torie finished.

"We want her to be less confident so she won't talk to our boys," Keisha said. "Somebody new come in, they threatened by what they are. Look at her, this and that. She's going to take my friends, she's going to take my man."

I asked, "Do girls want other girls to be confident in general?"

"*No*," came a chorus.

"No." It was Keisha.

Why not?

"Girls don't because they're threatened by what they are."

Every class, every school, pieces together its own definition of the girl who thinks she's all that. "All that" changes meaning depending on the events of the week. The school culture plays a role: in poorer schools, "all that" is often about luxury items like acrylic nails, hair extensions, and new sneakers. In wealthier schools, it may be more about flirtatiousness or conceit. The label cuts a wide swath across lines of class and race; no matter where I went, whether or not I brought it up, it always found its way into our discussions, and to great gusts of enthusiasm.

In spite of the legion definitions of "all that," there is one bottom line. There are rules, and the girl who thinks she's all that breaks them. They are the rules of femininity: girls must be modest, self-abnegating, and demure; girls must be nice and put others before themselves; girls get power by who likes them, who approves, who they know, but not by their own hand. Break these rules, and "all that" looms on the horizon.

Here is the common denominator for "all that," the one that never changes: The girl who thinks she's all that is the girl who expresses or projects an aura of assertiveness or self-confidence. She may assert her sexuality, her independence, her body, or her speech. She has appetite and desire. The girl who thinks she's all that is generally the one who resists the self-sacrifice and restraint that define "good girls." Her speech and body, even her clothes, suggest others are not foremost on her mind.

The "all that" label flummoxes girls. On the one hand, they know it's not cool to be conceited, to think you're better than others. On the other hand, they sometimes find themselves jealous of the ones who do. "It's bad if you think you're skinny because then you're full of yourself. But if you're fat? Then you're bad," said Sarah, a Marymount eighth grader.

Our culture has girls playing a perverse game of Twister, pushing and tangling themselves into increasingly strained, unnatural positions. We are telling girls to be bold and timid, voracious and slight, sexual and demure. We are telling them to hurry up and wait. But in the game of Twister, players eventually wind up in impossible positions and collapse.

Game over. In a culture that cannot decide who it wants them to be, girls are being asked to become the sum of our confusion. Girls make sense of our mixed messages by deciding to behave indirectly, deducing that manipulation—the sum of power and passivity—is the best route to power. The media reinforces this culture of indirection, prompting duplicity and evasion in girls.

The culture of indirection reflects a desire to have it both ways—to give girls the world but keep them on a leash. It is *yes, but: yes,* you may be anything you want, *but* only if you don't stray beyond the parameters of what is acceptable. *Yes,* girls can compete and win, *but* only while being modest, self-abnegating, and demure. Go too far, tip the scales, even without meaning to or knowing it, and you may be the next girl who thinks she's all that.

The culture of indirection permeates every corner of girls' lives. Deceit is eroticized in the media, where we are titillated by the prospect of a prim facade concealing a truer, dangerous passion. Think of the mousy librarian who tucks up her hair and conceals breasts, hips, and eyes beneath dowdy dresses and chunky glasses. This is the girl who "works it," who appears sweet while suggesting the boil of sin beneath the surface. The sexually indirect girl milks the good girl/bad girl dichotomy to the bone.

The sexiest among us, writes Elizabeth Wurtzel, is "the small town sweetheart who drips sugar and saccharine for all the world to see but is in fact full of lust and evil . . . and malice and bad thoughts."[27] The erotic value of this girl emanates directly from the layer of truth hidden beneath her false exterior. It is the very fact of her lie that arouses us. As the tagline for the film *Sorority* drawls, "When they're bad, they're very, very good."

Manipulation, especially when it's sexual, is often shown to girls as the path to power. This woman can't get what she wants by earning it, so instead she deceives and manipulates everyone around her. The classic female villainess, Wurtzel argues, "rarely holds up a bank, and she gets to be seductive and sweet until that creepy moment when, suddenly, she just isn't. She is conniving and manipulative and tempting and treacherous."

Glorifying female duplicity is not limited to Hollywood. A multi-billion-dollar market that has sprung up to cater to girls has also cashed in on the appeal of duplicity. In a July 2000 issue of *Teen* magazine, two photographs of the same young teenager were displayed: on the left, she was pierced and in leather, wearing heavy red and black makeup and a black tank top with lace bra. Her hands were clasped over her breasts, lips parted suggestively. On the right, the same girl was chastely clad in a cardigan, demurely hugging her schoolbooks, a Shirley Temple smile on her face. Above the racy photograph: "3:00—THE MALL." Above the other: one: "3:15—FOR MOM." The product? Jane Cosmetics' makeup remover, promising to "clean up your act."

Other advertisements portray indirection as a form of beauty. These images suggest that the ideal girl should be indirect or duplicitous. The ads help reinforce the culture's message that being too assertive is unattractive in girls. Some feminists have argued that the image of the sexual temptress is a sign of empowerment, since it allows women to call the shots by saying when and where they'll become intimate. However, the temptress suggests that female power is palatable only when it's used for sex, and even then when it's defined by insincere or manipulative acts.

jealousy and competition

The culture of indirection places a massive psychological burden on the girls who internalize it. When girls call each other "all that," they are showing us the friction produced by a culture that is confused, a world that at once prohibits and promotes a language of body and voice in which girls can be confident.

Fifteen-year-old Tasha Keller told me about an attractive classmate who triggered her clique's anger because of her forthright behavior with boys. "You see her go up to the guys and it scares [the girls]. . . . [In a movie] you see this girl going up to a guy and you've never been with a guy before. It's not like that. It never happens like that.

"They say you're supposed to get the guy and stuff, but the one who's closest to getting it is the one who's actually trying. And you're not supposed to try.

"Now that it's all about girls taking initiative and power and stuff, you get all these mixed messages. The media says girls should take control, like Nike ads," she continued. "The people on TV, they show you these scenarios, but they never show you how life is."

And how is life? I asked her. "It's this whole competition," she replied wistfully. "At school you don't have this perfect world around you.... There's so much jealousy. There's so much insecurity."

Two steps forward, one step back. It's not that we've done a bad job in teaching girls to reach for the stars. If they're privileged enough to enjoy a girl-positive school, American girls are overrun with a pastiche of powerful images past and present: Amelia Earhart, Sojourner Truth, Rigoberta Menchu, Lisa Leslie. They know women outnumber men in law school and college, that they are on the road to evening the scales in other fields. They ask, "Who will be the first woman president in my lifetime?"

The problem is with the means to get there. So fiercely have we focused on winning girls the right to dream that we have overlooked the cruder reality of what it will take to get them from point A to B and make their dreams come true. We have, in effect, put the cart before the horse.

What do I mean by this? The fear of being called "all that" and the demonization of girls who appear assertive or self-satisfied force underground the very behaviors girls need to become successful. Confidence and competition are critical tools for success, yet they break the rules of femininity. Openly competitive behavior undermines the "good girl" personality. Consider, for example, how competitive people aren't "nice" and oriented to others. Competition suggests a desire to be better than others. Competition and winning are about denying others what you wish to take for yourself.

As a result, being competitive, a sixth grader told me, becomes "a silent battle between the two girls. They don't say to their friends,

'I'm better' or 'I am competing with so-and-so,' but they kind of challenge each other, like 'beat this' through looks and actions.... They do it all in front of their competitor. That way the other person will see how great they are." Do you want to pinpoint the popular girls at school? The ones who shrug, "There is no popular group," or insist that "everybody's friends with each other" are your popular girls. As with aggression, as with conceit, competition violates the terms of femininity and so must be carefully shielded from others.[28]

The same goes for jealousy. To be jealous is to desire more than we have been given, to wish to take rather than to give. Jealousy is unbridled desire. Jealousy transforms friends into mere objects, as girls obsess over whatever part of them—body, hair, boyfriend, skin—they want for themselves. A group of ninth graders talked to me about sitting around comparing bodies during free time at school. "If we're not doing anything," one said, "we're like, 'I want her legs,' and 'I like her height' and 'I love her hair.'"

Girls are loosely aware of the way feeling jealous violates the expectation that they must be both perfect and self-sacrificing. One-on-one jealousy "bothers us," a Ridgewood ninth grader told me. "If we're jealous of somebody, I think it's because they're admirable, and maybe they have physical features that we like or something like that, and we don't want people to think that we don't accept ourselves." For some girls, jealousy is selfish, a refusal to embrace the caregiving qualities of a grown woman. "Well, I feel immature [when I'm jealous]," a ninth grader told me. "You feel like a little— you're not supposed to feel like that. You're acting like a baby."

As with aggression, girls learn to mute feelings of jealousy and competition. As with aggression, jealousy and competition do not disappear but instead morph into "acceptable" forms. And as with aggression, to remain steadfastly "good" and "nice," girls must resort to hidden codes. They learn, in other words, to express competition and jealousy indirectly.

"All that" is the hub of a hidden code that allows girls to displace feelings of competition, jealousy, anger, and desire. "Sometimes," a ninth grader told me, "I'll get angry about some little thing, and then," she said, switching to a fake-crying voice, "I'm like, 'I'm just jealous of you!'" A classmate offered, "I mean, you don't go around saying, 'She's so pretty.' Instead you say something bad to make you feel better."

speaking in code

Code words, I found, are scattered all over girls' lives. They are often used to set standards of behavior. "All that," for example, inscribes a border around girls' assertiveness. It is a social red zone used to telegraph to girls they have drifted beyond what is acceptably feminine, a vehicle allowing girls to police each other into passivity when they become too much of something—when, in other words, they become too assertive.

The remarks that earn you the title "all that" are often not even explicit: "You like my shoes?" can be perceived by the listener as bragging. "I don't know which party to go to this weekend!" is heard as conceit. "Do you like my hair?" or "Are my nails okay?"— even frequent checks of makeup or hair combing are taken as signs the girl thinks she's thin or pretty. There are cruder signs, too: the girl who thinks she's all that may dare to suggest she thinks she's pretty. She may not speak to and smile at everyone throughout the day. She may attract and flirt with boys, even the ones already spoken for.

All of this is not to say the "all that" girls aren't actually conceited. Plenty of them may be. But "all that" is less a fixed identity than it is a hidden repository in which girls can store uncomfortable feelings of anger, jealousy, and competitiveness. Quite often the distance between "all that" and jealousy is really a matter of degrees.

Indeed, the girls who get ostracized are usually the ones who have what most girls are expected to want: looks, the guy, money, and cool clothes. When I ask girls what they get jealous of, a Mississippi freshman summed it up: "Who they go out with, what they wear, how much money they have, who likes them, who hangs out with them, and in some cases the grades they get." What is "all that," really, but *acting like* you've got some or all of these things instead of just quietly owning them, in an aw-shucks sort of way.

Jacqueline, a sophomore, explained that a girl who thinks she's all that "flaunts everything. Like if she's smart, you know, she always has the answers around the teachers. She knows she always gets praise or whatever." When I asked why it bothers girls so much, she said, "Because if you have a lot of stuff, you have it. . . . My mother always told me nobody's better than anybody." I pressed harder. Why does it make girls so insecure? "Because we want that and we don't like the fact that she has it. We want to be like that. . . . You don't have to show the whole world you have good grades. That makes other people feel bad."

Another code word between girls is "flirt." You might think girls aspire to be attractive to guys, but calling someone a flirt is rarely a compliment. Many girls think flirting with a guy is tantamount to being physically intimate with him, and if a girl happens to be seen flirting with a guy who's already spoken for, her social life may be in danger.

The trouble is that no one can say for sure exactly what flirting is. Like "all that," just about anything qualifies, as long as it's with a guy. As Stephanie discovered, a girl could be talking to a guy, looking at him, working with him, responding to him, writing him a note, instant messaging with him, playing around—or she could be seen doing any of these things. The definition of flirting depends not on the doer, but the viewer. A ninth grader illustrated the murkiness of "flirt" in a story she told.

"This girl in our school, she was liking this boy. He was always coming up and talking to me. I didn't like him like that. He was my friend. One day I was talking to him and he grabbed my waist and pushed me back and pulled me and I'm screaming and she was thinking that I was flirting with him and then the next day at school she put White-Out in my hair. I asked her why she did that and she said, 'Because you're flirting with my dude.' I was like, 'No.' She went and asked him and he was like, 'No, we're just friends.' And then she apologized."

Needless to say, it is a short walk from "flirt" to "slut." Although most adults believe a slut is a promiscuous girl, often the opposite is true. The accused girl is often only assertive, not active; because she wears tight-fitting clothes and approaches boys fearlessly, she is labeled a slut. It is not her sexual behavior that earns ire, but her departure from the norms of feminine sexual modesty.

A girl who refuses to be "nice" all the time and to everyone may also get called a slut. She may flirt with a guy who is dating someone else or have a crush on a boy who is already spoken for. As Lyn Mikel Brown observed in her study of girls' anger, "a 'slut' is not someone who is sexually active per se, but rather someone who is disconnected from her partner or from other girls."[29] Psychologist Deborah Tolman writes that "the fact of girls' sexual activity is explained in terms of relationships: girls have sex in the service of relationships."[30] When a girl's sexuality becomes indiscriminate, performed to entertain or pleasure only herself, it has broken the rules.

In Mississippi, girls often used the word "skank" in a similar way. Like a slut, a skank is sexually brash, but she's also conceited. "[A skank] talks about [herself] more than anything else," a ninth grader said, imitating her: " 'Well, I can do this. I can get any person.' " A skank may sit with her legs open, wearing baggy, skater clothes, or she may wear wear skintight, "slutty" clothes. She may talk in slang, not use proper language, or get into fights; or she might be excessively sexual with her boyfriend in public.

Some code words have multiple meanings. "I'm so fat" is a common lament with at least three separate translations. When I first started meeting with girls, middle-class students complained constantly of peers who overused the phrase. In fact, in a study called "Fat Talk," researchers noted that most girls who said "I'm so fat" weren't fat at all.[31]

First, "I'm so fat" is used as a tool of indirect one-upping. "Girls ask each other if they are fat, and that is a way of competing with each other," an eighth grader explained to me. "If they are skinny and ask themselves if they are fat, what does that say about me? It's a passive aggressive way of saying the other person's not skinny." In

"Fat Talk," girls described "how their friends practically 'accused' them of being thin, 'as if it were my fault or something.' "

"I'm so fat" is also used as a roundabout way to seek positive reinforcement from a peer. "I'm so fat is fishing for compliments," thirteen-year-old Nicole said. "[Girls] want attention." The researchers confirmed that "for many girls, the motivation in saying 'I'm so fat' is to gauge what other people think about them. Girls are really competitive but they don't make it seem that way," Mary Duke explained. "Like, 'I'm so fat.' When they say that it's because they want attention."

Finally, girls use "I'm so fat" to short-circuit the possibility of getting labeled "all that." The researchers found that if a girl didn't say she thought she was fat, she would imply that she was perfect. "In other words, saying she doesn't need to diet would be an admission that she didn't need to work on herself—that she was satisfied." Instead, they found, the "good girl" must put herself down, and so wind her way to the compliment she is seeking.

Another code word is the accusation of "copying." At Marymount, an eighth-grade girl threw out her shorts in tears after Lisa, a popular girl, was enraged by her wearing the same pair that Lisa had purchased at a special outlet. After alliances were built and the whole grade was talking, the "copier" wrote Lisa an anguished note and barricaded herself in the guidance counselor's office. I am astonished by the fever-pitch rage that flies across cliques when one girl is copying the look or behavior of another. Whether they're eight or in the eighth grade, the response is clearly disproportionate, suggesting "copying" has a hidden meaning.

Like "all that," "copying" is an accusation in which girls sometimes hide competition and jealousy. Often girls will say they detest copiers because they want to have their own unique style. Press a little harder, and you hear this: "If she copied me, people would think she looked better than me." A sixth grader explained over e-mail that "it feels like they're stealing my ideas. . . . I guess because we kind of compete with each other." The copying accusation takes a girl from being on the defensive, feeling discomfort about jealousy and competition, and changes the terms of the conflict. Now, righteously indignant, the copied one can deflect attention from the messier feelings fueling her reaction, directing her anger toward someone else.

What about the popular girl who gets angry that a wanna-be is dressing like her? The copying accusation is extremely effective. "Copying" gives the popular girl a concrete fault to attack. It deflects attention from the real issue: the wanna-be's attempt to get into the popular clique. Because being accused of copying can be such a heavy blow to a girl's social status, the popular girl manages to defuse the threat entirely and isolate the wanna-be from the group.

girl passive

Girls are expected to be passive and powerful at the same time. I never understood this more clearly than an afternoon I spent at a leadership workshop for girls. The twenty-eight girls were between thirteen and seventeen; one quarter were nonwhite. Standing before a pad perched on a wooden easel, watched by fourteen pairs of eyes, I began.

"Caroline"—I pointed over to a younger counselor—"is going to be Vanna White." They giggled. "I want you guys to call out the qualities you think the ideal or perfect girl has. Then I want you to tell me who the anti-girl is—the girl no one wants to be. Think of a girl you know, or one you see represented in the media." I nodded at Caroline, who uncapped a red marker. And here is what they said (boldface added):

IDEAL GIRL	ANTI-GIRL
Very thin	**Mean**
Pretty	Ugly
Blond	Excessively cheerful
Fake	Athletic
Stupid	**Brainy**

ODD *girl* OUT

Tall

Blue eyes

Big boobs

Fit

Expensive clothes

Unproportional

Naked

Trendy

Popular

Boyfriends

Smiling

Happy

Helpless

Talking on phone
  (has friends)

**Superficial conflicts
  (solved easily)**

Looks older

Girlie

Dependent

Impractical clothes

Manipulative

Sex = power

Rich

Good teeth/clear skin

Smart

Perfect

**Romantically attached to
  someone with status**

Opinionated

Pushy

Dark features

Not skinny

Imperfections

Promiscuity (slut)

Professional

Insecure

Dorky

Unhappy/depressed

Masculine

Serious

Strong

Independent

Gay/lesbian

Artsy

PMSish

Unrestrained

Egocentric

Not social

Hard to get along with

Bookish

What I noticed first was how the ideal girl was *physically* perfect, a Caucasian Barbie doll: bone thin, tall, pretty, blond, blue eyes, big boobs, good teeth, clear skin—in other words, what you'd expect. Moments later, I realized that what these girls also find perfect is not

just a flawless body, but also an indirect, middle-of-the-road character. For them, the ideal girl's true perfection was her ability to hold
herself back from the world, expressing herself through manipulation.

Look again at the lists. The ideal girl is stupid, yet manipulative.
She is dependent and helpless, yet she uses sex and romantic attach-
ments to get power. She is popular yet superficial. She is fit, but not
athletic, or strong. She is happy, but not excessively cheerful. She is
fake. She is tiptoeing around the lines that will trigger the alarm of
"all that."

The anti-girl, on the other hand, lacks the ideal girl's sophisticated
indirection. She is the polar opposite of the "nice," other-oriented,
relational girl. The non-ideal girl is mean, opinionated, and pushy.
She is egocentric and selfish. She is not the sweet girl everyone wants
to be around; she is unhappy and insecure. She is not social. She is
not in control of her emotions. She is moody and hard to get along
with.

The anti-girl doesn't blend in. She doesn't agree and she doesn't
get along. Yet persistence, maverick thinking, and a fighting spirit are
precisely the qualities girls are taught to embrace in the heroines they
grow up to admire. The competing messages translate into conflict-
ing visions of the women they are supposed to become. That day, I
was confused and disheartened.

American culture is built on dual pillars of independence and competition, values that run directly counter to the passionate intimacy,
care, and friendship between girls. Giving girls a chance at success
means giving them full, equal access to the tools of the game: to the
acts of competition and desire required to excel and to the knowledge that relationships can survive them. When competition and desire cannot be enacted in healthy ways and when girls are expected to
give priority to care and relationship, resentment, confusion, and retribution follow shortly behind.

For the past twenty-five years, a growing number of psychologists
have celebrated different cultures of play and work among boys and

girls. Their portrayals carry the legacy of science's refusal to explore female aggression, and they end up idealizing female relationships. Where boys "stress position and hierarchy...girls emphasize the construction of intimacy and connection. Girls affirm solidarity and commonality, expressing what has been called an 'egalitarian ethos.'" Sadly, this work has reinforced the image of girls' lives as idyllic, free of impulses toward unrestrained competition and desire.

It's not just girls who must learn to be comfortable with competition. Our culture stigmatizes assertive, professional women, casting them as cold, frigid bitches doomed to failure in their personal lives. I want to emphasize how this particular stereotype communicates to girls their worst fear: that to become assertive in any way will terminate their relationships and disqualify them from the primary social currency in their lives, tenderness and nurturing.

As we push girls harder and expect more, girlhood's codes will continue to divide them from one another. These codes have confused, shifting meanings. They are built on a second layer of truth hidden beneath a deceptive exterior. They leave girls ever suspicious of what is really being said and who will be branded next, leaving deep fissures of trust between them. "Someone can be a really good friend," an eighth grader told me, "but she won't be happy for you. She'll be jealous. It's not spoken, but you can feel it." Friendships are corroded in the silence that is a weak substitute for what must be expressed, for what is real and human and yet feels so sinful. Girlhood's stigma against competition and desire can never allow girls a healthy outlet for their feelings or the kind of straightforward truth telling to which every human being is entitled.

It would be nice to think we live in a time of cultural transition, of flux, of a world that is learning to give its girls equality in the ways it finds hardest. But by not socializing girls into healthy, supported acts of competition and desire, we consign them to a culture that refuses to put its money on the table and wager who and what it wants girls to be. We ask them to suffer the "tension when the ideals of womanhood and femininity are those of 'selflessness,' and the ideals of maturity and adulthood are those of separation and independence."[32] Do we want to give girls the freedoms boys enjoy or don't we? If we as a culture haven't yet decided, girls most certainly have not. And if girls can never be sure who they are supposed to be, they will play out their (and our) anxieties on each other, policing themselves into the ground, punishing and bullying and fighting to know the answer for themselves.

CHAPTER *five*

the bully

in the mirror

Popularity, like trigonometry, was something I never quite grasped. It was like reaching under my bed to grab an errant shoe, willing my fingers to stretch out of their joints, feeling my fingertips closing in, and yet always coming up short. Sure, I had plenty of access, could count the popular girls as friends, sat at lunch and passed notes, went to parties. But there was something that separated us. It was unnamable, invisible, and yet utterly obvious. The knowledge sat in me like a sandbag. It followed me wherever I went. I was an addendum, an extra. What I wouldn't have given or done to be on the inside.

When Anne and I met one evening for drinks in Washington, I hadn't planned to talk about the day I stopped speaking to her over a decade before. Anne had been my best friend in the fifth grade, and our love for each other was irrepressible. We were frequent visitors to Mrs. Katz's time-out chair, where we nearly fainted choking silently on our laughter, squawking "Dead dogs! Dead dogs!" to get control. We named each other the Booger Twins, after the animated Wonder Twins. We passed notes marked with skull and crossbones, labeled "BBL" for "Booger Breath Lives."

Anne lived in Washington's Cleveland Park, and because of her I got to ride the subway for the first time. We spent nights in her huge bed listening to the Top Ten at Ten on the radio and days making bracelets with beaded safety pins bound with elastic. For a while that year she was like me, gingerly toeing the borders of the popular clique. Then, one day, without ceremony, she was swallowed inside.

By ninth grade, Anne, Rebecca, Sandy, and Julie were the powerful four. They were the usual: best dressed, prettiest, got the most guys. I hung out with them, as I had for the last four years. Rebecca and Anne both liked Geoffrey, a freckled, ginger-haired sophomore. One day, before the last bell, someone passed me a note. "Omigod!" it said. "Rebecca dumped Anne!"

That day, Rebecca had decided she didn't want to be friends with Anne anymore and over sandwiches and juice boxes had told her as much. Within minutes, the popular clique stopped speaking to Anne. And so did I.

I remember very little beyond that day. For a while Anne floated through the hallways, sallow and empty eyed. Eventually, we saw her eating lunch or on the bus with other girls, unpopular, of course. By year's end, she and Rebecca had reconciled, but the lines connecting us were torn. The last time I saw her, she was cleaning out her locker. She never returned to school the next fall. Three years later, during my first week of college, I bumped into her seeking shade beneath a maple tree. It took years before we were able to talk for more than a few strained moments. Each time I saw her, I felt something curdle inside me. I remembered what happened the way I might wake from a dream in the night, in pieces that didn't fit together but still left me uneasy. Shortly after college, we both took jobs in politics and became friends. With enormous relief, I felt sure I had earned the right to let go of what I had done.

Now as adults, twenty-five years old, we were sipping drinks in an elegant D.C. lounge. So removed had I become, so fiercely had I clung to our present friendship, that I cheerfully summed up my project on girls and bullying without a single thought to our past.

Anne played absently with the ashtray. "Remember ninth grade?" she
asked. I froze in my chair. As she began talking, I pulled out my tape
recorder. She nodded as I placed it on the table. I listened. Toward
the end of her remembering, she said, "I just spent that whole year
like a *wounded animal*. Like I just didn't know how to collect myself. It was so . . . God. You just feel like you have no way to protect
yourself. You feel like there's nobody there to help you. You feel like
naked in a room filled with people pointing and laughing at you and
nobody will hand you a blanket to cover yourself with. It's that feeling all the time, all this vulnerability. You don't have the tools at that
age to pick yourself up and wipe yourself off."

There was a long silence. "You were part of it, too. You witnessed
it," she said. She took a sip of her water and looked at me. "What do
you think it was?"

It felt like someone had dropped an anchor in my stomach. How
could I have done this? How could I, always the outsider, once a victim—how could I have done this?

Easily.

When I pulled into the horseshoe-shaped driveway at Linden,
Megan was hanging out with her friends. She waved and hopped in
the backseat, followed by another girl, who slid in next to me. "Hey,
I'm Taylor," she said. "Can I come, too? Cool music," she added,
nodding to my Jill Scott CD.

We headed to Starbucks and grabbed a table. While they scoped
out the other girls there, I got us a snack. Then Megan began to tell
me her story.

In fifth grade, at her small Catholic school, Megan got into an exclusive clique for the first time. Though she loved being popular, it
was hardly the paradise people made it out to be. It was work. "I always worried that they would do something without me," she said.
"That I'd be left out. I wasn't like one of the main people. I wasn't
the one that all the guys liked." She strove for the attention of Jackie,
the queen of the grade. If she liked you, you would be safe. Apparently it had always been that way.

Megan paused. I knew she was here to talk with me about being a bully; she'd told me as much over e-mail. I stared at my coffee so she wouldn't feel self-conscious, wondering if like so many girls, Megan would clam up, deny what she had done, claim she'd forgotten, play dumb. "I was kind of like, the nice person, kind of. I wasn't really anything special," she said, beginning to backpedal.

"There was this one girl named Liane Chapin," she said, exhaling. The group had always thought she was kind of weird, and in fifth grade, Liane started acting like she was friends with their clique. "She was *such* a follower," Megan said. "She tried to be like us in every way." Liane copied them. It was annoying.

One day, hanging out after school, someone had an idea. What if they invented a rock band to see if Liane would act like she knew it, to see if she'd copy them to the point of lying? "So we were like, 'Liane, have you ever heard of Jawbreaker?' And she's like, 'Yeah!' And we were like, 'Really!'" It went from there. The girls wrote lyrics to songs, sang them in front of her, and snickered when Liane tried singing along. "She'd be like, 'Yeah, I heard that on the radio yesterday,' and we'd be like, 'Really?'"

It was a joke that never lost steam, and a genuine opportunity for Megan. She applied herself diligently, composing several songs. Jackie loved them. By year's end, Jawbreaker had an album's worth of material and a half-choreographed video. Megan was the closest she'd been to the inner circle. "It kind of made me feel like I had a more secure place in the group," Megan explained. "It made me feel like—when I would write the songs, they'd be like, 'Yeah, that's so funny!' It made me feel like, 'Wow, I can be mean, too, kind of.'"

It all felt easy, like the transition from ice skates to Rollerblades. People say you'll be good at it, but you never quite understand why until you feel yourself rolling forward. That's how being mean was. Plus, the girls never said an unkind word to Liane. To the contrary: "We acted nice to her. Like, we acted nice to her face, but we totally just like talked about her so much behind her back. We totally like destroyed her." It was easy to keep Liane hanging around because she had considered Megan a really good friend since the previous summer when they had gone to camp together, long before Megan had gotten really popular.

One day, for no good reason, Megan felt something within her catch as abruptly as a sweater on a nail. At her old school, Megan told me, her best friend, Anna, had used her as bait for the popular clique, abandoning and insulting her publicly. As she told me this, Megan was trying intently to fish ice out of her plastic cup with her straw. "It was so bad," she remembered quietly. She gave up on the ice and started chewing a cuticle. "It was horrible. I didn't have any friends. I would look in the mirror and, 'Oh, I'm just like an ugly person, inside and outside. I'm just disgusting.' Like nothing was shining." After recalling her own victimization, Megan said that being mean to Liane felt easy and hard at the same time. "We would be laughing at her, in her face, and, like, I'd be thinking this is exactly what Anna did to me, and I'm doing it to her right now."

But Jackie was the sun, and the other girls orbited around her, each maneuvering to move closer in. In the girls' bathroom, Megan and Jackie were fixing their hair. Megan glanced compulsively under the stalls and saw platforms belonging to Jenny, the second-most-popular, just as Jackie started berating her. Megan nodded and uh-huhed, glancing furtively at the platforms that stood still as stone. "I didn't make her stop," Megan explained, "because I knew Jenny was listening."

As Megan had predicted, the conversation triggered a six-month war between the girls, and the hostility never dissipated. Megan's silence led to a tectonic shift in their social universe. "Everyone was like, 'What happened?' And I was like, 'Oh, my God.' I could exaggerate however much I wanted. I was in the bathroom with Jackie and Jenny who were the most popular girls. That was really big." People Megan didn't even know approached her for information. "If you're involved in something," she told me, "you know what's going on and you're a part of it." Simple as that.

But the betrayals Megan witnessed and experienced have filled her with social anxiety. "I still feel this way," she said. "I'll get kind of like panic attacks. My personal thing is that everyone's talking about me, so when I see two people whispering, I'll just be like, I'll kind of read their lips and catch part of their conversation. People are talking about me. I hate it when people do things without me, and I'm like, 'Oh, I'm going to miss all these inside jokes, or they'll be talking about me.' We have another best friend, and whenever I miss going somewhere, I'm even like, 'Shit, I'm going to miss all these inside jokes.'"

Taylor, who was nodding gently throughout her friend's interview, described the surprise party she and Monica threw Megan last month. Taylor had been stealthy in the planning, and the day before the party, she'd tried to plot details with Monica during soccer practice. When Megan approached, the two girls stopped talking. Megan stood frozen watching them, then ran to the locker room, got her things, and went home. "I was sobbing. I had a panic attack. I was like, 'Oh my God, I don't have any friends.'" Taylor smiled sheepishly at her friend and rolled her eyes.

In a social world where anger explodes unannounced, anxiety is the norm and security a luxury. For Megan, the sudden, inexplicable abandonment of her best friend taught her that people and feelings are not always what they seem. Never knowing for sure if she was truly liked by others made the need to exclude someone else a fact of life. "I guess I wanted someone else to feel bad," she said simply.

It's often said that one girl alone is rarely a problem, but get two or three together and they're different creatures entirely. Because girls often aggress as a group, exclusion and its cruel trappings can be a perversely good opportunity for secure companionship. An odd girl out is undeniably so; her exclusion is made possible by the banding together of many. When it happens, all bets are off and the borders are unpatrolled. Anyone with guts can make a run for status and acceptance by attacking the designated target. For Megan, writing songs and positioning herself in the middle of a fight were chances to stand out. They were a way in and a step up. They may have been fleeting opportunities, but they felt very real and very safe.

But if the gratification is as temporary as it is cruel, it begs the question: What takes someone over when she surrenders to these impulses? What did I stand to gain when I turned my back on Anne and left her to wither?

If I had to name one trait many girl bullies and victims share, I'd say that both draw a potent mix of power and security from the close relationships in their lives. And they are terrified of being alone. When the dark cloud of relational instability dominates girls' *everyday* social worlds, the threat of isolation hangs over them. For some, it is a gripping fear; for others, an emotional white noise. It's true that popularity is a gravitational force, inexorably pulling girls into behaviors that in a normal world would seem outrageous. But in some cases, the ambition for popularity may be secondary, even beside the point. The girls I met described an equally powerful drive to avoid the desolation of solitude.

Solitude, after all, undermines the essence of the girl identity. Girls know we expect them to be sociable creatures, to be in nurturing relationships, especially with other girls. The constant sense that isolation is imminent and the ground unsettled can make girls feel desperate. Without the luxury of social security, a girl will do anything to survive at school—whatever will get her through the homeroom, the lunch hour, the hallway. Acts of exclusion in these instances assure a girl that she is acting as part of a group and won't be the one left behind.

Indeed, some girls describe a kind of exhilaration derived from excluding one of their own, which bears a disturbing similarity to the joy of close friendship. Michelle, profiled in chapter three, described the mesmerizing hold Erin had on her when they first met. Erin was like "a drug almost. . . . She says everything that you want her to say and she acts like she's such a good friend and acts like you're the best thing ever to happen to her, and you're kind of excited because you're like insecure and you're her everything. That's what people generally want to be. They want to be important to somebody else."

Later, Michelle explained her clique's retaliation against Erin in nearly identical terms. "It was amazing to be able to let it go when everybody else was, so you weren't by yourself. It was like you had control over her which was just like the best feeling." She added, "I know that it had to do with having a sense of power that I'd never felt before. . . . I think it was mostly just like, nobody can get mad at me for something. I was the good friend. I wasn't the problem. . . . I have everything that she thought she had. It was just like a sense of empowerment. I didn't need anybody, like I had everything I needed."

Both of Michelle's accounts emphasize the rush she felt when her connections to others seemed unbreakable, when the specter of isolation was at bay. In these moments, friendship feels pure, unthreatened, and free of insecurity.

musical chairs

Lisa was early, in time to watch me spill coffee on myself jiggering the key in the door to the room where we'd planned to meet. Athletic and dark-eyed, with a ponytail of raven hair that curled and frayed at the ends, she watched me quietly from beneath a thick arc of bangs. As we sat down to chat in a parlor on her college campus, her words were as spare and sharp as her looks.

Lisa spent her first three years in school as the girl everyone pretended not to see. From the first days of kindergarten at a small Catholic school in New Jersey, she was alone on the playground. At recess she would tarry behind a large metal box and stare at her reflection, holding her coat at different angles. "If my coat touched the ground," she recalled to me, "I would be a princess, but if it didn't, I wasn't. That was my whole world. I was either a princess or nothing." Through the end of second grade, Lisa would go home after school and cry in her room. She performed poorly in class, and teachers warned her parents of possible developmental delays.

Lisa convinced her parents to transfer her to a public school, where she got straight A's and found social respite. Two years later, she moved on to a large middle school, a feeder for several area public elementaries. Barely a day passed before Lisa's stomach tightened in that familiar knot. "I saw the same stuff happening. Girls being mean to other girls. But this time," she said evenly, eyes fixed on me, "I was going to be the one to be mean."

Lisa met Karen the second week, when she successfully faked needing a tissue to pass Karen a note from Jason. Karen smiled gratefully and passed her a note. It said, "Thanks! What school are you from?" with a smiley face and bubble letters. When the girls sat together that day at lunch, it was clear Karen had been popular at her old school. You couldn't deny the special electricity she gave off. Lisa felt an uncomfortable sense of—what was it? luck? guilty pleasure?—whenever they were together.

"I always thought she was cooler than me, and being mean was something we did together," Lisa told me. "It made us better than everyone else." The girls filled their lunches and study halls with notes, gossip, giggling, and furtive glances at other girls. They started the We All Hate Vicki Club, drafted a petition, and convinced the whole school to sign it. The chubby girl in chorus was next; they wrote a song about how she was fat and unloved, called her a prostitute, wouldn't look at her while she sang. The girl didn't come back to school after spring break.

For Lisa, meanness was as much a part of middle school as meals and morning announcements, as basic and oppressive as the stale air and annoying tick of classroom clocks. Yet Lisa clung to Karen by gossamer threads at best. She could bet everything that others were talking about her, too. The constant hum of under-the-breath remarks and whispers and notes and nasty looks swirled together and filled the air around them. Even if she stopped being mean, it was clear there would always be someone to slide into her place. As Lisa explained, "Maybe there were twenty girls in the class, and all of them would be talking about each other behind their backs. Because you sort of felt like everyone was your friend, but if everyone else was like you, they were talking about you because you were talking about them. It was just terrible. I remember feeling terrible all the time. Because I knew my friends were talking about me, and I was talking about them."

The constant manipulation and ganging up, the uneasy sense that no one was who she seemed or said she was, was dizzying. In her frenzy of betrayal and insincerity, Lisa constantly wondered who her real friends were and at times, if she had any at all.

Meanness was Lisa's social amulet. Still, she said, "the only thing I wanted was for somebody to be my friend. Someone I could depend on. And there wasn't anyone like that." In spite of her efforts, her relationships felt increasingly unsteady. "It was a time," she explained, "when I didn't really feel like I had anybody except the girls that I was being mean to someone else with." She couldn't win. No matter what, "I always thought there was something wrong with me. I felt like a bad person. I was either a dork for being the victim or a mean, horrible bitch for being the bully." And anyone could beat up the dork. Her mother had begged her not to be the girl who bullied. "But I couldn't do that," she said simply. "I didn't want to be the dork."

When she graduated eighth grade, Lisa felt worn and beaten. She was convinced she was, as she put it, "a dork and a loser and a bitch." As a joke, her class voted her most likely to become a nun, but she was crushed by the prude label.

Two years later it all began again. When she'd turned down some boys who asked her out, they called her a lesbian. News spread, and Lisa felt her sorrow relapse. She found solace in writing poetry and was asked that spring to read an original piece at assembly. The next day, she was pegged a feminist, at her school the equivalent of being a lesbian. It was the last poem she wrote.

Today, Lisa describes herself as "really defensive. It's made me not willing to share myself with other people. It's made me hard to become friends with." Her first year at college, most people called her "Ice Queen" because she never told anyone anything about herself. At the end of freshman year, she met someone who encouraged her to trust others: her boyfriend. "I hate to say that," she told me. "It isn't true that it was him who saved me. It was me that saved me. He loved me for who I am and it didn't matter that in school I was a bitch or a dork. I am who I am now."

———

There is a kind of musical-chairs quality to Lisa's middle-school experience. Winners and losers are easily interchangeable, and for no compelling reason. Some women and girls I spoke with described weeks when they were the odd girl out, only to be on top the following week when it was someone else's turn. "It was all about having somebody be 'out,'" Maggie recalled. "If there were three of you hanging out, two of you would make a plan to 'go off' and just have inside jokes and tease the other person and just make them feel bad." Just who rotates into the odd-girl position is arbitrary. As one guidance counselor remarked to me, "The same girls who are ostensibly the doers will be in here crying about what others are doing to them."

Lisa's story is about the intense hunger for retaliation. The desire to take an eye for an eye is a common fantasy for many victimized girls. "For all the times I'd been excluded and cried, I wanted her to know what it felt like to cry," Emily, a ninth grader, told me. "I was so angry at this person. I got joy from seeing her upset because she had gotten joy from seeing me upset." Said sixth-grader Jessica: "I want to get back at them. I want them to experience what it's like not being wanted." Again, the punishment envisioned is isolation and the loss of human connection.

Research indicates that girls who are victimized are significantly more likely to become bullies themselves.[33] Indeed, memories of being the odd girl out figured prominently in the stories of girls willing to identify themselves to me as bullies or mean.[34] Like Lisa, these girls framed their behavior in terms of avoiding injury and maximizing security. In other words, they bullied because they felt threatened, because in their minds there was no other choice.

memories of betrayal

It was Thursday, and Kathy Liu had forgotten about our interview. Again. Clearly she had me on her to-do list between "alphabetize canned foods" and "start stamp collection." I took this as a good sign.

When she finally answered the door to her Washington home, she was clutching tissues and wearing flannels. Aha, I thought. Too sick to ditch me. Kathy let me in, smiling and apologizing. A senior at Georgetown University, she was living in what can best be described as a girl frat house. Indie movie posters plastered the walls. I'd like to say the carpet was once green, but I wouldn't bet the farm on it. It was furry, an inadvertent shag, closer to brown now. The kitchen was gnarled with hanging rusted pots and piles of bottles and dishes and spice jars. An errant Hoyas sweatshirt was draped on an easy chair that was leaking stuffing. "Sorry about the mess," she said sheepishly. "Oh no!" I told her, remembering my apartment in college, "I feel right at home."

A first-generation Korean-American, Kathy was twenty-three. "So," she said, raising an eyebrow. "Do I get to quit school if I make it into your book? Make lots of money?" We laughed. She pulled out a cigarette.

Kathy grew up in South Carolina. Her parents, Korean-born, emigrated to New York following their wedding. Kathy's father was accepted to study engineering in South Carolina and upon graduation was hired locally.

Theirs was the only Asian family in the small community, and they were among the first Asians many there had ever seen. At age three and four in the grocery store with her mother, Kathy noticed the pointing fingers, eyes pulling back, nudging elbows, and whispering. By middle school, people saw no problem with making "chink" jokes in her presence. She was even nicknamed Suzy Wan at school. In the hallways, she was often trailed by high-pitched "ching chong" noises. Most people, including her friends, thought this was hilarious.

Kathy did not. Fitting in meant everything to her. She felt something was wrong with her, that she looked funny and wasn't normal. She loved going over to friends' houses and begged her mom not to cook Korean food when her friends were around. They thought the kitchen smelled funny, that the food looked weird. She hated it. Kathy was stylish and cute, able to wear, as she put it, the "right brands." She spent a great deal of time on her hair and makeup (no small expenditure in the late 1980s South). She was second-tier popular, B-level: a hair breadth from the top. In other words, she had potential.

By eighth grade, Kathy had been best friends with Nancy for three years. They were passionately close and spent class time writing long notes to each other, folding them in funky shapes and squeezing them in each other's lockers throughout the day.

One afternoon, Nancy wrote a letter about one of the popular girls being snotty. "I agree," Kathy started to scribble, then stopped midsentence, pen in the air. "I realized," she told me, "that wait, I could win favor with the popular kids if I told them what Nancy had said." Kathy gave them Nancy's notes. The popular girls promised not to tell.

The next morning, in the auditorium where everyone hung out before the bell, Nancy walked in holding a few wrinkled pieces of paper. Her face was red, her eyes swollen. Kathy asked what was wrong, "even though," she told me, "I knew exactly what was wrong, why she would be crying, why she would be upset." Nancy looked at her with blank, defeated eyes.

"How did they get these?" she asked.

"I don't know."

"How did they get these?" she repeated.

Over the thin sound of her own voice, Kathy suddenly felt the weight of the damage she had caused. "I couldn't bear to assume that responsibility," she told me, curling her legs under her, sucking hard on her second cigarette. "I couldn't bear to say, 'I did this to you. This is what I did.'" All day long, people bombarded her in the hallways, pumping her for information. She pleaded ignorance. "I kept trying to get the blame off me, to create this phantom third party so I could get out of it," she said, blowing her nose.

Their friendship was over, of course. "It was a complete betrayal." Kathy sighed. "It's almost unimaginable why the desire to be popular and accepted would make me do something that's so malicious. To betray someone so close to me." She cleared her throat, her voice deeper. "I was—I'm sure that—I'm sure that it has significantly scarred her." Kathy said she wants to forget what happened. "But you can't forget when you've caused so much hurt to someone."

She grew quiet. Her cigarette smoke hung in the air before us. "It is a little hard to talk about." She flicked her ash into a chipped bowl overflowing with butts. This was the second time she had ever spoken of what happened. I asked her why popularity was so important.

"I guess I thought that it kind of represented acceptance and belonging and desirability," she said. "I was feeling degraded from other instances of being bullied. If I were to be accepted by them, it would be to kind of get myself out of the degraded position. It wasn't really so much that I wanted to be friends with them. I felt like, then it wouldn't matter that I was Asian."

Nancy was one of several girls Kathy bullied. In one instance, she demeaned a close friend constantly out of jealousy over the attention she was getting. "I remember thinking, 'Why can't I stop this? Why can't I just sit back and let her have her time in the spotlight?'" Looking back at that time, she said, "I felt like there were so many people above me, to know that there was someone below me was comforting."

Kathy asked me again if I would definitely change her name in the book, and I said, yes, of course. "Well," she muttered, "if somebody can learn from my experience . . ."

"What would you like them to learn?" I asked.

"I guess to make them understand the impact that they're having potentially on another person's life," Kathy replied. "I can tell them for years and years I couldn't be friends with that person anymore. I was questioning my own loyalties to people. I was kind of like, 'Wow, if I'm capable of doing this, I'm capable of completely betraying somebody close to me for the possible favor of someone that doesn't really care about me at all.' I basically sold her out. You're giving up what's real for something that you see as more desirable, a higher social status or something."

The knowledge that she could so coldly hurt her friend, in spite of her values, was "very disturbing. I was old enough to know what's right and wrong. It was almost like I felt I wasn't really in control," she said.

"I can barely explain how much guilt I feel from this one situation," Kathy continued. "I don't know where to begin to make up for what I did. I always hoped that maybe my feelings of guilt would subside as time went on, but I don't feel like they have. I feel like on some level I can identify with soldiers that go back to villages that twenty years ago they had completely destroyed and ransacked, those soldiers that go back and apologize to the people they harmed, their kids and grandkids. And maybe in the future I will do something like that and talk to her about it."

A few months after we spoke, she did. Nancy was surprised to hear from her. Kathy e-mailed me:

> I lost the friendship and trust of the one person who meant the most to me. We are now friends again, but we lost the level of trust that we once had, in addition to the time that we weren't friends. What I lost through the thoughtlessness of my actions can never be regained, and if I could have understood that the state of our relationship today is the consequence of my actions, I think things would have been different. I never realized that I could potentially destroy my friendship with my best friend, and if I could have realized that, I would never have imagined that it would bear this much influence on my life these years later.

Kathy believes the experience has made her more compassionate and empathetic. Nevertheless, the memory of her betrayal has never faded. "What good does it do to say I'm sorry?" she asked me.

in control

Like Samantha, whose relationship with Annie is described in chapter two, some girls may be unaware of their cruel behavior. When I first started interviewing people for my book, I began speaking with my friends. Roma, whom I met in college, told me about being abused by one of her best childhood friends. Jane's aggression ranged from telling Roma she hoped she died in a fire to forming elaborate clubs that Roma wasn't allowed to join. Jane prank-called her, called her clothes cheap and her mother a hippie, frequently exercised her ability to turn her other friends against her, and ridiculed Roma's intense affection for friends. At the same time, Roma remembered, "She was a charmer. That was the other part of her. When you were in her favor, it was so great. She was fun and silly and just really sweet." The torment lasted eight years. It was ninth grade when the two finally let go of each other.

When Roma was twenty-three, Jane's mom called Roma's mom, Ellen, searching for Roma's number. Jane wanted to talk to Roma. Ellen explained that her daughter was not interested. "What do you mean?" Jane's mom asked incredulously. "They were such good friends." When Ellen told Jane's mother about her daughter's behavior, she was astonished.

Shortly afterward, Roma and her best friend Sally were home for the holidays and hanging out in a café when Jane came in. Roma remembered, "She started talking to Sally like I wasn't there, saying things like, 'I live in San Francisco now. Doesn't your best friend live in San Francisco?'" Finally, Roma asked Jane if she had something to say. Jane turned to Roma and said, "Why did you tell your mother that we were never friends?" She began to weep. "If we were never friends," Jane cried, "how do I know that you like to sleep with your feet above the blanket and that you don't like peanut butter?" Jane ran through a list of personal facts about Roma as Roma listened stiffly. The two women recalled such vastly different stories of their friendship that Roma didn't know how to respond.

Danielle, a sophomore at Linden, met me over lunch to tell me about how controlling she was of two girlfriends between third and seventh grade. She struggled to describe her behavior. "I don't know how to . . . explain it," she said haltingly. "I wanted to control them and who they hung out with. I wanted to make sure they were never closer to the other girls than I was. And that they never did stuff with them when I wasn't there."

Danielle wanted to be the girls' only friend, although she allowed herself as many friends as she wanted. She was afraid the other girls would be more liked than she was. "I think that's basically why I did it," she said, remembering Jessica in a low, strained voice that sounded far older than her fifteen years. "She was really nice and everyone loved her. I guess I wanted to have control over that."

Later on in our interview, which was filled with increasingly long periods of awkward silence, Danielle admitted that Emma also made her jealous. "I remember when we'd just be hanging out and people would be like, 'Oh my God, I love your hair.' I was so jealous. And I used to be like, 'That's so annoying.'"

Mostly, however, Danielle remembered her need for control. "I never wanted her to do things. I wanted to be with her doing things, like going out. I didn't want her to have a sleepover somewhere and me not be there. That's the main thing," she said. That way, she explained, "I would have someone to fall back on, who would always be there for me and never be like, 'Oh, I'm doing something with someone else.'"

Danielle lived with her parents, both professionals, in an affluent Northeastern community. Her mother and father were invested in her social life, and her dad was especially interested. She told me, "I always feel like he wants me to live through him and be more—I'm definitely more outgoing than both of my parents. So I guess they feel like, um, they always make sure that I have tons of friends and that I'm happy."

After a long pause, she added, "I don't tell my dad when I'm having problems with friends because I think he would be disappointed in me. I'm just afraid he's going to look down on me, like why are you having problems? Or if I'm not friends with someone anymore."

I had never known Danielle, normally exuberant, to be this quiet. "I look back on it now and I realize it was so mean and cruel," she said. And then, somewhere after sixth grade, she said her personality did a "complete change." It was as simple as understanding that control isn't the right way to make friends. "I should gain my friends by being nice rather than . . ." She didn't finish. She could hardly imagine herself behaving in those ways today, and it was hard to remember the other times.

Listening to Danielle, we are returned again to the centrality of relationship and connection in girls' lives. As the fear of isolation has fueled some girls' decisions to stay in bad friendships, here it inspired Danielle's controlling behavior. Adrienne Rich has written that a person who does not tell the truth "lives in fear of losing control. She cannot even desire a relationship without manipulation, since to be vulnerable to another person means for her the loss of control."[35] A fear of isolation or abandonment, then, may be key to understanding some alternative aggressions.

the wages of repression

"When my parents divorced, I was mad a lot," said Molly, who was sitting opposite me on the yellowed grass in the sun outside her junior high. Pale and lanky, she had a mop of brown hair, green eyes, braces, and the awkward, slightly stretched features of a girl on the cusp of a growth spurt. "I was mad at my friends," she explained, "because, you know, everybody has two parents and I don't."

Molly was in eighth grade and living in Ridgewood with her mother, who has a degenerative disease. Although her mother was not wheelchair bound, her walking was impaired and she was in chronic pain. Molly's father, whom Molly saw every other weekend, lived in another town. Her mother's illness made her father's absence even more difficult.

Molly thought her friends often bragged about their nuclear families. They talked about going to the mall with their mothers, a trip Molly's mom had never been well enough to make. Recently, a friend had a birthday party and invited all the girls and their mothers to shop together. Molly couldn't go. When her friends asked why Molly's mother did not volunteer at church, or mother-daughter ac-

tivities, Molly felt embarrassed and left out. "I'm like, 'Well, that's
kind of hard for me,' and they're like, 'Well, I can't help it,' and I'm
like, 'Well, I can't either.'" Molly looked at me. "It's not fair. It's like
they're laughin' at you or something."

I asked Molly if they have laughed about it to her face.

"I don't think they exactly laugh at me," she said slowly, thinking.
"I'm sure most people feel sorry for me. I just think that maybe
when I say stuff like that, they kind of look at each other, look
around, just try to get off the subject or something. And that really
hurts my feelings."

When she gets angry, Molly said, she tries to ignore it and stop
thinking about it. "I try to look on the bright side," she said, "and
think, at least I have a mother, some people don't have a mother."
She listed a few things that could be worse. But sometimes, when
she can't ignore the anger, she feels it inside all day "till it drives me
crazy." Then she cries. During those times, she said, her father is not
around when she needs him, so she may get angry at her friends or
their parents. "It's not their fault," she said, "but the anger has to go
somewhere so it goes to whoever I'm around."

She had only "blown up" once at her mother for the ways her disease constrains Molly's life, and especially for not having a boyfriend.
"I didn't mean to," Molly said, twisting a clump of grass into rope.
"Now I'm just kind of sorry I did." After Molly yelled, her mother
was silent for a long time. "She goes, 'Well, I can't help it. I'm disabled. Nobody wants me, you know.'" Surely there was someone
out there, Molly pleaded. "And she just sort of looked at me funny."
The conflict "sort of blew away," she said, because they never spoke
of the subject, or the fight, again.

In general, Molly tried to keep her mother at arm's length. Molly
was always having to take down posters in her room when they offended her mother's fervent Baptist beliefs, even the Backstreet
Boys pictures. Her mother wouldn't buy her rock-and-roll music
and preferred to hear Christian music in their home. Out with her
friends once, Molly mentioned her mother didn't like her browsing
through the rock posters. "They look at me like I'm crazy. And that

makes me mad because I'm like, y'all, it's just the way she is, I can't say anything about it."

Molly said she has made fun of girls over the years: "Their clothes, hair, just anything that came to mind." Afterward she'd feel bad and try unsuccessfully to be friends. Other times she's gotten in fights. "I was so mad," she explained, "and I wanted to start a fight." She threatened a girl, so they went outside, but nothing happened. Like the conflict with her mother, "it sort of blew off."

I asked Molly what it feels like to be angry. "You feel hatred toward somebody and you try not to, but it's like they've been pulling on you and it's kind of hard to stop yourself when someone's pulling," she said. "You keep thinking about it and the more you think about it, the worse it makes you feel." When she finally decides to act, "Going after somebody, you have the intention to tear into them. You build all these emotions up into this steam like you want to run that person over. And you feel hateful, you feel hate towards them, and a lot of times you want to go at them. A lot of times you can't stop yourself. You want to but you can't stop yourself. It's hard to stop yourself once you start." Like the aggression Anne Campbell observed in women, Molly's aggression only emerges unpredictably, when she no longer has the strength to resist it.

Molly cherished her best friend, but lately there had been a lot of tension between them. "She gets mad at me and I'll do anything to be her friend again. I'll do anything," she said urgently. But Kate has rarely said why she was angry at Molly, so Molly has asked, waited patiently, written "nice letters." Then, she explained, "just one day, the next day, she'll start talking to me, and we'll start talking, and it just all goes away. I don't think about it anymore."

"I can't say anything about it": these words, Molly's own, were the story of her life. On her plate were more restriction, more stress, than most reasonable adults could handle. Divorce, disability, economic hardship, religious restrictions—the list went on and on. Molly was, against the odds, trying to be a "good girl," to "look at the bright side," to care for her ailing mother, to swallow life without an attentive father, to be understanding of the disease that debilitated her mother and bridled her own life, a disease that made even things like car pooling and play dates and clothes shopping embarrassing.

Like so many girls, Molly lets go only when she can't stop herself, when the anger pops, although most times, as she said, the conflict "blows away." Her passive tone belies the truth she feels: that in fact she is not entitled to conflict, to anger, to expressing her intense emotions. Her mother, who asks Molly to empathize and nurture, cannot bear the burden of her frustration. Nor can her father, whose rare company must be treasured, whom she must please. Under these circumstances, aggression will seep through only the most permeable wall, and it is likely Molly feels most herself, and least restricted, when she is with her friends.

Molly is as passionate and fierce as graffiti, telling me hurriedly that she wants to be better than others, to be the best student, the prettiest, and "all that stuff." She has run for class president and homecoming queen (this last one is frustrating; she never wins because she isn't popular at all). Even as she told me of her penchant to cut people down who compete with her, to make fun of girls' families and friends, to spread rumors and talk behind people's backs, she told me, "I try to be nice to everyone. I just want to be everyone's friend. I want everyone to like me, and if I do anything to hurt somebody's feelings I want them to know that I didn't mean to do it or anything."

Perhaps more than anyone else I interviewed, Molly exemplifies the girl who has been taught not to know aggression, and yet is incapable of *not* knowing it. That she is clearly not a conventional bully makes her story a powerful example of how keeping girls away from natural feelings of anger can lead them to cruel or inappropriate acts. For Molly, anger is both foreign and central to her self, and the combination leaves her at once blinded and submerged by it.

When I asked women and girls to talk about times they had bullied or been mean to other girls, they were suddenly indisposed. There were closets to be cleaned, homework to get done, cavities to be filled. After reading some of my interview questions, one girl blocked me from e-mailing her ever again.

At first I thought my inability to track down girl bullies would be a fatal flaw in my research, but it turned out to be the research itself. If girls were going to such great lengths to hide their aggression, they'd hardly be breaking down my door to talk about it. Girls think being "mean"—conveying open, individual expressions of negative feelings—is just as bad as being fat, ugly, or uncool. So, for that matter, do most women. "Mean" undermines the core of the feminine identity: to be nice, to nurture, to say yes. As it turned out, I was coming up against the same problems as the first aggression researchers, who took women at their word when they refused to be aggressive under the microscope.

I can see things more clearly now. I can remember girls widely acknowledged to be bullies, girls whose multiple victims had interviewed individually with me for hours, who assure me that, "When I get angry, I'll read my Bible" or "When I'm mad, I'll get sad. It doesn't feel good to be angry." I waited for a disclosure that would never come.

The same thing had happened the first time I asked a group of mostly white, middle-class girls to volunteer stories of being mean. They'd looked at me as though I'd asked them to swallow live goldfish. The next time, I took the hint. I asked the girls to role-play a hypothetical situation with girl bullies and victims they didn't know. The floodgates opened. As long as they didn't have to personally identify as mean, they had plenty to say.

The weirdest thing was, I had done the same thing. When I first started hanging out with girls, I never identified myself as a former mean girl. My victimization in third grade was a trump card that had embedded itself comfortably into my life's narrative. People nodded gravely when they heard why I was writing the book. "Oh, of course," they said, their eyes serious and sympathetic. The truth is, I approached writing this chapter the same way I'd sauntered into that

Washington lounge to meet Anne: without a thought to my own capacity for cruelty. That wasn't me, I thought; *I* did what I had to do. I was merely an accomplice, an enabler. I was different than Abby, than Rebecca: *they* were demons. *They* were evil.

Then, after writing up the stories of Kathy, Megan, and the others, something felt wrong to me. I couldn't put my finger on it, but eventually I knew: I couldn't deliver the demon. There was no evil child here, no bad apple. These girls were good people who had done bad things, and for understandable, if not good, reasons. They were not the cold, cunning creatures girl bullies are so often made out to be.

The belief that we are only victims or only bullies has caricatured the memories and discussions of girls' meanness. It has also helped many of us dismiss the complexity of our own behavior. The upshot is that it's transformed "us against them" into "us against us."

By washing our hands of our own capacity to injure, we perpetuate the stereotype that females are nonaggressive. We become accomplices in the culture's repression of assertive women and girls by making aggression pathological, private, and hidden. We also help silence the public discussion of the ways and reasons girls are mean to each other. Most disturbingly, we become strangers to each other. By leaving these episodes in the private, emotional realm, by continuing to imagine those who have bullied us living in the gutter and falling off cliffs—and trust me, I have—we deprive alternative aggressions of a fair hearing and ourselves of a more honest sisterhood, because to put it out there would mean we have to admit to ourselves that inside we are all mean, that inside we are all aggressive. And girlfriends, we *are*.

"Oh, yeah," I'd hear in cafés, at parties, on grocery lines. "It happened to me." Nearly everyone I met had a story to tell, a wretched moment to remember. But meanness, anger, impulsive, thoughtless behavior—it's in each of us. Even my conscience cannot throw itself fast enough before the speeding train of my meanness: I have indulged in the knowledge of a shared secret, in eyes locking exclusively with someone else's or rolling in furtive annoyance. I have said I wasn't angry when I was, then degraded people behind their backs. I have gossiped. I have relished that rush of inclusion at the expense of an odd girl out. Have you?

The question bears answering.

It is time to own our own feelings—to own up, as author Rosalind Wiseman would say.[36] It is time, in all seriousness, to get in touch with our inner bully.

When we hide natural feelings of competition, jealousy, anger, and resentment, we lie to each other and ourselves. Our friendships, as so many of us know, pay the price. When I started living with my close friend and college roommate Jenny, our first big fight swelled rotten and quiet inside our small apartment until one day it cracked wide open. "You make me feel badly because I wake up at eleven in the morning!" she said. "Your boyfriend's too loud when he comes in at night," I shot back. We went back and forth, beckoning each other toward the edge, where we finally teetered perilously. I seesawed between rage and panic. I knew I was being defensive, even irrational, but I could hardly contain my anger. "I'm just not sure if this is going to work out," she said quietly. She sounded resigned and sad. "I just don't know if we can do this."

My head felt gummy. I was holding my breath, tingling with fear. "What is it?" I finally shouted. "What is so bad here that we have to end our friendship?"

Then, abruptly, she asked, "Don't you think you're arrogant?" I froze. Was this a trick question?

"Yes?" I half asked, mental fingers crossed.

"Good," she said. "Because if you hadn't said that, I wouldn't be able to trust you."

Now we said it: I was jealous. I was jealous of her beautiful body and her irresistible sexual allure. I was jealous of her spiritual enlightenment, the ease with which she loved and was loved. Jenny was jealous, too: of my steely self-discipline, my grasp of current events. She envied my social life and my regular gym schedule.

Here we were, two young women standing tremulous before the Great and Powerful Oz. The curtain had been pulled back, and jealousy, expelled between us on the black couch, was laid bare. Now that we had confessed it, face to face, now that it had been yanked from its hiding place, jealousy was nothing special, nothing insurmountable. In fact, as we looked at each other, still sitting there intact, jealousy felt like nothing much, not even half of what we thought it would be.

Thinking back to that day, I remember the summer I learned to kayak. The guide instructed me to lean into the rush of the river's current, but when I began to lean in that first time I jerked back, muscles taut. No way: I was going to capsize. My body's instinct was to lean *against* the weight of the water to create balance. If you do that, the instructor warned, you're going to flip over.

Jealousy feels this way: that it must be sequestered, that it will be the end of our friendships if we show it the light of day. But what saved Jenny and me that day was that the jealousy and anger became ours—not mine, not hers, not inside of us as it was, silent as a tumor, corroding us from within. When we acknowledged it, when we named it, it lost its dark, baleful hugeness. We gave it a place inside our relationship, made it a part of us, for better or for worse. And we were released.

How close I came to saying I wasn't arrogant but instead humble and sweet, ever respectful of others. How easy it was to forget Anne, to let my betrayal fade away from my consciousness. Our culture has made truth telling and anger, indeed, everything that is "not nice," feel very wrong to girls. We have been taught that the right answer is the one that hurts the least. As Brown and Gilligan have shown us, it is critical that girls learn how to expose their most uncomfortable feelings to "the air and the light of relationship."[37] For at the core of us are natural feelings of anger and desire, the messy, uncomfortable truths that make us, our relationships, our friends and lovers, imperfect.

Denying those feelings locks us away from ourselves and so from authentic relationships with others. Denying those feelings doesn't make them go away but somewhere else, leaving the people around us unsure of what we mean, who we are, and how we feel. Denying them takes us to a place others sense but do not see. It is a place no girl deserves to be.

CHAPTER *six*

popular

I have been invited to hang out at a birthday sleepover. The girls, who are all students at an exclusive same-sex school in the Northeast, barely notice my entrance. They are scattered like flower petals across the birthday girl's bedroom floor. Each has dutifully brought a makeup bag that spills over with glittering gels, lipsticks, shadows, and glosses. Some sit contentedly in front of friends as their hair is braided and smeared with sparkly goo. They have yet to eat dinner, but a few have already changed into pajamas. Soft cotton tank tops with short bottoms that furl up seem to dominate. Hair is long and blown dry, nails manicured and polished.

After a light dinner, the girls move to the living room, where they spontaneously begin painting toenails. The television flickers and hums. Foam toe separators have been supplied by the host. As images of Marc Anthony and Christina Aguilera flash through the room, a girl chirps, "Oh, he is soooo hot!" "Totally!" a few voices rise up from the couch. An ad for a film with Matt Damon appears. "I'm *so* excited he's single again!" coos a girl who has momentarily stopped buffing.

Almost as soon as her toes are done, one girl, willowy as a reed, hops on the stationary bike and shouts, "I'm going to work off my dinner!" A few others jump up and begin clamoring for a turn. For the next hour, the girls climb on and off the bike, making sure to announce the number of calories they are burning with the regularity of train conductors.

They are nine years old.

Researchers have nailed down some broad ideas about what makes girls popular, but they remind me of my mom out to dinner without her reading glasses: She knows what restaurant we're at, but she can't read the menu. When a prominent research team observed students at an Ohio public elementary school, they witnessed the most pronounced sex differences in popularity politics. For girls, they concluded, success was having money, good looks, and "social development," which they defined as the "early attainment of adult social characteristics."[38] Which most mothers could have told them without the trouble of a formal study.

As parents with a pulse know, popular girls get maximum access to the booty of womanhood. The cool girls are the first to discover makeup and boys. They get the parents born without genes for party supervision, bedtime setting, and credit card control. They look and act like they just stepped off the pages of a Delia's catalog. They do just about everything and anything to simulate womanhood.

But here is the truth about girls and popularity: It is a cutthroat contest into which girls pour boundless energy and anxiety. It is an addiction, a siren call, a prize for which some would pay any price. Popularity changes girls, causes a great many of them to lie and cheat and steal. They lie to be accepted, cheat their friends by using them, steal people's secrets to resell at a higher social price. It is an accepted fact of life, an eleven-year-old advised me, that "if girls have a chance to be popular, they will take it, and they wouldn't really care who they were hurting."

Women have long relied upon their affiliations with others to enhance social status, and at its core, popularity is a mean and merciless competition for relationships. When women lacked earning power and equality, they were especially inclined to "marry up: to marry men who are taller, richer, older, stronger, with at least the promise of more social clout."[39] Despite the advent of girl power, many girls today cut their friendships from the same cloth. Lexie remembers the thrill of having a popular friend. "It meant so much for me and my self-esteem," she told me. "I used to drop her name in conversation with friends or write her name in my schoolbooks because I wanted people to know that Susan K., one of the cool girls, liked *me*!" Jessie Johnston, a sixth grader, explained, "It's pressure you put on yourself. I wish she was my best friend because she's really popular and that would make me popular, too." A high school junior put it more bluntly: "You use people to advance up the hierarchy."

With scientific precision, girls track their bearings on the relational landscape. They chart alliances in professional-looking graphs, monitoring the balance of power. One sixth-grade graph I saw positioned peers along an axis that began with *A* ("Acquaintance") and ended at *BF* ("Best Friend"). In the diary of seventh grade she lent me, Lily Carter's story of her life is always told in terms of relationships. "It is really hard for me to write about my life," she begins, "but I'll try."

> Today Arlyn was talking about Asia and how she didn't have her own personality. It got me thinking about myself. Julia has stopped talking to me since her Bat Mitzvah. It really bothers me. Liz is nice to me except she never calls me, I call her. It makes me feel inferior or something. Anyway I was thinking that maybe Liz has stopped being as nice to me as she was at the beginning of the year.

With relationships in constant flux, girls pressure peers to evaluate their friendships, their looks, their personalities. Emily's friend presided over a weekly ritual in which she seated their clique in a secret circle and gave each girl a grade out of one hundred. Such events are anything but frivolous. In the uncertain world of girls' relationships, the need to know anything for certain is urgent. The number may be the one thing you can hold on to.

"People ask, who do you like more as a best friend, me or so-and-so?" Ashley Vernon said, just after telling me shyly that she is the most popular girl in her grade. When she told her friend that she likes people equally, the girl replied, "Well, you gotta like one of us more. You gotta have a really, really good friend." Once, when the girl learned she was liked more than someone else in their clique, she left a gloating note in the "less liked" girl's locker. Ashley's friends compete to sit next to her, often making her pick a number; the closest guesser gets the lucky seat. "They think it's a privilege to be there or something," she said sheepishly.

In the race for popularity, girls take on as many friends as they can, trying to balance them like so many saucers stacked and swaying on a tray. America Online hit the jackpot with its Instant Messenger technology, which allows girls to exchange cybermessages with their peers in real time—actually, about as many online buddies as can fit on a single screen. Girls can have a hundred people or more on their buddy lists. They can exchange messages with five people at once, have someone over at their house, and still be on the phone, thus managing multiple relationships at once. "It's like being able to be on the phone but with six individual conversations!" crowed eighth-grader Shelley McCullough. "It's a way to extend your friendships." IM, as it's called, is dominated by girls, no doubt because it's a girl gizmo that fits their social specs to a tee. Perhaps that's why one junior chortled to me cheerfully, "IM is God's gift to teenagers!"

Lily's diary tracks shifting alliances with growing panic. "Today was awful," she writes in January 1998. "Julia hasn't been nice to me all this week and I don't know why. Julia is taking over Liz and the two of them are completely excluding me. The same thing is happening to Asia with Arlyn and Julia." At soccer practice, she notes anxiously that Liz and Arlyn are mysteriously sitting in another row. "Neither Liz nor Arlyn waited for me or Asia after the game. . . . Arlyn turned her back on me the WHOLE PRACTICE! AAAAAHHHHH!"

Girls' fierce attachment to their friends illustrates the powerful influence relationship exerts over their lives. As they grow more socially sophisticated, the love between girls takes them into new, enchanting territory. But for girls on the popularity treadmill, friendship is rarely just friendship; it's a ticket, a tool, an opportunity—or a deadweight. You can own everything Abercrombie ever made, but if you don't have the right friends, you're nobody.

In the 1989 film *Heathers,* it is the threat and promise of relationships that drive the characters' jockeying to become "Heather #1," the most popular girl in school. Jason Dean is the dark new student who seduces the protagonist Veronica, helping her weave her repressed anger toward her friends into vengeful acts of violence. He forces one of the Heathers into his service by waving around an old photograph of her with Martha "Dumptruck," the biggest loser in school. Heather gasps. A long-expired relationship with a "lesser" person would be enough to bring her down, and she knows it.

After Veronica embarrasses Heather Chandler by throwing up at a college party, the ringleader corners her and snarls, "You were nothing before you met me. You were playing Barbies with Betty Finn. You were a Bluebird. You were a Brownie. You were a Girl Scout cookie." Without me, she crows, "Monday morning you're history. I'll tell everyone about tonight."

Relationships are the Rosetta stone of girls' social status. Not surprisingly, they often inspire suspicion: *Why is she my friend? Why did she buy her that gift? What does she want from me? Or I from her?* The popularity contest leaves many girls dubious of their peers' intentions. Daniella mused, "When you're separately with your friends, they're like, 'Oh, you're so much better than [the others], the way you do that is so great.' You get all these compliments but they're not always meaningful. Or, like, [they say] you have better hair, or you're *so* much better than they are. But what they're saying to you is meaningless. . . . it's to make you think you should go to them."

At Marymount, Emily listed some of the relational calculations she and her friends have made. "She's going to be invited to the next party, so I'll be friends with her, or I'll be friends with her because she's rich." The strategy also works in reverse. A fifth grader in

Mississippi explained, "They can act like you're the most important person and then they'll leave you. When you need them the most, they dump you....When they're popular enough, they just move on." Jessie Johnston said, "I'd rather just go around 'cause if you're in the popular group and something happened, suddenly no one really likes you. With their influence you can just plummet to the bottom."

Authentic connections between girls are the first to go in the race for popularity. Getting popular requires strategy and calculation, that affection be shown selectively, that some be left behind, that others be attended to in private, and that the rules change from day to day. "It's not a contest," warned the ad for *Popular*, the WB's hit television show. "It's a war."

friends, sometimes

The sudden loss of a close friend to popularity is one of the most wrenching and common experiences I observed. The course of things is simple enough: one girl's window to popularity opens and she jumps through it, leaving her close or best friend behind. The abandoned find themselves alone with the knowledge they don't have what it takes to be cool.

The aftermath of the change is far more complicated. The break is often not clean but gradual, and there are a variety of scenarios. Some girls are mean in public and nice in private. Others are the reverse. Some girls simply behave as though their friends no longer exist.

But when the ditched girls cling to broken pieces of friendship with those who have only partially abandoned them, they suffer well beyond the moment of initial loss. By staying friends with these girls, they learn that they will be cared for at times and under circumstances beyond their control. There is no language to articulate this behavior, and especially the confusion and sadness that result. As they lose control of their relationships, girls feel privately responsible for their loss.

As any witnessing parent knows, these are not simply part-time friendships. They are abusive. They are a training ground in which vulnerability and disempowerment are learned and the ability to identify abuse is lost. One girl described the situation this way: "It's kind of like a new friendship begins and then it ends three hours later. And then it begins the next week and it ends three hours later." But there can be little self-respect when a girl learns to be loved on someone else's terms. The willingness to give oneself over to another's omnipotence in a friendship bears disturbing similarities to the willingness of a victim to remain in a violent relationship. I worry that if we do not teach girls early on to know and resist these dynamics, we may be permitting the groundwork to be laid for violence in their adult lives.

For children, there is something almost profane about being abandoned by a close friend. It undermines the few assumptions they are old enough to make—that friends are nice, that love and care will be reciprocated in kind—at a critical developmental moment. The impact of such a loss should not be underestimated.

Lucia and Haley had been best friends at Sackler since third grade, and this year, in fifth grade, they'd been placed in the same class with the lion's share of the popular girls. During the second week of school, Haley got the uneasy feeling that Lucia was ignoring her. She decided to check and asked Lucia a few times to play at recess. Sure enough, Lucia apologized and refused, telling Haley she was playing with someone else. It was always one of the cooler girls. In no time it was clear that Lucia was getting popular, playing soccer at lunchtime and being partners with new girls during class.

Haley and I were rocking gently on a damp wooden swing outside her house in the balmy April air. As she dipped her sneaker down to kick up chips of mud, I swung my legs around and leaned back against the armrest. I noticed the contrast her pale skin made against the tiny freckles pooling under her eyes. Haley's coffee-colored hair was broomstick straight, and her eyes were serious behind wire-rim glasses as she watched the mud. She reminded me of Harriet the Spy. I asked Haley how she was feeling.

"I feel hurt," she said, her words slow and measured. "I feel she's got other things to do and that I'm not as important as other people. Sometimes I just try and brush it off, but I really can't, and I have that feeling that you know, it's gonna end soon, our friendship. We never had a fight, and then all of a sudden, she's in another crowd, she doesn't care about me anymore. We stopped talking, it's finished."

I asked the obvious question. "Did you talk to Lucia about it?" Haley's eyes widened and she thrust her chin forward, indignant at the stupidity of the question. Of course she had. Lucia denied anything had changed in their friendship.

"So . . . who's right?" I asked hesitantly, bracing for another reprimand. Haley's voice tightened with frustration.

"Sometimes I know that I'm right because I know who's hurting me. But I mean, then who is? I would know who's hurting my feelings! I say, 'You're hurting my feelings,' and people go back and say, 'What are you talking about? I'm not doing anything.' That's what I get a lot of: 'No I'm not!'"

For a brief moment there was nothing but the muted creak of the damp swing. "I think that maybe I'm not sure about my feelings," she said more evenly. "I don't know! I question my feelings. I'm like, 'Is she really saying this?' Because I was really sure that yesterday she was *ignoring* me, or yesterday she wouldn't talk to me at recess or something like that. And I really question the fact."

Haley echoed the remarks of so many girls: the feeling of "being crazy," of not being able to know for sure the realness of one's own feelings or version of events in the world. Haley knew she was being ignored, yet the girl she loved and trusted was telling her otherwise. For Haley, it was as though Lucia said the sky was brown with as much certainty as Haley felt when she saw it as blue, yet Haley could not decide who was right. Lucia was pulling Haley away from what Haley knew was true about herself, her feelings, and her life, and into a place where she would doubt the worth of all of these, offering them up to Lucia for definition. Lucia had managed to hurt Haley while assuring her that, in fact, she was not hurt at all, that she was imagining all of this.

Anyway, Haley told me, kicking her legs up and swinging us forward, Lucia was still a good friend.

"When?" Did I miss something?

"Sometimes, every Thursday after school, I stay till five and have dance class till six. So I stay for an hour and thirty minutes. Then we're friends." I sat quietly, unsure what to say, listening to us swing.

"Look," she said. "You have to make very sure you're not going to yell at them for no reason, and make a mistake."

"Why?" I asked.

And here was the real reason Haley was afraid to press the case. It was the thread of fear that runs through so many girls' relationships: the fear that conflict of any kind will result in relational loss. "Because then you would lose—they would be like, 'No, why are you doing this to me? Maybe I shouldn't be your friend.' So you could lose somebody."

"They can break you down," she explained, "until you're like, 'Oh, I shouldn't speak to anyone else. I should just curl up in the corner during recess and just not talk to anybody anymore.' Sometimes it makes you think you've got no friends even if you do. And it makes you hurt other people sometimes."

As Haley saw it, she had two choices: put up with the best she can get or speak up and lose everything. Hold on to the tatters of a relationship because it was preferable to no relationship at all. At ten, with her best friend Lucia, Haley was learning to settle for much, much less, and so to feel disposable and used. She was learning, as many girls do, to carve a tiny space for herself in this relationship—in this case ninety minutes a week during dance class—where she would tell herself that she was happy, that indeed this may be the most she deserves. And she would come to blame herself for the way she was being treated.

Haley would draw the line, she said, when Lucia was no longer nice in private. "I mean, I know she's always going to be a good friend to me and that I can talk to her. It's just the fact that when we're in class or..." She trailed off. "I don't know. I don't know."

Haley was still unsure. She veered between what she knew was true and what Lucia wanted her to believe. "Maybe she feels she spends too much time with me, and she needs to spend time with other people. I just don't wanna—I'm just—I'm just afraid—I don't want to try it—try risking a friendship outside. I'm just going to leave it because I've got other friends." She exhaled loudly, spluttering with frustration.

Like Haley, many girls describe their feelings in part-time friendships as simply "bad." There is a hint of resignation in their voices, a somber recognition that this is the way of their world. As Jessica told me, "Even though you feel like girls only want to be your friends for a few hours, they have to [do what it takes to] be popular."

the price of popularity

Some girls can't get popular unless they pay for it. Call it a dowry or hazing, a cover charge or a sacrificial offering of loyalty: however you look at it, sometimes a girl has to squash a friend to rise above the mortals. Girls told me two versions of this story: in the first, the supplicant, as I'll call her, publicly bullies her friend while she is nice to her in private. In the illustration to this story, I see the bully blowing on a single dandelion, her friend. Some wisps of friendship cling to the stem while others flutter to the ground, leaving parts of the core bald, bare, and struggling, yet still alive. In the second story, the victim is offered up as booty to the popular clique, and the shroud of friendship falls away completely.

Now in her forties and living with her partner in the Northwest, Janet says her mind wanders often to the memory of Cheryl, her best and often only friend from third through eighth grade. Every day after school, the two girls talked on the phone or played together. They spent nights holding elaborate dance contests at each other's homes, which were only two blocks apart. In the winter, they iceskated and drew maps of the sinewy streams that ran through their southern Illinois college town.

But when the homeroom bell rang, Janet never knew if Cheryl would be her friend. Cheryl wanted to be in the popular group, and Janet, short and awkward with thick glasses, was a liability. Cheryl was bigger and taller than Janet, a lightning-fast runner. At school, she always looked right in her clothes. Around the cool kids, Cheryl called Janet names and told her to get away. She nicknamed her "Bottle Eyes" and ordered the other girls to steal her glasses. She laughed the loudest while Janet, frightened and blinded, felt her way on bended knee along the black tar playground, searching for the school door. Whenever the cooler girls left Cheryl out, she would run back to Janet, who never protested.

Janet found comfort in academic success and relied on it to distract her through the rough days. Often the only one to raise her hand in class, Janet remembers a powerful intent to be good and do the right thing. Despite her success, Janet confided that "my doing better in school didn't count in my eyes that way. She dominated me. She wanted to be in control." When Cheryl asked Janet why she'd gotten a better grade on a test, Janet answered, "I think I'm more focused than you are." Cheryl teased her mercilessly about using the word "focused." In her junior high yearbook, Cheryl wrote, "To one of the dumbest people I know. Oh well, maybe you'll grow out of it. Your friend, Cheryl." Janet was crushed but remained silent.

Eventually, Cheryl's attacks moved beyond the perimeter of the school. Little was visible to others as she hollowed out the center of their friendship and filled it with meanness and hate. To anyone looking from the kitchen window into the backyard the girls were the picture of loving friendship, while outside on the grass Cheryl dominated Janet, demanding that she obey her every wish. The murmur behind Janet's door was the familiar hum of chattering girls, while on the rug Cheryl snarled that Janet's shoes were stupid and pushed her to wear her first bra, pantyhose, and other "cool" accessories. Janet was broken and quiet, attached to and abused by her only friend.

Today, in counseling, Janet feels certain that resolving her feelings about Cheryl will help her cope with lifelong feelings of low self-esteem. Not surprisingly, the hardest part has been renaming the friendship as the abuse that it truly was. "I'm still struggling to know that it was abusive," she told me. "At the time I thought there was something wrong with me, that I deserved this treatment. I thought of her as a real friend. I thought this is what friendship was. I'm still working on extracting myself from that point of view.

"I don't remember ever thinking she shouldn't be treating me like this, that this is not what a friend does. I really didn't know that," she said. "I took whatever friend was willing to play with me. When she was mean to me I thought I deserved it because somewhere down in there I believed I was a bad person who hurt people, so if someone was angry at me or hurting me, that was what I deserved."

As a child, Janet was sexually abused. Now, looking back, she sees shadows of her friendship with Cheryl in her experience as a survivor of sexual abuse. Both episodes, she told me, deprived her of power and control. "Someone has the right to do whatever they want to me and it doesn't occur to me to say no. There is the feeling that it must be right for this to happen to me just because someone else is doing it," she said.

Janet cannot explain why she endured Cheryl's treatment in the first place. "That's still a mystery to me." Thinking of Cheryl today, she remembers "a very vivid image of her looking at me, her eyes hard and slitted." Yet she also remembers a best friend that she loved.

Janet surrendered her version of reality to her tormentor. Her need to remain in the relationship became destructive as she steeled

herself at the greatest costs to know this relationship as friendly. The
impulse of some girls to cling to a damaged relationship at any cost
demands our attention. Its link to the trials of bullying remains
largely unexplored.

Elizabeth had no trouble telling me that Deirdre was no friend, that she ruined fifth and sixth grade. Elizabeth e-mailed me that she'd like to talk, so I called her one day in Indiana, where she was in graduate school for psychology. Elizabeth said she became an outcast in third grade, though it was really only the popular girls who disliked her. Although she had always been well-liked at summer camp and during afterschool activities, she became the main target at school. Every September, Elizabeth prayed for a new girl to come to school. "It was my only hope," she said, laughing ruefully. "Anytime there was a new girl in school I would try my damnedest to sit next to her and talk to her and get to her before they did, because then I might be able to prove that I was worthy of being her friend before she found out I wasn't cool to be friends with."

In sixth grade Elizabeth had her chance with Deirdre, who slid behind a desk next to Elizabeth on the first day. It was friends at first sight, and they had a blissful month of busy sleepovers and lunchtimes and recesses. On the day of the Oktoberfest festival, Deirdre signed up to sit at a table during lunch selling baked goods with two popular girls, and their friendship was over as quickly as it started.

"She must have realized she was jeopardizing any chance she had of being popular by hanging out with me," Elizabeth told me. "She found out it just wasn't cool. She began to realize this would not bode well for her future. All of a sudden, she just switched, like night and day, and she was in with the popular girls and torturing me. She became the ringleader of the girls who did this."

Deirdre carried out flashy demonstrations of cruelty to show off to her new friends. She pointed and laughed from the lunch table and insulted Elizabeth at recess, often using what she knew intimately of Elizabeth to sharpen her barbs. The popular girls circled Deirdre like the petals on a single flower, and Elizabeth watched, stunned and silent. She steeled herself at school, refusing to let the girls see her break down, and collapsed on the couch at home to cry to her mother every night. "I had no self-esteem. I didn't trust anybody. I cried myself to sleep most nights," she said.

Once she was safely ensconced in the folds of the clique, Deirdre let up, but their group's disdain vibrated around them like a force-field. By the time Elizabeth graduated eighth grade, she said, "I had a wall a mile thick around me. I was the most defensive little ball, no one could get into me. Everyone had hurt me. Everyone I had trusted had abandoned me and made me feel like shit. I would trust people and think they were my friends, and then they would turn around and stab me in the back." Elizabeth began viewing herself as her own twin, inventing stories about her other life to new kids in the neighborhood. "I thought that maybe if I didn't tell them anything about who I really was, they might like me."

Like many women I spoke with, Elizabeth is certain the experience permanently altered her development as a person. "I had always been mellow and easygoing and all of a sudden I was hostile and sarcastic and bitter," she said. I can almost see her shrugging resignedly through the phone. "I had never been that before." Today Elizabeth studies psychology in part to understand how she was changed and how, as she put it, "could someone do this? It's just so wrong. It just didn't work in my head. It didn't compute."

In high school, Elizabeth's sudden popularity shocked her. She was amazed that people could like her just for who she was. Nevertheless, she said drily, "I'm still reaping the benefits of all this." She has only now, in her late twenties, begun to reconnect with women. Elizabeth felt safer around guys because, as she put it—echoing countless women I spoke with—"there was no bullshit, there was no cattiness, there was no competitiveness, there was nothing." She attended a women's college to avoid fraternities, only then realizing how fearful she still was of other women. "I put myself at a distance. I wouldn't trust them right off the bat. I always felt like there was a hidden agenda." Even now she can never shake the feeling of being an "outsider, feeling like I will never truly belong and also feeling like not wanting to."

secrets and lies

The popularity race shines a harsh, relentless spotlight on its contenders, raising the stakes on everything they say and do, making every utterance and outfit subject to peer punishment, reward, or worse, indifference. A girl at Linden explained, "Girls are judging me every second, examining me and thinking if they want to be my friend or not." A classmate added, "You don't see girls for who they are. You see girls for what they wear, who they hang out with. It's a package." The feeling of constant scrutiny creates an unpredictable social landscape that frequently causes sudden changes in behavior, so that many girls become different people depending on who they're with.

Chloe Kaplan, a fifth grader at Sackler Day School, and I were hanging out one afternoon on her tall twin canopy bed, white ruffles and stuffed animals spilling out beneath us. The wall above her desk was plastered with gummy, curling magazine cutouts of *NSync and Backstreet Boys, and a wicker dresser was scattered with tubes of glitter cream and disks of lip gloss. We sat cross-legged, shoes off, facing each other and unwrapping sticks of bubble gum.

For a ten-year-old, Chloe had an astonishing grasp of the politics of popularity and betrayal. She learned the hard way. In the first weeks of third grade, Alisa had approached and asked to be best friends. Delighted, Chloe said yes. At the time, she told me, "I didn't have the most friends in the third grade and I was making as many friends as I could." Chloe and Alisa played and spent recess together every day, chatting, playing jacks, trading stickers, and—their favorite—having upside-down contests on the monkey bars.

Some months later, Chloe found out that Alisa had been making up lies about her and telling her secrets to the popular girls. Chloe said she felt "really bad. It was like if you write in a diary, and someone reads it and they tell their friends what was in it and they tell their friends." When you've trusted someone that way, it hurts a lot. Chloe was afraid to say anything about it, she said, because "most of the friends I had came from her. If I lost her, I lost the rest."

Two years later, Chloe was still sad and perplexed that someone who seemed to care for her so much could also coldly violate her trust. But in the time she'd had to think about it, she'd figured out a couple of things.

For one thing, Chloe said, she notices now that some girls can change themselves depending on whom they're with. When her mom, who's president of the PTA, takes her to ice-cream socials, there are popular girls there who "act totally different—like they've been friends with you for a long time," and when they see her at school, "act like they don't know you and don't care about you." She told me about a popular classmate who's cruel and critical in school, but at sleepaway camp becomes a "whole different person . . . so much more nicer there."

The other thing, Chloe told me, is that she knows now that everything she did and said was being assessed and reported by Alisa. That it was, above all, currency to be traded with more popular girls. This year, she could sense the feeling of being judged following her around like a shadow, and it made her uncomfortable. The other girls watch and talk about everything: what she eats and wears, whom she plays with. "They care about everything but your personality," she said glumly. I asked what she meant. Well, she said, there was a girl in her class who wore capri pants with hearts and a matching shirt. "Everyone's gonna remember that," she explained, "because that's like baby and everything. Everyone will know that came from Kids 'R' Us. Everyone popular will be embarrassed to be her friend because they wear the updated clothes."

Chloe told me that fifth grade was a minefield: one misstep and you were done for. "If you do one stupid thing," she explained, "people will never forget that. Then they know you could not *ever* be a cool person. If you change, they don't realize it because they think of that stupid thing you did before." It's not worth it.

I asked her for an example of a "stupid thing."

"Like if you say a dumb comment," she said, blowing a bubble.

"Such as?"

"Such as if we're out telling jokes in school and everything, and you make a stupid joke, like why did the chicken cross the road, when they're making mean jokes. Or we're all in music [class], and the teacher leaves the room, and everyone's like, 'Oh, that's a really stupid song,' and you're like, 'Some parts of it are nice,' and they're like, 'Well, we're all saying it's stupid and you're talking about it being nice.' And everyone will say that together.

"It's just weird," she explained, squeezing a Beanie Baby, "because the quieter you are, the better off you are, because no one's going to find out or have rumors about you or anything. And the quieter you are, no one's gonna find out who you like and everything. And then you're better off because you're quiet and no one's going to find anything out about you. You don't tell. So no rumors about you and they only think of you as a quiet, nice person."

She placed her palms in back of her and dropped her head back, staring at the ceiling. "It's like each girl has a file, and everything you wear—if you wear like one off thing—goes in it," she said. "They don't even care about you anymore. And they throw the file away."

Chloe told me that her best friend's duplicity had changed everything for her. At the moment her capacity for emotional intimacy was deepening, as she shared the first quiet feelings of her heart, she was betrayed. What she shared with Alisa was laid bare to be dissected and mocked by everyone else. She could no longer completely trust that a friend was a friend, even if she appeared that way.

There is a movement within feminism that believes the female orientation to relationship and connection—to nurturing and caregiving—gives women a uniquely wise approach to their world. Popularity, however, turns this phenomenon on its head. In the race to be cool, some girls transform friendship into a series of deals and calculations, using relationship as much to destroy as to build. Relationship is no longer simply an end; it is also a means.

If popularity is a competition for relationships, getting ahead socially means new relationships must be targeted and formed, old ones dismissed and shed. Juliet, a ninth grader from Linden, explained why she and her two best friends used code names to describe the peers they ridiculed in fifth grade. "We wanted to be with our friends. We didn't want anybody to get in the way. We didn't want other people we didn't like hanging out with us. There were three of us and we knew so much about each other, and we didn't want that to break up or something. We didn't get pleasure out of making people feel bad. But we had to protect ourselves."

If girls' relationships are distinguished by secret telling and intimacy, the popularity seeker—or in girlspeak, the "wanna-be"—will use the accoutrements of relationship to her advantage. In a relational race, the winner will use intimacy as the mortar to wedge herself most tightly among the "right" people. She will communicate in words or actions that she can be depended on and trusted. To signal her loyalty, she may appear to abandon other relationships in her life; hence the mean-in-public, nice-in-private behavior. To shore up her position or edge out another girl, the wanna-be may have to minimize, even eliminate the relationships of someone else; hence the tormenting and secret telling in the presence of popular girls. In the typically tangled parlance of a teenager, a Mississippi ninth grader explained, "A lot of people may really like Melissa, but maybe the person [a girl is] talking to doesn't like [her]. To keep friends with both of them, she talks bad to the one who doesn't like [Melissa]."

In friendship, girls share secrets to grow closer. Relational competitions corrupt this process, transforming secrets into social currency and, later, ammunition. These girls spread gossip: they tell other people's secrets. They spread rumors: they invent other people's secrets. They gain calculated access to each other using intimate information.

Despite their dreams of glory, plenty of wanna-bes still fear direct conflict. A girl who, like Plunkett of Tammany Hall, "seen her opportunities and took 'em" is equally likely to abandon her lower-status friends without explanation. Rather than face an uncomfortable conflict where she has to announce her intention to move up and on, the wanna-be may assure her old friends that nothing at all is wrong; hence, Lucia's repeated assurances and Haley's feeling of craziness.

Girls bullied by their best or close friends often find themselves in these situations. Many parents have asked me to decipher the power these girls exercise over their daughters. The only answer I have is the one the girls give me: the bully controls her victim by controlling her version of events. For instance, when Michelle protested Erin's behavior, Michelle was told that she was almost always wrong, that it really happened this way, or not at all. "She would always get mad," Michelle recalled. "If you were mad at her about something, she would turn it around so that it was your fault. It would always be my fault, my fault, my fault."

When I suggested to Natalie that she confront Reese, Natalie retorted, "When you talk to her, she'll tell you a different story, and she's going to have all these explanations that make sense to you!" For these girls, it feels easier to believe someone else's story rather than their own. If they can know themselves as at fault and in need of forgiveness, they can continue to believe in the relationship rather than feel that they have been cast out of the circle of friendship.

the truth about popularity

It may come as a surprise, but once a girl gets her coveted status, popularity is no walk in the park. Competition and insecurity are rampant. When popular girls talk about their social lives, many of them talk about losing themselves. Their feelings closely mirror the symptoms psychologists associate with girls' loss of self-esteem.

Corinna, a sixth grader, was devastated when she lost one of her close friends to the popular clique. The girl and her new friends would "talk and walk very close together, and if one of their other good friends said hi, they won't, they don't, they can't hear," she remembered. Corinna set out to be included in the popular group and eventually won her way in. Once she was the one excluding her other friends from the popular crowd, Corinna felt dislocated and strange. "I know that I am kind of excluding [my other less popular friends] and I don't want to do that. But I feel like it's literally a bubble or something, and you get sucked in and then when you go out and stuff, it's just like so weird." She paused. "It's like, you go in, it's like, all of this talk and I don't know what else. They talk about boys and all these things. They have inside jokes that I don't really get."

I asked what it felt like inside the bubble.

"It kind of feels good because I'm like included, but then again I know these aren't the best friends for me," she explained. Here Corinna echoes the observations of Lyn Mikel Brown and Carol Gilligan: she has sacrificed her connection to her true feelings in order to remain in less authentic relationships with others.[40] In the process, she becomes disconnected from herself.

"I belong but I don't belong," she continued. "I fit into a lot of groups but I'm not part of any group. I'm walking around alone at recess. Sometimes I feel like I have so many friends but sometimes I feel like I have none, and everyone likes me or maybe they're just being nice." And sometimes, she said later, "sometimes I'll get sad and go into a shell even though I'm a happy-go-lucky person."

At Linden, Alexis, an extremely popular freshman, confided how hard it can be to keep up with other girls. "You don't trust anyone. You're totally insecure. To everyone you look fine, but it's very fake." Her friend Sarah agreed. "Are you my friend because of me or because I know this guy? False friendships are kept up for image all the time."

Now a sophomore, Lily Carter told me, "It takes so much more effort to be a part of that group than not to because when you're in that group it's so intense. It's like every second of every day you have to be perfect. You need to be perfect, your makeup needs to be perfect, you need to be wearing the perfect clothes. Your whole presence needs to be perfect, the way people look at you, the way you look at yourself. You know, I mean, what you say, everything you say, how the guys treat you, everything has to *be perfect*....[The hardest part] is that you're not perfect. That you're not doing everything perfectly. And that one day, you're going to wake up and you're just not going to be popular. And you're not going to have those friends anymore."

The closer they edge toward the center of the clique, the more some girls are urged to silence their own authentic voices. A few spoke to me wistfully of wanting to appear less "hyper," while some mentioned friends who warned that boisterous play was inappropriate and unattractive. These girls feel like they are no longer entitled to "be myself."

Heathers was the first in a string of movies depicting the clandestine politics of popular girl cliques. By the late 1990s, however, something had changed. A new fairy tale was being spun, and this time the prince was beside the point. In films like *She's All That* and *Cruel Intentions,* the romance was with popularity, the transformation of the girl from school geek to clique goddess. Popularity became so popular that it got its own show on the WB channel. In the film *Jawbreaker,* Courtney is part fairy godmother and mostly witch as she offers Fern the chance of a lifetime: "You're nothing. We're everything. You're the shadow, we're the sun. But I'm here to offer you something you never dared dream of. Something you were never meant to be. We're going to make you one of us. Beautiful and popular."

For better or worse, popularity is accepted by researchers and schools alike as a tool children use to group themselves socially. But the sheer volume of incidents of aggression spawned by the race for popularity deserves a closer investigation. Why is it so many of us are well trained to spot destructive images portraying girls as thin and beautiful, but we overlook the subtext of the race for popularity: that girls must be liked, even worshiped by their peers, often at the expense of authentic relationships? If some girls who want to be skinny starve themselves, some girls trying to be popular destroy one another. This makes popularity, and the race for it, as dangerous an issue for girls as weight, appearance, or sexuality.

When the politics of popularity devastate girls' relationships, the loss is multilayered. A girl is abandoned by someone she loves and trusts. The loss signals her low social value, an event that shrinks her self-esteem and for which she blames herself. She learns a new, dark understanding of relationship as a tool. And where the abandonment is public and followed by cruelty, there is public scorn and shame. For the newly popular girl, there is the danger of losing herself as she moves on and up into the "bubble."

The rules of popularity require that the girl who has arrived police herself as harshly as others do to maintain her status. The myth that popular girls are blissfully content couldn't be more wrong. The closer you get to the epicenter of popularity, the more perilous it gets. "Even though it looks secure, it's the most insecure thing in the world," Erin told me. "Everything changes in there. You compete with those five people every day: who does things first, who looks the best. It's hard and competitive. There's so much insecurity and fighting because you're selfish."

Lounging in a circle, sixteen eighth-grade girls were speaking informally with me about the feeling of being judged by others. Leslie, lying on her back, head propped up under clasped hands, had had it with me. I could tell. If her brown eyes rolled any higher they would disappear. She rocked her body up, exasperated. "Look, we can't stop talking about each other, okay?" she said. "We're addicted! As soon as we walk out of this room we're going to talk about what everyone said."

Bronwyn, a popular girl who had been sitting quietly for thirty minutes, finally raised her hand. "I just wish that people wouldn't judge each other, saying this person's not good enough. I hang around some people who just sit there and make fun of what people wear. I sit there and listen to it because I consider them my friends, but it bothers me. If they talk about other people, what are they saying about me?"

No one answered. They were thinking.

CHAPTER *seven*

resistance

For some girls, silence and indirection are neither attractive nor an option. They are instead signs of weakness. I found this to be true especially among the girls I met whose lives were marked by oppression. For them, assertiveness and anger were tools of spiritual strength. These young women might encounter the misogyny of families and neighbors, the racism of teachers, and threats of violence in their neighborhoods. Where economic struggle and disenfranchisement prevail, self-assertion and aggression become as much a part of the social landscape as playgrounds and ice-cream trucks. In this world, silence can mean invisibility and danger.

Lyn Mikel Brown and Carol Gilligan have found that girls on the margins of their school communities, whether because of race or class, "were more likely to stay in touch with their thoughts and feelings and to have close, confiding relationships."[41] Researchers studying the self-esteem and emotional health of some working-class girls and girls of color report findings that run directly counter to the signs of loss so epidemic in white middle-class girls.

Indeed, the now-famous American Association of University Women's 1990 report on girls found that black girls scored highest on self-esteem measures throughout adolescence.[42] In interviews with urban adolescents, psychologist Niobe Way discovered a unique tendency to "speak one's mind" in relationships. The girls she interviewed, who came from predominantly working-class African American families, described relationships empowered, not dissolved, by conflict.[43]

These girls are exceptional. The heart of their resistance appears to be an ease with truth telling, a willingness to know and voice their negative emotions. When girls make a choice to value their emotions, they value themselves. They tell the truth because their survival may depend on raising their voices in a hostile culture.

How might the face of girls' anger take on a different appearance, and why? Not all girls resort to alternative aggressions as a primary means of releasing negative feelings. In this chapter, I explore the use and origins of truth telling as a means of resisting silence and oppression. I conclude with the story of a victim of bullying, whose despair prompted her to fight back.

My own white middle-class background made me especially aware of my difference when I spoke with girls in less-privileged communities. At times, I was positively floored by some girls' courage and outspokenness, which felt so different from my own. In spite of this, I repeated to myself—and now share with you, the reader—the words of bell hooks, who cautions us to avoid romanticizing the truth telling of African American girls. Truth telling and assertiveness, she argues, are "not necessarily traits associated with building self-esteem. An outspoken girl might still feel worthless because her skin was not light enough or the right texture."

hooks urges us to remember that "[t]here is no one story of black girlhood."[44] Indeed, now that the white, middle-class experience is being dislodged as the exclusive model for research, it is especially important to heed hooks's words. To imagine a universal minority female experience would be to repeat exclusive patterns of research. Girls from all walks of life have different experiences. Not all white, middle-class girls avoid conflict, and not all other girls embrace it. Every child is her own person, with her own unique set of life circumstances.

Indeed, dominant middle-class notions of femininity are foreign to the experience of many white girls. "I know where I come from," writes author and essayist Dorothy Allison, "and it is not that part of the world."[45] Research confirms that some working-class white children are socialized by their parents to use physical aggression to protect themselves from peers. After spending a year in the working-class Maine town of Mansfield, Lyn Mikel Brown noticed how the girls she studied resisted some aspects of the middle-class model of femininity while embracing others.

> Although these girls are care-givers and nurturers, they reveal, often with pride, that part of themselves that is outspoken and direct, that knows and expresses deep, passionate anger, even that part of themselves prone to uncontrollable rage. . . . While their experience of themselves and their perception of relationships contest the selflessness and purity typically associated with white middle-class notions of motherhood and femininity, care-taking, nurturance, and responsiveness hold a central place in their lives.

Although Brown would find, as I did, many working-class girls who were unwilling to bring anger into their close relationships, she concludes that "they do so, not because anger is a culturally inappropriate emotion, but because they need their friends."[46] The Mansfield girls at once appreciate and elude anger, presenting an alternative picture of girls' relationship to aggression.

getting physical

The e-mail came a few days after the 2000 New Year. "I am a Caucasian female who often experienced physical confrontations by African American and Mexican American females. *I was not the aggressor.* I protected myself and my two sisters were always looking out for me. We did not tolerate any crap, we knocked the shit out of these girls. Do not get me wrong, though, I never looked for, or wanted to fight."

Bonnie was twenty-eight and studying at a midwestern university for her masters in social work. "I was in so many fights," she wrote in her e-mail, "that I was expelled from the entire county school district. Basically my high school education was ruined. I finally graduated with a GED from the Job Corps in 1989." The youngest of three girls and a boy, she grew up in rural Southern California. Shortly after her brother died, the family moved to a working-class neighborhood in San Jose, "a suburb-city," she noted, "but it certainly didn't seem like [a suburb] to me."

The family was raised by Bonnie's mother, a survivor of multiple violent relationships with men, including a husband who beat Bonnie and her sisters. When Bonnie began her freshman year, her two sisters were already upperclassmen. They were everything to her. If anything truly anchored Bonnie during this stormy time, it was the almost religious devotion the sisters had to one another. "If there was some sort of crisis," she explained, "we would always know about it and be right there for each other. . . . We were very tight. No matter how angry we were." She recalls one sister as a guardian angel. "She would appear at these strange moments when I was in trouble."

Bonnie's new school was a confusing patchwork of the cliques and fervent musical subcultures that marked 1980s America. African American students were embracing hip-hop, while Bonnie was swept up in the culture of Lita Ford–style rock and roll. Pictures show Bonnie's hair blond and feathered back, her Levi's tight and tapered down the leg. She struggled through her first year, and by January was failing nearly all of her classes. She was cutting school more than she attended it.

Bonnie clashed often with her African American peers. Nasty looks were exchanged in the halls, insults were traded about clothing and style. Remembering the hostility, Bonnie was unrepentant about her own role in the conflicts, refusing to take responsibility for provoking anyone's anger. "I never considered myself to be a bully," she insisted, "or someone that would harass or assault anybody, although if someone assaulted me, I was going to protect myself and what I perceived as my own honor."

Bonnie does concede that her social skills weren't great, but she is quick to point out that she prized friendship above all else. "That was one of the things we prided ourselves on—making friends. Being accepting of others," she said. "I wasn't lacking in the fact that I knew how to treat people, and that you don't hit people unless you expect to be hit back."

One day, along the south side of the school, the rock-and-roll and heavy-metal crowd mingled on their part of the block, colonizing their patch of curb. An acquaintance of Bonnie's ran up, breathless. She had turned away an interested African American boy, and another girl who had been interested in him, also African American, was angry.

Twenty minutes later, the girls saw a crowd of African American girls coming toward them up Elm Street. "White trash!" they shouted. One of the girls came dangerously close to Bonnie. She told me she still can't remember who grabbed who first. "I think it was us—we grabbed her and threw her on the ground and jumped on top of her." A melee ensued. Bonnie looked up and saw one of her sisters surrounded by three girls, one of whom began swinging.

Once again, she couldn't remember what came next. "I went blank. I must have flipped out," she told me. "My friend said I threw the girls up against fences and went crazy."

Bonnie was expelled and sent to another high school. She could return to her old school if she went without a fight for six months. At the new school, determined as she was to return to her sisters, there were more fights. Bonnie was sent to yet another school for troubled youth, or, as Bonnie put it, "where all the fuckups went." Bonnie grew angrier and skipped even more school.

Cat had been Bonnie's best friend for two years. Pugnacious, rowdy, and an inveterate rule breaker, Cat inspired suspicion in everyone around her. Bonnie was no exception, not least when she finally got her first serious boyfriend. "I said, 'You can do anything you want. You can have anyone you want, but don't fuck with me and don't fuck my boyfriend.' . . . I said, 'Listen to me. You sleep with my boyfriend, I will kick your ass. I will do this to you.' "

When she heard that Cat had hooked up with her boyfriend, Bonnie marched up to Cat in the hallway at school. "I didn't want to," Bonnie told me, "but people had known that I said that, and I had a reputation to protect. I was forced to. I had no choice but to put my hands on her. I said, 'What the fuck do you think you're doing? I don't even want to kick your ass and now I have to.'" Bonnie led her off school property to avoid further disciplinary action.

"I knew if I didn't, people were going to lose respect for me," she said, "and that opened me to more potential threats, disrespect. I told her straight out, over and over again, 'Don't do this or these will be the consequences.' I guess," she added, probably for my sake, "I was being a bully but in a way I was showing consequence to her."

Bonnie knew if she didn't fight Cat, she would disgrace her sisters' reputation, something she could not live with. "We had a real reputation for not taking anyone's shit," she explained. "If I would have backed down, everyone would have felt free to walk all over us." Bonnie stood opposite Cat, having repeated for the last time the terms of the deal. Cat had broken the rule. Bonnie grabbed Cat and punched her in the chest. Cat didn't move. Bonnie punched her four or five times, in the arm, in the stomach. Cat fell limply on the ground and lay there silent, refusing to fight.

"Don't you get it?" Bonnie yelled. "You do this, and this is what happens. I *told* you."

Cat didn't answer.

"I didn't want to hurt her," Bonnie said, "but I felt like I was in too deep."

Where many white middle-class girls dispense justice in covert ways, Bonnie described a world in which anger and vengeance are inscribed deeply into the school culture. Here, aggression is not ignored or avoided but is a tool used to confer or maintain social status. Moreover, conflict for Bonnie and her sisters was an essential part of preserving their dignity.

Bonnie's comfort with physical aggression was the product of a life of struggle, including a childhood spent in a home marked by family violence. Her defiance of feminine social norms was not a matter of conscious, political resistance. Her ferocity was balanced by a cautious, at times socially avoidant, personality. She told me, "It's hard when someone's not there for you, when you hardly ever need anybody. I'm very independent minded, strong. Very much do-it-myself. I won't introduce myself to you. I won't show you who I am and I won't be honest.... I see people very clearly sometimes. I see people the way I do because I've been conditioned. I've lived in a hostile environment and I can recognize potential threats."

Bonnie's self-imposed isolation has been observed in some working-class girls and girls of color, especially those who feel showing emotion or vulnerability is a sign of weakness. "Even among those who feel more free to express their anger, power, or sexual interest," write Jill McLean Taylor and her colleagues, "the overriding move is to 'stay to myself,' 'not talk to anybody,' 'keep my feelings bottled up,' and 'not tell anybody about anything.'"[47] Long-term isolation can impede cognitive and emotional development.

keeping it real

Waiting outside Ridgewood Junior High for my next interview, I noticed a tall, thin African American girl sitting bone straight on a stone bench by the main doors. She was so still I could hardly see her breathing. It was twenty minutes after the last yellow bus had pulled out of the parking lot. A white pickup truck approached, stopping in front of the main doors and raising orbs of milky brown dust. An elderly African American woman emerged. She was stately and gray, regal looking. She strode toward the girl on the slab, raising a thick arm.

"I *told* you, girl, whenever anyone hits you, you hit 'em back! You should have took off your sneaker and hit her in the face!" The girl stared straight ahead as her grandmother swished past through the school's main doors. The passenger door of the truck swung open and another girl hopped out. She ran toward the first girl, shouting, "I'm gonna get her! I'm gonna get her!"

"You're going to get me *expelled*!" the tall girl cried, suddenly standing. "Is that what you want?"

"Then after school," she replied, winded, "when it's nobody's business."

The tall girl sat back down on the bench, mouth pursed in defiance, tapping her sneaker. The girls' soccer team was trickling into the parking lot, and I barely noticed the assistant principal, Pam Bank, suddenly standing next to me. She apologized for being late and jerked her head over at the sisters, now silent. "She tried to beat up the sister of the boy who was pickin' on her brother. She got the shit beat out of her, and she wants to fight again. I told her, girl, you got your shirt torn off!"

The front door swung open and the principal, pale and wispy as his comb over, moseyed out, followed by Keisha, a frequent contributor to my freshman group discussions. Buxom and strong, Keisha was dressed stylishly in black capris and a purple button-down shirt with matching sandals, one of which she was carrying in her hand. She was walking the way my grandmother always tells me to, chest forward, shoulders back.

"That's the girl who beat her up," Pam whispered.

Keisha followed the principal to a sedan and opened the passenger door as though she had done it before.

Pam sighed. "He's taking her home."

I met Keisha during my first week at Ridgewood. She seemed to love our group discussions, and she filled the room with laughter and stories. Her group, a random mix of girls from driver's education and study hall, was mostly African American. In response to the question, "When you are mad at someone, do you tell them about it?" she did not hesitate. "I do," she said. "I do let her know. If I'm sad, I'm going to act sad. I'm not going to put on a fake smile and walk around like everything's perfect every day. If I'm sad, don't talk to me. Be warned."

"Yeah, you better not!" Her friend Brittney confirmed, snickering and pretending to cower.

"Yeah, if I'm mad at you, I'll tell you what you did," Keisha continued. "I'm not going to keep it back. That would be childish, just to sit there and be mad at someone and not even—I mean, I don't know." Many of the girls nodded. When I asked them where they learned to confront the people that upset them, nearly all of them responded, "My mother."

African American mothers are renowned for their determination "to mold their daughters into whole and self-actualizing persons in a society that devalues black women." Research indicates that many parents socialize their daughters to use independence and self-confidence as a means to resist the oppression likely to touch their lives. Scholar Janie Ward observed that "parents provide their children with ways of thinking, seeing, and doing," a "psychological script" that is transmitted intergenerationally and intended to empower offspring. Girls learn to expect to work and use education to attain power.[48]

These mothers "know that if daughters fit too well into the limited opportunities offered black women, they become willing participants in their own subordination." Like some working-class girls, black girls may learn to walk a fine line between fitting in and speaking up. Ward also found that significant numbers of African American parents used personal experiences and feelings to introduce their progeny to the problems of racism. In one example, a parent told a researcher, "I don't teach it's an even playing field, all men are created equal, do what's right and you will be treated fairly."[49]

African American families typically enjoy extended kin networks; some children have "othermothers," women who share in child-rearing responsibilities. These women live out a "more generalized ethic of care where black women feel accountable to all the black community's children."[50] When a freshman at Clara Barton told me about trying to ignore a problem with a girl who was bothering her, her cousin Tanya wouldn't have it. "My cousin will be like, '*Tell her!*' You'll be like, 'No, I don't want to, I don't want to.' She'll be like, 'Tell her.' Then your cousin will come up and say, 'If you don't tell her, I'm gonna beat your behind.'"

The older women in her life, she explained, "tell you you're supposed to do it like this, do it like that. They just trying to teach you because out here it's like a game. It's just a big game. You got to play. You got players in the game. And the game is a player's game."

Such marked differences in parenting practices distinguish the socialization of some black girls in at least two important ways from many of their white middle-class counterparts. First, psychologists have linked the withering of girls' self-esteem to an avoidance of authentic relationships and feelings. Many African American parents, however, are apparently blunt about the pain and anger they have felt as black citizens. As a result, their daughters are in some senses shielded from the "idealized relationships" that signal the onset of a girl's alienation from her true self. Instead, many girls are urged to confront the realities of human behavior, especially aggression.

Second, the everyday threats of racism and oppression make it unsafe for some girls of color to put relationships first and be "nice" to everyone. The African American girls I met, from the middle and working class, used their own language to set boundaries between themselves and others and so resisted creating the social conditions that end up damaging many girls' friendships. In groups and private interviews, they differentiated between "friends," peers they trusted and were committed to, and "associates," or acquaintances. They used the words to demarcate clearly who was deemed trustworthy and who wasn't. On the other hand, like Brown and Gilligan, I heard white middle-class girls "distinguish between 'real, real good' friends, those they could trust not to whisper or talk about them behind their backs, and 'just' friends"—those who might.[51]

The concept of "associates" clarifies the status of those girls who have yet to prove themselves as true friends. It rejects the expectation that a girl must be everyone's friend, that she ought to be nice and accept everyone she meets. "Associates" empowers a girl by allowing the choice, rather than the assumption, of a relationship.

African American girls made further distinctions between associates and girls who are two-faced, that is, those who lie or are otherwise duplicitous. For some girls, being exposed as two-faced can be grounds for a confrontation. Where white girls often felt resigned about the frequency of behind-the-back whispering—"As soon as we walk out of this room we're going to talk about what everyone said!"—many African American girls spoke in unequivocal terms about avoiding relationships with such individuals and about having been raised by their mothers to do so.

When I talked with Danielle, a freshman at Clara Barton, she told me it's important to confront someone who is talking behind your back. "I learned that from the streets. I was raised in . . . two projects. In both places you got to learn how to stick up for yourself. You can't let people push you down. Supposed to tell people how you feel." A black fifth grader in Ridgewood told me when she hears someone is talking about her, "I'll say, 'If you have something to say, say it to my face.'"

Other girls referred to two-faced behavior as a deal breaker in a friendship, or a red flag. Tamika, a sixth grader, said, "If you have to act two different ways to be yourself, then your friends aren't your friends." Evelyn, her classmate, agreed. "I don't want to be her friend anymore." Chanel, a Ridgewood freshman, remarked, "When a girl goes behind another girl's back, that other girl don't know what the other girl is saying about her. When a girl goes behind another girl's back, I think it's to steal her boyfriend or do something to hurt her real bad."

Finally, African American girls from different class backgrounds commonly referred to trustworthy, true friends as "real." Someone who is real will never be two-faced but will always bring a problem directly to you for resolution.

Many of the African American girls I met demonstrated the effectiveness of developing a vocabulary for girls' relationships. They provided a glimpse of an alternative scenario for girls, one in which relationship may be chosen and the need for aggression acknowledged. A shared language anchored the girls as they negotiated their increasingly complex relationships, giving voice to the betrayals that are so often swept under the rug. In addition to the cultural permission that enabled them to express overt aggression, language acted as an additional buffer to the social pressure that would move these girls into false, conflict-free connections with others. Language helped girls stay with their feelings simply by providing a means to communicate them.

In some urban Hispanic and black communities, the language of relationship is common. Losing or avoiding a conflict can brand a girl a "punk," leaving her exposed to further violence. "Punking out" means choosing not to fight back when attacked, which is "staying hit," a cardinal sin in some households. "I believe if a girl hits me," Nydia, a Puerto Rican sophomore told me, "I'm not going to stay hit. If I do stay hit, everybody's going to think that they could tease me." Lauren, a black sixth grader at Ridgewood, explained, "Sometimes people will call you, they'll say, 'Oh, you're so ugly.' You can't just say, 'Well, thank you very much.' You have to say, 'Okay, your mom's so fat she can't fit in the doorway of her car!'"

Fifteen-year-old Jacqueline Ruiz, a Puerto Rican freshman at Sojourner Truth, said a punk "don't speak up for herself. She doesn't think. She doesn't stick up for herself. Somebody's yelling at her or cursing at her, she'll just stay really quiet all the time." Although Jacqueline sometimes felt the impulse to avoid confrontation, she had concluded she was better off being direct in the long run. "What

I learned through experience," Jacqueline explained, "is that you have to say it, and there are ways of saying it. If you attack the problem when it starts, you can avoid future problems. By not saying anything, people call you a punk or you feel like a punk because you don't never say anything to that person and she continues doing what she does. That just makes everything worse."

when cultures collide

An awareness of their feelings, the ability to distinguish between levels of relationship, and a willingness to speak out do not necessarily insulate black, urban, or working-class girls from losing self-esteem at adolescence. Nor do they refrain from alternative aggressions. Researchers point out that "[b]eing able to speak out in some situations, however, did not necessarily suggest a confidence or willingness to speak out in all relationships."[52] For instance, high-achieving African American girls can dissociate psychologically and become silent as they move deeper into mainstream white academic culture, attempting to avoid raising the ire of others who might resent their success. Other black girls may resort to a self-destructive form of resistance, in which a girl's outspoken behavior endangers herself and her future.[53]

The middle-class African American girls I met reported difficulties thriving in a white social universe. With uncanny regularity, girls confided frustration when their attempts at truth telling were rebuffed and even punished. "I'm trying to tell the truth," Michelle explained to me in one such instance, "but they think I'm a bitch." These girls struggle in a social desert between "nice," where no anger is shared, and "bitch"; they inhabit female identities of assertiveness and truth telling, identities that the culture, and consequently most girls, pathologize as "mean," "bitchy," or "skanky."

Some of the urban Latina girls I met expressed a willingness to engage in conflict that would be considered problematic in certain

Hispanic communities. The socialization of Latina girls most resembles that of their white middle-class counterparts. Latin American culture is family centered, and parents socialize children along traditional gender lines. Wives and daughters are expected to be nonaggressive and honor the authority of men. Women are "traditionally idealized as pure and self-sacrificing, like the Virgin Mary," and rules of behavior for girls can be extremely restrictive.[54]

The Dominican and Puerto Rican girls I met were mostly working class or poor first-generation Americans. They came from homes where parents spoke little or no English, where the girls had to translate notes and report cards sent home. These girls live in two worlds: the one more traditional and sheltered, and the other a contrary world of youthful license and temptation. Their personalities reflect the convergence of different cultural forces: the legacy of obedience imposed by their community, alongside the self-protective armor necessary to survive in lower-income communities.

Thirteen-year-old Jasmine found herself in a world of privilege that contrasted sharply with her working-class upbringing. When I came to Arden Country Day, where she was on full scholarship, Jasmine sat close to me, raising her hand often, eager to participate. We met a few weeks after school let out for the summer at a pizza joint near school. Jasmine had long black kinky hair and a full beautiful face, which she made up expertly every day. After seven years as the only Latina in an all-black public school in her neighborhood, Jasmine transferred to Arden to begin seventh grade.

Jasmine's mother is an immigrant from the Dominican Republic. "I can describe my family," Jasmine told me plaintively, "as loose strings held together by a knot. That knot was my grandmother." The family congregated at her grandmother's small apartment every weekend for meals and conversation. When she died, Jasmine said, "all these strings went every which way. They disintegrated. The whole family." Jasmine had been growing closer with her grandmother at the time of her death, and the loss weighed heavily on her.

Jasmine's grief felt especially keen, since she had seen so much of herself reflected in her grandmother's stewardship of the family. Jasmine's own mother, she told me, could be "weak-minded." The contrast between this and her own strength made Jasmine uneasy. "She's always been the kind of person that listens to what other people tell her a lot." Jasmine perceived her mother as inconsistent, allowing Jasmine something once and then forbidding it without explanation. When mother and daughter argued, Jasmine was sometimes told she didn't deserve what was being lobbied for. Jasmine vehemently disagreed.

"I feel that I do [deserve] a lot. I wake up at five in the morning to get to school. I get home at 6:30. I do my homework. Iron my clothes, take a shower, go to sleep. I end up going to sleep at one or two, and I get up at five." Jasmine complained that her mother wanted her to clean the apartment too much on the weekends. "She forgets that I just turned thirteen. She's so used to me having like an older mentality that she kind of thinks I can take more things and responsibility."

Her mother's inability to make her own decisions frustrated her, especially when there seemed to be so many to make right at the time. Perhaps because of this, Jasmine told me that "my mother doesn't know me as much as my friends do."

In one sense, Jasmine's complaints have the texture of typical adolescent angst—my mother doesn't get me; she makes me do too much. Jasmine's frustration, however, ran deeper, and her anger pointed to a gulf between herself and her mother that paralleled the two worlds she was living in. Her mother didn't speak English, and her mind, Jasmine said gingerly, "is kind of set back to the culture in DR (Dominican Republic). She doesn't understand the way things are now." The values Jasmine was learning at school—of competition, ambition, and individual success—conflicted with her mother's attempts to socialize her into interdependence. To survive the confusion, Jasmine turned to herself, holding fast to her own voice.

From the first days at the new private school, Jasmine told me she steeled herself to remember certain things. "I came in with a certain attitude. That this is me. You like me, that's it; you don't like me, that's it, too. I'm not going to try and change myself because someone doesn't like me." She was surprised to attract more friends than she could handle, but some girls viewed her with animosity. "I'm not going to be trying to impress people because I want them to like me. I think that kind of intimidates people that I'm sort of more assertive and more aggressive in what I do. In my thinking I'm not weak-minded. I consider myself a very strong person. That scares them because they're not like that."

Jasmine described public school as a place where "you can't show weakness," and private school as a hotbed for emotions. Yet she was confused and insecure about the duplicity she noticed in some of her new peers. "A lot of people are hypocritical," she told me. "They pretend to be your good friend. They pretend nothing's changed. That's just worse." When she tried to tell people how she felt, they often thought she was being "mean." They were offended by her directness. "Can't you just take what I'm saying as coming to you?" Jasmine remarked. "Don't try and change it. I'm just saying, this is it."

Jasmine struggled with the unexplained abandonment and silences from the girls she loved most, and the friction in her group of friends had Jasmine questioning herself. Bewildered and sad, having tried fiercely to keep her relationships intact, she remembered thinking, "What is it that I do that pushes people away? Why is it that so many of my friendships are failures? What do I keep on doing wrong? When you see a pattern in your life, you look to yourself for the problem." Eventually, however, she realized that trying and hoping and wanting would not be enough. "There's only so much you can do in a friendship," she said simply. "You can't give 110 percent and another person gives 5 percent." Eventually, she told me, some of the friends who had stopped speaking to her confessed they had been jealous.

Jasmine resented it. "I have had to work really hard for everything I have in my life. Nothing's been handed to me. A lot of girls in this school have. It's a really expensive school. I'm on scholarship. I'm not paying for anything for this school. And it's like they don't grasp the fact that you have to work for things. You're not always going to be given things in your hand." She later told me, "I've been through a lot in my life and I've learned that in certain situations you have to be more aggressive because, if not, people are going to take advantage of you."

Jasmine's marked self-reliance complicated her relationships with her friends. She found competition with other girls so jarring that she preferred friendships with boys. She balked at the disdain she felt emanating from girls who seemed to resent her academic success. "I have to keep my grades up!" she said in protest. "It's a must or I won't be attending [the school] or any school like that. They just don't understand that."

Jasmine was perplexed by the need of her girlfriends to rely on each other so much, especially their endless barrage of questions about how they looked and what they should do. "It's not like, 'Oh, my God, I hang on the opinions of my friends all the time.' I do depend on opinions. I always ask, What do you think? But it's not like I'm going to change something about myself because someone doesn't like it. If I really feel I should do it, I'm going to do it."

Whether at her old public school or Arden, Jasmine had always been a minority, and she found particular comfort in her identity at her mostly white school. Yet she found that "people kind of forget who they are and they start acting a certain way." At school, minorities rarely attended gatherings for students of color. "Like you know?" she asked. "They're forgetting their heritage. They kind of get lost in all that. My friend Ray is a Dominican. It's so sad. He doesn't speak Spanish." She told me she was ashamed that she could write only a little Spanish. "What are you trying to be?" she asked no one in particular. "Don't forget who you are."

She noticed her white peers trying on "ghetto" fashions like bandannas, imitating Jasmine's Spanish slang and Dominican inflection. One classmate shared her address with the caveat that she "lives in the ghetto," and Jasmine silently imagined her coming to visit her neighborhood sometime. There, Jasmine said, she can't wear a bandanna because it signals gang affiliations.

When I asked Jasmine who she turns to for help, she echoed many urban girls observed by researchers. "Mostly I don't talk to anyone. Sometimes I'll talk about stuff. Most of the stuff I deal with on my own."

As a working-class Latina, Jasmine's transition into white middle-class culture had left her a stranger in both worlds. She was caught in the space between, and to adapt, to avoid the overload and confusion of mixed messages, Jasmine was digging in her heels and holding fast to the memory of her grandmother. Where the messages of her world collided, she chose to rely on herself and her own voice, the only sound she could hear clearly.

Parents' attempts to empower their children were evident in my discussions with urban girls. I was struck by the extent to which many of them were socialized to defend themselves physically. In some instances, girls reported being struck by their parents for returning home beaten. One urban African American girl who lost a fistfight was given some credit by her mother. "My mother says at least you tried. My mother doesn't want me to be no sucker, nobody's fool." It is important to emphasize that these girls are not expected to be aggressive generally, but to defend themselves when they have been provoked. Their comments confirm the observations of researchers who found parents training their children to expect affronts on their dignity.[55]

Martin Luther King Elementary's students are predominantly African American, Puerto Rican, and Dominican. Twice a week, when I arrived for our group discussions, the open expanse of the first floor hovered over a cliff of afterschool chaos, thick-skinned maroon balls crashing out of the gym and into lockers, children's voices raised in laughter and shouts as they moved toward their activities.

Ntozake, the head of the after-school program, had chosen a mix of known bullies and victims to speak with me. These fifth- and sixth-grade girls were assembled around a conference table used by teachers. In the dim, smoky light flowing through crisp venetian blinds, the girls fidgeted in too-large chairs, looking apprehensively at Ntozake.

At this school, Ntozake said, shaking her head in wonder, the girls fight as often as and sometimes more than the boys. Standing at the front of the room on our first day together, she asked a simple question. She said she wanted to know the answer as much as I did, and I was grateful for the comforting effect her presence clearly had on the girls. "Why," she asked pointedly, eyes narrowing, "is there so much fighting?"

"The reason why we fight so much is because when they spread rumors, and you tell them to come to your face, they change it around and talk about your mother and dead family members," Rosa said.

"We have fights because sometimes we say to say it to our face to show that if you want to talk, talk to my face!" Marisol added. "My sister told me, 'If someone calls you a word, you say it back. If they say something, don't take it because it's not true.'"

"My mother says to bust 'em up if someone hits you," Tiffany volunteered.

"You can't stay hit," Latoya explained. "If you don't hit, they gon' say, 'Oh, why don't you hit, you a punk?'"

Rosa gestured at Ntozake. "Even though you tell us not to fight, our parents tell us not to stay hit."

"In third grade," Jessica began, "I used to be a punk. There was a boy. He hit me and I wouldn't do nothing. I'd go home crying. My mother would be like, 'What happened?' One time he punched me in the mouth. My mother said, 'If you don't hurt him, I'm gonna hit you.'" The girls erupted in cheers and shared similar rules from their homes.

Later, after the discussion had ended and only a few students lingered, Rosa approached. "I don't want to be in fights," she said, "but I feel like I have to. My dad says, 'Beat their behind up.' But I don't want to. I'd come home with bruises and my father would yell at me. So I had to fight."

Some physical fights between girls bear a powerful likeness to nonviolent alliance building, explored in chapter three. Tiffany, an African American ninth grader in Mississippi, explained that fistfights between girls are often prolonged by the need to get other girls involved in a supportive backup, not unlike the way girls build alliances.

"They gotta go get their clique," she explained. "They gotta take all their time. The girls have to get their clique because ... they're likely to jump in and just have your back, just like that." Notably, although girls in the Northeast and Mississippi described girls standing behind a friend to back her up, they said it was extremely rare for witnesses to enter the fracas themselves.

Nevertheless, Tiffany explained, their presence "tells you who your real friends are," adding that "you feel much stronger" with them by your side. Tiffany alluded to R & B singer Jill Scott's video "Gettin' in the Way," in which Scott decides she must resort to physical violence to convince her boyfriend's ex to stop trying to sabotage his new relationship. Scott charges up the scorned woman's front steps, trailed by her closest friends (and most of the neighborhood), and tears off the woman's wig, to the delight of the crowd.

Jacqueline explained, "If you have your friends there, it's kind of a threat. If you're just talking to the girl, she probably won't be as nervous to say what she has to say. Or she probably won't get as loud. But if you have another friend there, you're dominating her because it's two of you." Like the middle-class girls who use emotional alliances, these girls make pacts to defend each other physically.

Fourteen-year-old Amanda shared intriguing insights when I asked her about her observations of boys fighting in her Puerto Rican neighborhood. Amanda had watched boys move up the social ladder when they won a fight one-on-one. "If he would win, he's stronger than that boy. . . . They're like, 'Oh, I beat him up. He knows the next time not to say nothing.'" The rules of masculinity demand displays of individual strength. Girlfights, she tells me, have different goals.

Girls "continue arguing. Usually when girls do that...she's beat up, she'll be scared of her, or she'll bring more people into the fight. Boys, they'll fight, they won, and leave it alone. If girls fight, it's just constant." Girls who lose fights often wait for the next moment they will be able to fight again. "It's like back and forth."

As with Jenny in chapter one who waited years to retaliate against her bully, feuds can last for years between girls as they seek opportunities to avenge their loss. Tiffany explained, "After a fistfight, girls feel like they need to get that girl back. Whoever beat that other girl up is going to have to watch her back all the time."

Similar to alliance building, in which middlegirls may have a stake in causing a fight, girls who fight physically also describe those who instigate. "Somebody'll pump it up. They're gonna say, 'Oh, she said this about you.' They're gonna come back in your face, and then, you know, they don't want to hear what you got to say."

Keisha explained, "They get stuff started. That's how it all happens."

unbidden resistance

Inner strength reveals itself at unlikely moments, often when we are at the end of our rope. For some girls, rock bottom points the way up and out. A fusillade of bullying can batter someone into hopelessness, and yet the same extreme situation can lay the groundwork for extraordinary acts of personal strength, like when a stunned father hoists a car off a trapped child.

The girls who decide to fight back seem to confront moments like these. Like girls living under economic and social stress, the girls who resist find themselves with few other choices. These girls, however, are not usually prepared for it the way their counterparts are. Rather, they come into an instinct to defend themselves and preserve their integrity, one that is only semiconscious, born more of desperation than desire.

Where they may have once drawn self-esteem and strength from their friends, solitude augurs new perspective and self-awareness. As my friend Astrid recalled, "Having it happen stripped me of all external sources of confidence, and I had only what I had internally to draw on. I realized I had a lot of strength and integrity." Shelley McCullough learned about her own limits, and especially the things she needs in her relationships with others. That insight has been critical to her friendships today. "I know how I react to things. I know more about myself. I learned more how to deal with stuff."

Alizah moved from California to live with her father in New Jersey when it was clear that the cruel campaign of the popular girls would not let up. The last straw came when one of the girls stole her sneaker and refused to return it. Alizah confronted her, the girl still refused, and when Alizah pushed her up against the lockers, the girl claimed Alizah had pulled a knife. When she was suspended, Alizah was furious, ready to go anywhere, even three thousand miles away.

In New Jersey, Alizah resolved to remake her image. She spent hours assembling a wardrobe that would fit in, and when she spoke to me, nearly fifteen years later, she could describe the first-day outfit down to the angle of her shirt collar. As she stood in line at the cafeteria, the cool girls swarmed. "What's up with the shoes? My father wears those shoes. You can't afford socks? Why does she have a triangle on her ass? What the hell is Guess? Why do you have a horse on your shirt?"

At that point, Alizah said, "I can't do anything else. I can't try any harder. I'm not even getting a chance here. I thought, screw you. I'm going to do what I want to do, and I'm going to wear what I want to wear." The next day Alizah wore the camouflage print pants she loved, with a tight black sleeveless top. She spiked her hair. "The girls said I had fishing lures in my ears and I glared at them."

Alizah befriended a girl who looked like her in the cafeteria. "Everyone said she was drinking bleach out of her thermos because she wanted to die. I sat down, introduced myself, and that was it. I thought, she's as much of an outcast as I am and we're going to get along just fine. We were best friends and are close to this day."

As I tried to understand what made the difference, Alizah explained, "I think I just didn't care anymore. I thought, I'm not going to try and be your friend. If you want to hang out with me, that's cool, but I'm not going to overextend myself and tell you my secrets and put myself out on the line."

Alizah had tried so hard to make people like her in California that she had been involved in few school activities. Her world revolved around trying to win others' affection. So she made changes. She started making her own clothes in high school and joined journalism, yearbook, and theater clubs. She became the first junior to edit the school newspaper.

"I became my own person. I was determined that I wasn't going to fall into it again. I didn't want the pain. I thought, even if I don't have a lot of friends, I'm going to keep myself busy and do the things I like to do. And I made friends that way, through my activities, as opposed to following everyone around and doing what everyone else was doing."

For some girls, being cast out is a blessing in disguise, as many are guided into a more centered, authentic self-awareness. Being the odd girl out helped Naomi off a treadmill of want and disappointment. "I felt like nothing, like no matter what I did it wasn't going to be okay, because nobody cared. I didn't have to live up to the standard other people had to live up to. I looked at these popular girls and they had these boyfriends that were like those cafeteria boyfriends. I felt like there was—these people, they had to be pretty, beautiful but not too sexy. They had to be desirable but not slutty, they had to be an ideal but always an unreachable ideal. Whereas I felt that as nothing, I had the freedom to be what I really was because nobody was looking to me for anything."

For twelve-year-old Alix, being bullied empowered her to demand respect in her relationships for who she is and to settle for nothing less. "It taught me to always be myself. I want people to respect me for who I am, not who I'm pretending to be." Ruth, now in her twenties, said, "My communication style became fiercer because I had to fight to earn it." And, she added, "It taught me compassion and independence. I can be alone and not feel insecure."

Girls who survive bullying can emerge from the experience with new strength. They can grow into women who learn to choose the right relationships and avoid abusive ones. They incorporate from their experience the ability to recognize harmful people long before harm can find them. If girls can go through their pain in a culture that validates it, more and more girls will get to walk away with silver linings.

When it is expressed, the overt aggression of girls is pathologized as unfeminine or worse. Minority and low-income girls are often stereotyped as aggressive, loud, and disruptive, and therefore "at risk." "Those loud black girls" is a term used to demean the brassy presence of African American female youth. When Jill McLean Taylor and her colleagues asked urban girls to fill out a questionnaire, they found that over half answered the question "What gets me into trouble?" with "my mouth" or "my big mouth." The girls spoke "as if repeating a mantra given them by some higher authority."[56]

Scuffles between boys, though met with swift punishment, are nevertheless seen as a predictable side effect of male adolescence. Yet when girls fight physically, their aggression is seen as a sign of deviant behavior. This double standard has grave consequences, suggesting to girls that their aggression will be more acceptable if only they keep it indirect or covert. Moreover, physically aggressive girls appear to be disproportionately working-class girls and girls of color; when they are punished disproportionately, officials perpetuate stereotypes about them, suggesting it is only they who break the rules. Not surprisingly, when girls of color are studied, it's often to identify high-risk behavior, individual deviancy, or social problems.

Our culture has long pathologized the black female as a willful matriarch. Black mothers are portrayed as domineering disciplinarians who promote disobedience in their children. The culture's anger toward the black female can be traced, in large part, to her mouth. The black woman crystallizes the culture's discomfort with female strength, voice, and aggression: her willingness to raise her voice and defend herself publicly, to provide for her family irrespective of the presence of a man, and to speak her heart and mind—all of these disrupt the social and sexual order of society.

What little we know about girls' relationships is based mostly on studies of white middle-class girls. Indeed, most of the stories in this book come from that part of society. The rich diversity of female relationships found among other races, ethnicities, and class backgrounds has often been overlooked.

That the girls who engage in direct conflict may have little real social power is a sad irony, to say the least. The assertiveness shown by some minority girls may reflect not self-confidence but their vulnerability in the larger society. Their voices indeed challenge the picture of indirect aggression painted in other chapters of this book. Yet in many instances their forthrightness stems from the girls' sense that they can only make themselves heard by using physical force or dangerous speech. Because it is linked to their marginalization, their directness cannot serve as a model for overcoming girls' sense of powerlessness.

Dealing effectively with that feeling of powerlessness is essential to fighting the loss of girls' authentic selves. What we can learn about assertive girls would be undeniably useful in developing concrete strategies to fight the loss of girls' authentic selves. The more we know about these girls, the more we honor their voices, the closer we will get to developing concrete strategies to combat female bullying in all its forms.

CHAPTER *eight*

parents & teachers

Suzanne Cohen was preparing for an emergency conference with her six-year-old daughter's teacher when she was suddenly uneasy. Standing before the classroom's closed door, poised to discuss the abusive behavior of her daughter's classmate, "I realized that I was about to describe this child [as] extremely manipulative, competitive, and underhanded. And to say that about a six-year-old girl—you sound like a lunatic!"

She is right. A system that refuses to classify these behaviors as genuine aggression will look askance at complaints of indirect, social, and relational aggression. As a result, parents who confront girl bullying face an experience that, in its own way, can be as upsetting as their daughters'. In the absence of a public language to talk about bullying, it's hard to avoid inflammatory words like "liar," "sneaky," or "manipulator." As their daughters fear going public and facing retaliation, parents are afraid of being designated "hysterical" or "overinvested" by the school. And where girls must overcome the embarrassment of low social status, parents may quietly worry over the role their errors might have played in their daughter's experience.

The attempt of parents to tone down their demands on teachers is one of the most powerful subtexts in this chapter of the story of girl bullying. Sitting with four mothers who meet regularly to chat at a Washington coffee shop, I asked them to explain.

"As a parent, you're aware of the incredible amount of power the teacher has over your child's life," Ellen said. "You don't want to jeopardize that relationship in any way." Her friends nodded. Added Christine, "I think parents worry that teachers will take things out on their children because of how a parent acts." Because complaining about alternative aggressions is often perceived as overreacting to everyday school behavior, many mothers harbor a fear of becoming the classroom's "hysterical mother." The need to remain calm and dispassionate, they emphasized, is key.

Perhaps more than any other event in a child's life, bullying forces the question every parent struggles with: How much should I intercede on my child's behalf? While the answer to this question should depend on the child—is she ready to fend for herself? is she being prematurely exposed to danger?—too often the answer is determined by the anticipated response. Will other parents take offense? Will the school be responsive, or worse, punitive? With most schools strapped to accomplish the most basic extracurricular objectives, getting somewhere with a busy teacher can be an uphill battle.

Parents seeking justice for their daughters face cultural and personal obstacles. Most daunting is the fact that alternative aggressions are ignored or rarely considered a legitimate social problem. More often, school officials downplay the problem or blame the victim. Many parents described daughters being sent to psychological counseling for treatment when there was nothing wrong with them, encouraged to get costly social skills training when it was the perpetrator who in fact needed the help, or ignored because the perpetrator was stealthy and it came down to a case of she-said, she-said. Not surprisingly, plenty of parents opt for silence.

Shame is also a reality. The discovery that your daughter struggles socially is painful; finding out she's not to blame is hardly a consolation. Every family handles it differently. It took no small courage for

Linda to confide the shame that felt to her both searing and ridiculous. "There was this nagging piece, and I never went to this place," she told me. "This is even hard to say but I thought it sometimes. As much as everything I said to [my daughter] did not reflect this, deep down I thought, 'My kid isn't *popular*? She isn't one of the cool kids?' Even though I know that's not what I really want. But you want your kid to be wonderful." It took Suzanne Cohen great courage to overcome her instinct to block the whole incident out. As she waited for the teacher, she recalled, "I secretly harbored this fantasy that someone would turn around and say, 'Why can't Hannah stand up for herself? Why don't you teach her how to stand up for herself? Why is she letting this happen?'" Although these feelings are common to anyone coping with a child's misfortune, shame weighs more heavily when most people regard the problem as a trivial phase in child development.

When a child is found to be learning disabled, there is a specialist. The child's parent suspects the problem, often using accessible literature, and expresses her concern to a knowledgeable official. The parent is reassured her child's situation is neither her fault nor that unusual. In time, her child may receive specialized attention to provide her with tools to accommodate her different needs and perform to the best of her abilities.

When a child is the target of alternative aggressions, there is often nobody to help. Without rules to refer to or a language to narrate a child's pain, parents know the cards are stacked against them from the get-go. As Suzanne explained, "If I made too much of a fuss about her social issues, you know, it would be like, 'Well what's wrong with your kid if she can't deal with her issues? Why doesn't she just walk away and get over this?' And I was embarrassed—I was embarrassed to appear the way I felt."

Silence is a second skin for American families. We put our best foot forward and draw the curtains in times of trouble. From across the yard we quietly blame parents for their children's plight. Middle-class families in particular are committed to keeping children's social, emotional, and learning problems secret, especially psychological pain. One mother, confiding the pressure to stay silent about her daughter's problems, put it simply: "We're afraid our kids aren't perfect. And that it reflects our mothering abilities. That we're home too much or not home enough. It reflects on us."

With ever more opportunities to showcase children, parents compete vigorously to project an image of social bliss and indomitable health. They stack trophies and throw glamorous birthday parties. Sharing the experience of despair engendered by girl bullying is for many parents impossible. Margaret Kaplan explained, "If I go to this person and tell them this is what's happening, who are they going to tell? How many people are going to know? How distorted will it become? Will it be, 'Oh, the Kaplans: *They're* having problems. *We're* not. *We're* all perfect. We have this idyllic lifestyle.'" Despite her deft organizing of parents to demand extra art classes, Susan Sussman gave a bitter laugh when I suggested a group to combat alternative aggressions. "There is no way I am going to organize a group around my daughter's experience of cruelty," she said.

Susan Patterson said the smallest incidents can become the subject of lunchtime conversations in Ridgewood. At forty-one, with her daughter bullied by a close friend, she was resolved to lock the town out of her private life. She closed down at even the thought of coming forward, brushing me off with a bitterness that seems to contain a lifetime of disappointments. "This town talks about everybody," she seethed. "They can't hardly wait to get up in the morning and find out who's getting divorced, who's sleeping with who. I mean, that's just the way life has been here forever." She pushed fiercely for her daughter to handle her bully on her own. "I wanted her to be an independent woman. I kept thinking, this is not as bad as it is. I didn't want to think it was as bad as it was. But it was really, really bad."

Parents are bit players in the national conversation on bullying. Our attention is fastened on the perpetrators, their victims, and silent peers. Critics have faulted television and movies for stoking the culture of peer violence. The role of parents, however, is often reduced to bitter epilogues of disasters: parents who did too little, too late, or who did nothing at all.

In this chapter, I present five mothers talking about their girls' experiences with bullying and explore what teachers face in responding to them. Each parent has a unique story, and like her daughter, brings her own set of personal memories and beliefs to the episode. The stories illustrate parents' influence over their daughters' social choices. They reveal how a culture which silences and invalidates female aggression affects the way parents respond to their children's pain.

blame

Patricia runs a small child-care facility in Ridgewood. When I visited her at the end of the day, she was wearing a long, untucked collared shirt over rumpled khaki pants. Her tall sturdy frame suggested an ability to fix just about anything, from a shoelace to a lawn mower. Her voice was surprisingly gentle and low, and her eyes drifted across the playroom to where a lone child played quietly, awaiting her mother. We are both tall women, and as we plunked down to talk on tiny chairs at a round table, our knees popped halfway up to our chests. She grinned and shrugged, reddening slightly.

Patricia never expected that four years after moving here with Ben and their daughter, people in town would still treat them as though they'd just unloaded their truck. When Ben was hired as a senior pharmacist, an impressive promotion so early in his career, he had promptly moved the family to Ridgewood midway through Hope's third-grade year.

When Hope started school after the winter holidays, her sudden appearance troubled her peers. She was met with quick skepticism by the other girls and deemed a threat to existing cliques. What began as a brief shunning stretched into a yearlong hazing. Hope knew she was being challenged because she had not grown up in town, but the longer she lived in Ridgewood, the easier it became to blame herself.

By fifth grade Hope had fallen in with a group of girls from the church who attended choir and Sunday school. At school, the clique leader often asked Hope to go somewhere else for the day or made rude comments about Hope's looks or personality. When Patricia asked her daughter why she stayed friends with them, Hope insisted it was better when they were at church together.

One day in sixth grade, one of the girls informed Hope that the group did not want to be her friend anymore. For several weeks afterward, they refused to acknowledge her existence. "She was just left," Patricia said, her eyes filling with tears. "Every day after school, she'd come home crying. 'They don't like me today. They don't want to be my friend anymore. What do I do? Why don't they like me? What's wrong with me? Why can't I be friends? Why don't they want to be friends with me?' What do you say?" she asked pleadingly.

"What did you do?" I asked.

"Well, it was a very emotional time," Patricia said, clearing her throat, her shaken voice righting itself. She leaned back in the chair and stretched her long legs. "I'm sure a lot of it had to do with her growing up, you know, her period starting and all that stuff, a lot of emotions come with that, too." Listening to her, I wondered if Patricia was edging away from the center of her child's pain, ascribing it to the "legitimate" factors affecting child development.

Patricia asked her daughter if there was any truth to her clique's critical remarks. "I asked if there were some things within herself that she'd like to change." Hope tried to come up with a couple of ideas, then retorted that she didn't know what else she could do. I asked Patricia if she thought Hope should have changed herself.

"Hope has a very outgoing personality," Patricia explained, sounding almost apologetic. "She's very bubbly. And she can be silly. I guess I don't know the right word for her personality. But I think she could get on people's nerves. It might really rattle them. And they might get tired of it. She felt like she could calm down a little bit, you know, not be so boisterous or outspoken." In the absence of an explanation for her daughter's torment, Patricia could do little but suspect it was Hope's fault. She begged Hope to find other friends. Hope refused. She said they were her only friends.

Patricia tried to comfort her daughter by asking her to pray. "Even though it's very hard right now, we know that God can use this to bring good in your life somewhere. You may not see it today or tomorrow." She paused. "I'm trying not to cry."

We sat in silence.

"I wanted to go to those girls and say, 'Do you realize what you're doing!' I wanted to go and tell their mothers, you know, but then you stop and think, 'Okay, I'm hearing one side.' I trust Hope and I believe that she's honest with me, but you don't want always to think that my child will never do anything wrong.

"If it had turned into something where I thought Hope was really suffering or going into a depression, or you know, having really physical or health problems, I probably would have done things a little differently," Patricia said. "A lot of it I felt like, this is just part of life. You have to learn how to deal with people who don't always treat you fairly." And here, Patricia expressed society's approach to bullying through her parenting philosophy, even as she sat before me, shoulders slumped in a small chair, brushing tears away, questioning her own words.

When I asked what she would have done differently, she sighed and looked at me squarely. "I wish I had gone ahead and tried to get those mothers together and sat down with them for coffee or something," she said. "You know, in a nonthreatening way. I would never want them to think that I was saying my child is better. If we had worked though all that then, it might have helped them now. Their support system might have been stronger now."

Patricia's fear of angering other parents stifled her defense of Hope and helped her rationalize Hope's torment. For most mothers I spoke with, the fear of another parent's anger played an uncommonly large role in their response. The first unwritten rule of parenting, I learned, is that no one wants to be told how to raise their child; the second is that criticizing another person's child puts you in peril. Many people interpret criticism of their child's behavior as a veiled attack on their parenting, and they become defensive, sometimes irrationally so. Most parents of victims simply say they just "don't go there."

Mothers especially may harbor fears about engaging in direct conflict. In smaller communities, the social costs of confrontation rise. Mothers may work together, volunteer at school or church, run into each other often, even be friends. Fathers might be current or hoped-for clients. It may be difficult to approach another parent without some aftershocks that reverberate beyond the girls' universe.

At times, bully-victim dynamics can spring up between mothers of warring girls, kicking into gear a second tier of indirect aggression and anger. Parents of perpetrators are naturally protective of their daughters, and especially when their girls aggress in total secret, often challenge the accusation. The approaching mother, already timid, can be silenced and bullied herself.

Jill's experience of bullying brought back a flood of memories for her mother, who was suddenly dropped by her best friends in junior high. For Faye, watching what happened to Jill proved her theory that mean girls are universal and unavoidable. Jill had changed profoundly since being alternately ignored and attended to by her best friend. "She used to be the happiest kid," Faye told me. "She was so happy-go-lucky. She used to float and it was wonderful." Then around first grade, Jill became increasingly shy. When her first best friend dropped her "like a ton of bricks," her self-esteem shrank. Now that Jill's new best friend in fifth grade was treating her nicely only in private, Faye was not going to interfere. There was no sense, she'd concluded, in protecting your child from this. It's everywhere.

This time, the bully was the daughter of Faye's friend. This woman was, according to Faye, powerful, controlling, and socially connected. Because of that, her daughter had many friends. "We have had discussions [about the girls' friendship]," she said, "but you can't tell someone that your daughter is being a bitch." Since Jill had seen trouble in more than one friendship, Faye believed Jill's low self-esteem was to blame for her victimization. "If you don't feel good about yourself and people know it, and people know that this person doesn't like you, then no one else is going to like you."

When I asked her if she'd thought of pursuing her daughter's plight with the school, she balked. "Other mothers might have called the other mother and said, 'What's going on?' And it never occurred to me to do that. It never did. And now I say to myself, 'Should I have called?' Should I have, you know, found out what went on, you see, because my mom was really not involved at all. There were a lot of other issues in her life and this was not something she could clearly see as a problem. And then I think, you know, on a scale from one to ten you have people dying from cancer. This really is not a problem. You know, she will grow up and she will find her good friend. And she'll be okay."

After minutes of trying to minimize her daughter's ordeal, Faye abruptly gave herself over to hopelessness. "She'll have this for the rest of her life. We all do," she said simply.

fear

On an icy February morning, I was inching down a backed-up street in Washington, D.C., heading for a lunch interview with the wife of a friend I hadn't seen in many years. Trawling for parking in an underground garage, I remembered that Melissa was bringing along her mother, who was visiting from upstate New York.

When I entered the restaurant, Melissa was holding an armful of shopping bags and standing by the bar. She was about my age, with shiny, curly black hair, narrow shoulders, and a broad, pleasant smile. Barbara, who stood just behind her daughter, was stout and middle-aged, with long curly salt-and-pepper hair. Both greeted me warmly, though as we were seated I noticed Barbara studying the menu intently.

After diet Cokes and salads were ordered, Melissa began.

"I have to admit that popularity was very important to me," she said, as though she were getting some shameful fact out of the way, confession-style. "I think I was always in the popular group. From the outside, people thought I was great friends with this group. I was always—*always*—thought of as being with that group." The reality, she was quick to add, was different.

Camille had always been her closest friend. She lived in the neighborhood, which made it easy for the girls to carpool to the many after-school activities they shared. There was swimming, gymnastics, ballet, soccer, Hebrew school. Even when there was nothing to do, Melissa hung out at Camille's house after school.

Camille was cute and magnetic. She seemed to fill the rooms she entered, and though that meant lots of girls to play with, Melissa could not help but feel small in Camille's shadow. She was plagued by the constant hum of being too big, too homely, too uncool. Whenever Melissa liked a boy, the boy liked Camille. When Camille got around guys, she acted stupid and silly and ignored Melissa. At Hebrew school, Camille ditched Melissa if a more popular girl from another school was around. Melissa was often jealous and ashamed.

Camille was best friends with Nicola, who lived across the street, and whenever the two of them got together, they started to lie. They would pretend not to have plans, so that when Melissa asked Camille what she was doing that day, the answer would always be some variation on "Oh, I don't know what I'm doing yet." Undeterred, Melissa called Camille constantly. One time, riding her bike past Camille's house, she saw the two of them chalking the driveway. "Oh, we just got together!" Camille insisted. "We never knew you wanted to come over." Camille made you feel, Melissa told me, "like she would do these obnoxious, mean things so slyly that you couldn't really call her on it."

In seventh grade, Melissa's class was divided, and she was separated from all of her friends except Camille and Nicola. The shift would permanently alter the social chemistry. By October, the two girls had turned on her.

"They basically dropped me as a friend but very slyly," Melissa said, stirring her soda. "They would just not invite me. I was not invited to hang out after school, never included in plans. They were horrible. They made my life hell."

But the illusion of their friendship persisted, and so did Melissa. Only a sharp eye would have seen the truth. "Camille's instinct was to be nice to everyone and to never say a mean thing. She would just be very elusive, very sly." So Melissa still ate lunch with them, even though nobody talked to her. She would go to the bathroom with them, even though one time Camille whirled around and snapped, "Melissa, do you *ever* stop following us?" She would see them together at the movies and want to disappear under the seats.

"I was very social, very outgoing. It was traumatic. I would go home crying every night. But on the other hand, I felt compelled to be part of that group," Melissa remembered.

As she lingered among the girls who mostly ignored her, she recalled, "I got very good at listening to conversations. I remember spying, anything I could do to understand. I walked behind them to hear what they were saying. I got good at investigating."

"Um," Barbara said, clearing her throat. I looked over, for a moment having nearly forgotten she was there. She had been twisting her cocktail napkin into small pieces underneath her tall soda glass, staring at stringy lemon pulp floating near the bottom. Her face seemed frozen.

"Uh, I have to be honest," she said, eyes still downcast. "I encouraged Melissa to be friendly with Camille. I thought, you know, that it would be nice to have a Jewish girl to hang around with."

Melissa gave her mother a quick "that's nice" look. "I remember walking home by myself a lot. I felt very, very lonely. I felt insecure. I felt ugly. Disgusting. Depressed. I'd lay on my bed, thinking these awful thoughts, that people wouldn't even care if..." She trailed off.

"I thought I must be awful to have my friends hate me," she continued, shaking her head. "I must be pathetic. I don't have anything good to say. They think I'm annoying. I was the most annoying person this year. Everything you could think negative about yourself, I thought."

"You handled it very well," Barbara said. "When you talk about it, it makes me want to cry." And before I could move my head to see Melissa's reaction, Barbara was up and around the table, holding her sobbing daughter. Barbara's face was wet.

"I'm fine," Melissa sniffled, raising her palm slightly off the table. "I'm very in touch with my feelings. I have to say that the experience really made me such a better person. I learned such a lesson. I really learned what I'm looking for.

"I think it was just that having friends that were part of this cool group was the most important thing. I would have done anything, to some degree, to be friends with them. I don't know why."

Barbara returned to her seat. Our food had arrived and Melissa was wiping her eyes. I waited. I tried to seem casual. I did not want Melissa to feel embarrassed. Then Barbara exhaled loudly, half sigh, half raspy cough. This time, when she spoke, she looked straight at me. "When Melissa talks about this, it's very painful for me. I think I'm a little shut down on it. I can't really feel my feelings." She paused as the white noise of the restaurant rose in the background. "Because I feel I perpetrated this."

Barbara grew up an overweight child with few friends. She received the lion's share of girls' meanness. Even the memory of her large body hulking against a backdrop of delicate girls still made her cringe. She looked mournfully at her daughter. "I didn't want Melissa to know that pain." When Melissa was born, Barbara became determined that she would be popular. When Melissa was old enough, Barbara told me, "I encouraged her to be friendly with the kids in the neighborhood." She paused. "I pushed her toward these people."

I asked the inevitable, awkward question. Did she know what Melissa was going through?

"Yes," she said. I saw Melissa's head whip around to her mother. "I felt so inadequate as a person." Barbara's eyes were shining. "I felt so ugly and obese. When I had a child, it brought out all my old fears and insecurities. I had to keep saying, *Melissa is not me. Melissa is not me.* It brought back memories of my own childhood. And I did not want her to know my pain. I wanted her to be happy. I wanted her to be popular."

Barbara had met Camille's mother, Iris, at the community pool when their girls were young. With four attractive children, Iris exuded the easygoing confidence Barbara had always longed for. And yet, Barbara remembered, "Iris could also be very manipulative." But Barbara was in awe of how this woman managed to raise several well-adjusted children, and she wanted a piece of it. "If Melissa could hang out with Camille, then she'd have a good influence on Melissa," she reasoned. "Of course, Melissa didn't really need anyone to have a good influence on her."

I persisted. "Did you ever mention to Iris how Camille was treating Melissa?"

"I did try to talk to her," Barbara murmured. "I think that Iris could be very nice and yet then she could maybe talk behind your back." After a moment, she added, "I felt that I needed Iris to help me be a good mother. And if I had to do it again, if I was thirty today, it would have been different. I don't think I would have... pushed for Melissa to do all those things." Instead, Barbara went to see the school guidance counselor, who recommended Melissa see a therapist. The therapist told Barbara there was nothing wrong with her daughter.

"Part of it," Melissa said, "and I'm not blaming you at all, Mom, is that you would ask me, 'What are your plans? What are Camille and Nicola doing? What are your plans? Why aren't you playing with them?' You did that all the time." She turned to me. "I was getting it from my mom. I don't want you to feel bad," she said, looking back at Barbara, "but it's true."

"I can face it on my own," Barbara said.

"I don't blame you," Melissa insisted. "But as encouraging as you were, there were periods where I felt like I was being compared to them and not good enough." One time, Melissa recalled, she and her mother saw Camille with a new haircut at a café. "You took me to get my hair cut, and you wanted me to be like her," Melissa told her mother.

"You wanted the haircut," Barbara said.

"No," Melissa insisted, "it was right after we saw her."

Barbara and Melissa had never discussed their ordeal until our long lunch in Washington. Watching them, I knew immediately I had been given a great gift. So often when parents respond to a bullying situation, they instinctively focus their anger and blame on the bully. Despite the great difficulty of separating the feelings that surround these ordeals, Barbara's story underscores the need for parents to be mindful of their own role in their daughters' social choices.

Barbara and Melissa also helped me see the benefits of honest communication between parents and children. Through them, I realized that parents must be more than tear wipers and back patters. Barbara might have made a tremendous difference in her daughter's life had she been willing to share the vulnerability and pain that were causing her to pressure her child into popularity. From Melissa's standpoint, Barbara appeared invulnerable, which only reinforced Melissa's sense of fault.

Of course, Barbara's choice to make Melissa popular at any cost was conscious, and not all choices are. It is indeed a blessing and curse of human nature that we unwittingly create opportunities to repeat our own mistakes and to pass them on, like heirlooms, to the people we love the most.

generations

I met Donna and Tracy Wood through a college friend, and I spoke with mother and daughter in North Carolina separately by phone. Fifteen years after Tracy's ordeal, the two women narrated their stories with uncanny synchronicity, as well as generous openness.

Tracy spent her first years on a large farm near Raleigh, playing
mostly with her brother or her ponies. After Tracy's parents divorced, Donna won custody and moved the children into town. She
inherited a healing, protective network of brassy ya-ya ladies who
warmed the new home and treasured Tracy. When Tracy visited her
father he was physically and mentally abusive, his affection sporadic.
At times, Tracy was the apple of his eye; at others, it was as though
she didn't exist. Her unsupervised visitations were taxing.

In fourth grade, Tracy stunned her teachers by completing her
math workbook during the first week of school. She was promptly
skipped a grade into a class notorious for meanness. On the first day
of fifth grade, the girls refused her at the lunch table, sniping that she
wasn't really a fifth grader. They forced her to eat alone. After several
days of solitude in the cafeteria, Tracy brought nail polish to entertain herself, and a monitor reprimanded her, consigning her to another silent lunch.

The lunchtime isolation quickly became a school-day pastime for
the popular girls. They continued to ostracize Tracy throughout
middle school, telling her she was stupid, that her jokes were bad,
her clothes all wrong. They taunted her about not wearing a bra
when she was ten and flat as a board. In the bathroom one day, she
listened from inside the stall as the ringleader warned Tracy's only
friend not to hang out with her. The girl was stone cold the next
time Tracy saw her. One summer, she became best friends with a
popular girl who rode horses at an area barn. In September, the girl
pretended she didn't know her.

For years, Tracy suffered quietly. "I remember every day," Tracy
told me. "It was just awful. Nobody liked me there. And I couldn't
do anything right. Everything I did I got teased for. Nobody had the
compassion or the maturity, including the teachers, to say this isn't
cool, to say, stop it!"

Sitting on the sofa three years after she started fifth grade, talking
with her mother about the concept of courage, Tracy looked up and
said, "You don't know how much courage it takes me to go to
school every day."

Donna asked her daughter what she meant. Tracy replied, "The girls don't want to let me sit with them." Donna was shocked. She had maintained contact with the school for years about her daughter's progress. "In this small private school," she told me, still seething nearly two decades later, "they couldn't bother to tell me that this child wasn't allowed to sit with anybody at recess or lunch. And I was appalled. I was absolutely undone."

Naturally, now that the secret was out, Donna assumed her daughter would be relieved to switch schools.

She was not.

The popular girls had tossed confusing signals of kindness into the mix of cruelty, ensnaring Tracy in a cycle in which she repeatedly tried to win her tormentors over. Some days there would be a glimmer of hope: a kind look, a day without comment or taunt, a shared laugh at the water fountain. To Tracy it felt like enough. She explained to me, "I just sort of thought that was how it was, and that it was incumbent upon me to change it. At some point, I was just sure I was going to triumph over the odds and make them like me and get all the things I wanted at that age." Fleeting moments and scraps of friendship sustained her, leaving Donna to struggle against a daughter who dug in her heels and refused to give up. Donna tried to coax her daughter's teachers without alienating them. She strained to listen to Tracy and accommodate her needs, even as she realized with horror that home was the only place where her daughter would feel respected.

But Tracy's resistance eventually slackened into a depression. Migraine headaches kept her out of school an average of three days a week, and she had to take shots of Demerol for the pain. One day, she found herself reading the same paragraph in her history book over and over again. For three months, her dog curled against her as she drifted in and out of consciousness.

Suddenly, it was Sunday night and she had to return to school full time on Monday. "And I thought," Tracy said, "I'd just rather die than go back to school."

Tracy set her alarm for the middle of the night, awoke, and went downstairs. She got out some of the kitchen knives. "It just hurt," she said. "I sat down and fell asleep and woke up in the morning thinking I couldn't even do this right." Tracy went to her mother's bedroom, who assured her that she would not have to go to school. Tracy was hospitalized for several weeks. Nobody called.

Of her daughter deep in depression, Donna said, "I saw a huge sense of helplessness. Real discouragement. And really noticeable. She had an absolutely wicked and delicious sense of humor. A lot of that disappeared. I would think, what happened to my little girl? It was like she was disappearing. She was getting so depressed it was just not her anymore. She told me that even though I said loving and supportive things, I didn't really know the picture—that she wasn't smart, she wasn't pretty, she wasn't worthwhile." Donna felt waves of frustration as she tried vainly to sway her daughter. "There were times when I just wanted to shake her. She would just not be moved. She would become almost mute. You could just see her silent, thinking emotionally."

After several years of psychotherapy, Tracy understood that her steadfast refusal to leave the school was related to her relationship with her father. "I think my father's cycle of making me his favorite and then not having any interest in me created a cycle of wanting to win over people that didn't want to be won over," Tracy explained. "So it was like, if I could just be good enough or get the right pair of jeans, it was going to be okay again." Years later, Tracy remains awed by her own participation in her suffering. "I didn't have a sense of, my God, this is really messed up!" she told me, wonder palpable in her voice.

Although Donna was unaware of it at the time, she believes her own tolerance of bullying at the hands of an abusive husband helped communicate to Tracy that with enough effort, a person can adjust to anything, no matter how painful. "Here was Tracy caught in an abusive relationship that she refused to leave," Donna said. Having spent years recovering from a traumatic divorce in which she was abandoned by many of her friends, in which she struggled with two young children, little money, and alcoholism, Donna was realistic about why she didn't read between the lines. "I was still reeling from what had happened to me and what had happened to my children. I was dealing with my own issues," she said. She reacted to Tracy with the bottled rage, frustration, and anxiety that had been triggered by her own experience.

Sometimes families transmit dynamics of their relationships to girls. That girls identify with the caregiving practices of their mothers is often celebrated. Yet as we have seen, there can be great risk where relationship becomes the primary currency of one's life. The girls in this book who have remained in abusive friendships at any cost bear disturbing similarity to people like Donna, who are survivors of relationship violence. (The connections between bullying and relationship violence are further explored in the final chapter.) Just as daughters may learn to love like their mothers, they may also be learning not to terminate relationships that have become dangerous.

helplessness

Elaine was sitting with her daughter Joanna, and we were talking about Joanna's problems with Amy. "I have to tell you," Elaine said, leaning forward to rest an elbow on her knee, "that it is so much work the second time around. I was so betrayed by my best friend. She was really my very best friend. I know how [Joanna] feels and that there's not much I can do. It's bad enough experiencing it yourself, but when you experience your child feeling those feelings, it's the most painful thing in the world."

She gazed at her daughter, returning to the present. "With Joanna's [experience of bullying], I felt so defenseless and helpless, so hurt. I can't really say anything to make it better. At the very basic level, you want to protect your children from anything, do the best that you can. You keep them fed and you keep them sheltered and you give them love and all the things you think you can control, and from the moment you get a baby that is handed to you, it's the most incredible feeling and you love that child."

Not being able to help her daughter was devastating. "You're a mom, you're supposed to be able to fix everything," Elaine said, "even if you know that's not true intellectually. Emotionally, you want to. It may have been one of the first true moments when I realized that I wasn't able to protect her." Tears slid down her cheeks. Elaine told me about when Joanna got her vaccinations, about the involuntary tears that came at the sight of her daughter's pain. Thinking of Joanna's anguish over Amy, she could not help but wonder how her daughter was truly feeling inside. "These moments may define you," she said, her voice heavy with emotion.

Sorrow is a binding energy between mother and child, arguably the most visceral response a parent has when a child is hurt outside the home. But parents of victimized girls report feeling a range of emotions toward their daughters, including anger and frustration.

How is it, a mother wonders, that my child could endure such cruelty from her best friend all week and then skip cheerfully down the driveway to spend the night there on Friday? How could she have lain in my lap crying so hard she nearly tore my sweater gasping for breath, and now giggles on the computer as she instant messages and types her secrets into cyberspace? How could I have had my heart broken and stomped on as a witness to this pain, stayed up nights anxious in the dark, been inspired to cruel fantasies against another child, wanted even to wring her mother's neck, and today my child acts as though it is me who is crazy, unhinged, irrational, and unforgiving?

In particular, it's the girls hurt by their close friends who pull parents along on their emotional roller coaster. During the darker days, a parent is exhausted with the caregiving her daughter's sadness demands. Moments later, she rubs her eyes to ensure she sees correctly. Her child, full of smiles, behaves as though nothing is wrong. Understandably, her impulse is to seize the child by the collar and rattle some old-fashioned sense into her. But it's the daughter who often thinks her mother is crazy.

As girls grow older, moving with increasing self-reliance through the labyrinth of their social world, the gulf between mother and daughter widens. Mothers may struggle to understand the social choices of their daughters. The girls' tendency to return to their bullies, to tolerate the meanness—behaviors which strike their mothers as patently absurd—appear strangely logical to the girls. For some girls, anything is preferable to isolation, no matter how passionate their parents' entreaties.

What defies logic to a mother is unmistakably clear to her daughter. Thirteen-year-old Shelley practically punches the table, furious at her mother's cluelessness. "She doesn't understand that you don't just go and tell someone, 'I can't believe you've done something so mean to me.' It's just not how you handle a situation!" When Erin, profiled in chapter three, reconciled with her friends, her mother was dumbstruck. "I just really was worried. I was really angry at these kids. I didn't want them near her. I didn't trust them. I was afraid they would propel her back into this." She added, "People have said to me, 'You have to be forgiving.' People I respect! My reaction is, Wait, you weren't standing there! You didn't feel the hatred that their eyes were sending out and cutting the air with a knife!"

Of her daughter, Linda confided that "it was hard to live with her not taking my advice. I pushed too hard. She was passive. I wanted her to do something. It felt so awful that she wasn't doing anything. I knew someone was hurting her and she was not taking care of herself. But I couldn't do it for her anymore."

For some mothers, the sight of their daughter's surrender to abuse is an infuriating sign of weakness. One mother was astonished at her daughter's irrational behavior. Her two tormentors insisted they were born on the same day, in the same room. "Rebecca knew their birthdays were different but she *still* questioned her own belief!" she said. Especially when mothers have worked hard to model assertive behavior to their daughters, the frustration can be intense. Andrea, Maggie's mom, explained. "When I tried to push, she would just say helplessly, 'I can't, I can't.' There were times when I would feel angry at her because I'm such an outspoken person. It was hard for me to remember when I wasn't, so I would want her to speak up. I would give her the words and everything. Why couldn't she do it!" The weakening connection between mother and child during this difficult period makes approaching the crisis of bullying even harder.

fate

Stereotypes about females and aggression play a powerful role in the approach of some mothers to their daughter's ordeal. A girl who has a punishing experience can grow up to become a mother who is suspicious, anxious, and angry about her daughter's peers. These women watch their children's pain through the lens of their own suffering. Explaining her decision not to speak up when her daughter was victimized, Mary said, "I can't always jump in and pull her out of a bad situation. It doesn't change when you grow up. There are still adults who are just as backstabbing as little kids." She later became frustrated when I pressed her, and as her daughter looked on, she exploded. "I mean, girls are just—I don't have a lot of girlfriends! Because you have to know who to trust. And I don't think girls are as nice as boys in the long run. She has to learn how to choose her friends!"

One Sunday morning, Margaret led me through a swirl of children who raced around my waist, slid in socks across the foyer floor, and pounded up the stairs squealing. "It's a little crazy here," she said, rolling her eyes and smiling warmly, "but I hope we can find somewhere quiet." We headed into a room that looked like it was used about twice a year. Margaret had asked me here to talk about her daughter, Chloe (see chapter six). Her face clouded as we sat down.

"I don't know what it is," she told me, hands clenched in her lap. "I look at her and I see sparkling water. It's a clean slate. Every day is just a wonderful thing. She sees the world, she loves people. And she's run into some very strange things with girls.... It's just this backbiting, this jealousy, this I don't know what it is."

Margaret was as awed as she was alienated by her daughter's beauty and brass. "I was in a different position," she said simply. Nearly thirty years ago, her clique chose a new girl to be picked on every week, and it was almost always Margaret. Sometimes they would pretend she didn't exist, and Margaret would hide and eat lunch in the library. Her feelings of hurt were still fresh today. "You really depend on your friends for acknowledgment and recognition and normality," she said. "Then they suddenly change how you trust people and whether you do trust people." Since then, she said, she had been hesitant to make new connections with people. She was less trusting. She gravitated to men because with women, "How can you know who's on your side and who's not?" Margaret said she is the most lonely in a crowd. Even when friends come to dinner at her home, she finds herself lingering over dishes, alone.

"So I was the dark one," she told me. "Distrusting. I was not happy. But I don't want to prejudice my child into thinking that everyone's terrible." It's hard. The rules of girlhood are, if anything, more elusive today. Chloe had been punished by her girlfriends because she played football at recess with the boys. "In two years," Margaret said, "it may be normal to play football. And then has she missed the boat? The rules are always changing. You never know what's right and what's not right. Who's in and who's not in. What's good and what's not good."

She felt less than optimistic about Chloe's impending physical maturity. "My daughter," she said, "is going to be a knockout. And I am amazed by her confidence. She walks around, shoulders up, head out, and she seems like she loves herself. I never had that," she added. Margaret felt certain Chloe's confidence and beauty would intimidate everyone around her. I asked why.

Margaret had only her experience of women today, informed so powerfully by her plight as a child, to guide her thoughts about her daughter's future. What came most often to mind was the unshakeable feeling of being judged by other women. "We're always comparing whose roots are longer: 'Oh, she needs to go have her hair done. Oh, she's getting heavy.' We're always judging because we're

holding the mirror up to ourselves. Her roots are showing; are mine?
If my roots are showing, are they all talking about it?"

It was the same thing with her daughter's social life, she told me.
"Your kid has learning issues in school," she said, lowering her voice
to a whisper. "It's a family secret. You're having troubles with the
teachers. You're the only one who's having the trouble. You don't
tell anyone." Later, she confessed, "We all know you'll be looking at
the other person and judging them."

Margaret believed the women's movement failed to unite women
and, as a stay-at-home mom, felt patronized by working mothers.
She was often ashamed at social gatherings. She told me about a
friend who asked her in amazement, "What do you *do* all day?" She
grimaced. "We don't respect each other. Why can't we stop looking
at each other's roots? We're all going through it together, and we
should help each other out. If you're a working mom and I can help
you, let me help you! We're still racing against men," she said. "Why
do we have to race against each other?"

When I think about parents and bullying, I am reminded of the
safety instructions you hear on a plane: if cabin pressure is lost, put
on your own oxygen mask before helping your child. Currently,
parents face unacceptable barriers to supporting their daughters
through social crises. They need a new language to talk about girls'
aggression. With a vocabulary to approach schools and speak the
truths of girls' relationships, a parent can take back some of the control she needs. Empowered by the knowledge that so many of her
peers share this experience, she can raise her own voice. Parents will
raise stronger daughters who can know their own experiences as a
shared, common chapter, and still grow up to cherish other women.

teachers

One of our best hopes for changing the hidden culture of girls' aggression is teachers. A teacher can create a classroom culture that
understands the range of girls' aggressions, refuses to tolerate them,
invites girls' private and public discussion of them, and seeks solutions

wherever possible. It is in the classroom that a girl can be socialized into a consciousness of alternative aggressions as nonassertive acts. Teachers can show girls that indirection and manipulation are unsatisfactory ways to express negative feelings.

Yet pursuing alternative aggressions in or out of the classroom can be as treacherous for teachers as it is for girls and parents. Pushed and pulled by parents and principals, faced with impossibly high curricular standards, exhausted and undercompensated, teachers are hardly breaking down the door to discipline behavior that is usually as invisible as it is undisruptive. As Peggy Orenstein points out in *Schoolgirls,* teachers sometimes have only girls to thank for the few moments of order in class. Girls have long played the straight man to the boys' class clown; the American Association of University Women has documented the dwarfing of girls' voices in schools by more rambunctious boys. It is precisely girls' reputation for civility which provides the perfect cover for covert aggressors, giving them unrestricted movement beneath the radar.[57]

To complicate matters, girlfights lack the boldly drawn lines of battles between boys. Girls' conflicts run deep under the ground like the roots of an old tree. The lack of institutional support for awareness of these behaviors only reinforces the anxiety many adults feel toward girls' relational conflicts. "Girls' relationships make me nervous," one veteran teacher confided, "and I'm not qualified to recommend psychological help."

Many teachers who would otherwise be willing to lend a hand are adrift without a disciplinary infrastructure. Marilyn, who has taught elementary school for over twenty years, explained, "I mean, how do you say to a parent, 'Your child is a consummate liar'? They don't want to hear that from me!" A new vocabulary would report on children's behavior in less inflammatory terms. Parents could refer to acts of relational, indirect, or social aggression such as rumor spreading, alliance building, or nonverbal gesturing. In turn, teachers might feel less fearful about approaching parents.

It is in part the invisibility of girls' aggression that puts teachers on such shaky ground. Many refuse to discipline behavior they did not themselves see. Marilyn explained, "It's easier to stop the physical because it's visual, and if you come across it, if you see one child stick his foot out, or see somebody hit somebody, or move a chair out from behind someone, that's very easy to confront because it's right there. The innuendo or slight—you have to be present, and you have to be right on top of it."

Barring cameras in the classroom, teachers aren't going to get instant replay; behavior that is open to question may remain so. "I don't hesitate to confront a child if I know I have ground to stand on. But you don't want to put yourself in jeopardy or a situation where you're not quite sure what's going on." Later, Marilyn added, "Parents are always watching you. They can be your best ally and worst enemy."

Indeed. Even a note in a message box from a parent can be enough to make a teacher panic. An elementary school teacher described the intense anxiety she feels when confronting a parent over a child's problem. "You get a note and you go home [anxious], and you stay up all night talking to your husband. Teachers walk out of the building crying over things like this." Marilyn has concluded it's generally useless to inform parents about the misbehavior of their children. "There's no rationale. It's not an intellectual reaction. It's like the lioness and her cubs. They're going to protect them no matter what. As a teacher," she said, "you don't want to touch that.

"I'm not the enemy," she noted, "but at some point, you just back off and don't go there anymore."

These days, teachers have their noses to the grindstone to keep their students working at a demanding academic pace. A teacher in a top-rated public school district explained, "Girls bullying each other is the farthest thing from our minds. I'm sorry, but I wasn't looking for it. It doesn't happen in that fifty-minute [class period]. I'm not noticing it. I'm not focused on it. I'm too focused on instruction. I don't have time for that.

"We're not trained to look for that," she added. "We are trained to make sure they are doing their books." The idea that teachers should be attuned to students' body language exasperates her. "It's so hard to be up all the time. You have to be on top of everything and you're bombarded constantly. And now, on top of everything, you have to be aware of the situation they're going through, aware of body language—all of it!"

Not surprisingly, teachers are apt to misinterpret problems at school. Maryann, also a twenty-year veteran of the classroom, told me that sometimes girls "misunderstand" other girls. "There's two girls who have a secret together," she explained to me. "It could be a good secret or a bad secret, just something that the two of them want to keep to themselves." She told me the story of a third grader who became "hysterical" when her best friends stopped talking every time she approached. She was devastated that her two best friends had left her out.

"I don't know how they could have voiced [the need to exclude her] without hurting her feelings. Even if they had said, 'Look, this is something we need to keep private between us,' she would have still felt left out." Maryann took the three girls outside and tried to help the excluded girl understand that some people needed to keep secrets.

When I press Maryann about why she permitted the girls to do this, she admits she didn't know what the secret was, just that she respected their right to keep it. "They said it was private," she explains. Yet there is a difference between keeping information private between two people and flaunting the privacy itself. Making distinctions like this one is critical to understanding how subtle the aggression between girls can be.

There is a darker misunderstanding between teachers and students to explore. Teachers do not have access to a neutral language to name girls' aggression, and most are unaware of the social and psychological impact of stifling anger. As a result, it becomes easier to resent girls' behavior and give in to cruel stereotypes. One of my old teachers put it simply, echoing a remark I've heard more times than I care to count: "I'd much rather deal with men. They are generally straightforward and honest with you. With men, you know where you stand." The impact of such attitudes on teachers' work in the classroom is unknown.

None of this is to say teachers prefer ignorance. When I called Lynn, the same guidance counselor I wept to when Abby took me on in the third grade, she was thrilled to hear from me. A slight woman with a globe of brown curls, a freckled face, and the presence of a center forward, she hugged me, asked me about my brother (himself no stranger to this office), then settled back into her chair. "The biggest difficulty I encounter, the hardest thing to work through, is this awful thing that girls do to each other," she said, crossing her legs and frowning. "I have been waiting for twenty-five years for someone that would explain this to me."

Like Lynn, some teachers have chosen to confront alternative aggressions in spite of the shroud of silence that surrounds the topic. For Amber, it is the memory of her own victimization that moves her. An elementary teacher in Mississippi, she sat with me one day in her classroom and told me about it: "I was short, had buck teeth and glasses. I know how it feels, and it's not gone away, and it's been twenty years. It's never gone away. I'm the most insecure person in the whole world. No one in my classroom would probably know that because I'm always telling them that we can do anything. I still, you know, I still can hear those kids calling me names and not accepting me because of my looks, my physical appearance."

Amber hawkishly forbids verbal cruelty. She recalled escorting a boy and girl into the hall after they traded insults and speaking to them frankly about her own life. "It hurts, doesn't it?" she said. "I've been there. I had buck teeth. They may not be now, but [the teasing] hurt me." When she takes girls outside, she often gives them equal time to tell their stories.

Very little training would be required to train teachers to identify and discipline alternative aggressions. The question is whether or not we want them to. When I asked Kendra how she can tell it's happening in her classroom, she said it's obvious: "[Girls become] very withdrawn, their personalities change. Their facial expressions change. It's almost like a sadness, an intimidation. . . . Even their posture. It almost sounds silly. They just withdraw—from the teachers, their group of friends. . . . You can just look. I like for a child to smile. Lots of times I say, 'Give me a smile,' and if they really cannot smile, you know something is wrong."

Of course, even the most well-intentioned educators miss some covert aggression. Kendra cautioned, "They will try to hurt without anyone seeing it. You really have to see the expressions on their faces to know who's being left out or what's happening." Even Jenny, my roommate who is a teacher and victim of bullying herself, often comes home frustrated because she cannot fathom when it is Princess manages to psychologically flatten fragile Maya. In these situations, only the child can be relied upon to come forward and explain. And if she believes that her teacher will trivialize or ignore her pain, or approach the problem insensitively, she will remain silent.

No one should have to rely on ad hoc moments of compassion or personal experience to confront an epidemic. It is only through enforceable public rules that we will begin to scratch the surface of this problem. If we don't make alternative aggressions a clear responsibility of school officials, children will continue to be vulnerable to bullying and abuse.

CHAPTER *nine*

the road ahead

Throughout this book, I have tried to offer glimpses of the back alleys and hidden corners of girl bullying, to begin the process of naming and understanding it. I have come to believe that the alternative aggressions in which girls engage are halfhearted, unsatisfying forms of communication, that they do not satiate the universal human need to express anger, and that they should not be the only avenue of expression available to girls.

Girls need to make peace with conflict, and they need our help. This means providing girls not only with a healthier relationship to aggression, but with permission to experience the uncomfortable feelings that often precede anger and conflict. We need to stop rewarding manipulation. We must encourage girls to embrace respectful acts of assertion and provide them with representations of female aggression that are neither sensationalized nor the stuff of fantasy. The responsibility begins at the moment of socialization, and it belongs to all of us—parents, teachers, and girls.

In this chapter, I offer strategies to combat alternative aggressions, including new directions for policy making and teaching. Most of the suggestions came directly from the parents, school officials, and survivors of bullying I met while researching this book.

for parents

I asked every woman and girl I interviewed to assess her parents' response to her ordeal. Overwhelmingly, the most effective parents were the ones who actively listened. These mothers and fathers inquired every day about how school went. They held their daughters when they cried and accommodated special requests, whether it was going to school later, being picked up within seconds of the last bell, or preparing a special meal. Elizabeth, from chapter six, confided that "if it weren't for my mom, I'd probably be demented. She respected my need not to say anything and my need for her silent presence. [I needed her to] just hug me, hold me." Hard as it may be to accept, there is not a great deal you can do to make the problem go away. Your contribution here may feel passive, but it's also by far the most vital.

Long after the crisis has passed, girls grow into women who remember the refuge of home and family as the one thing that helped them survive. So turn your home into a sanctuary for your daughter. Let it be the place where she can fill herself up with unconditional love and support to replenish what she is losing day after difficult day. Talk quietly to her siblings about how they can help.

All of this is not to say your hands are tied. There are things to do and questions to ask. When you talk to your daughter, get the facts as a journalist would: find out who's doing it, how long it's been happening, what they're doing to her, and if the teacher knows. Then plot some strategies, with her and on your own.

If the bully is a classmate, ask your daughter if she wants to have her seat moved, or better yet, if it would help to switch out of the bully's class. If she's in elementary school, you'll notice social groups often forming along classroom lines. If she can move out, perhaps she can move on or at least form protective social bonds with other kids.

Does she want to switch schools? Several women I met transferred to make a fresh start and never looked back. The change may seem disruptive, but it can make a huge difference. Like a storm, girl bullying is often little more than different social elements swirling together in a particular climate. There's a reason why tornadoes touch down in Kansas more often than in California, and social chemistry among girls is often the same way. The stories I heard confirm that girls who are whittled down in one environment can thrive in the next.

If changing schools is a financial burden, there are other options. Elizabeth entered a weeklong youth program at the low point of her suffering in eighth grade. Angry, suspicious, and defensive at the time, she was practically dragged in by her parents. To her great surprise, Elizabeth recalled, "These perfect stranger kids would walk up and give me a hug and say, 'It's nice to meet you. I'm so-and-so.' And I was like, 'Oh my God. Are you for real? Are you serious?' But by the end of the week I skipped out of there.... They wanted to know me and there was no catch. They weren't going to stab me in the back."

That experience, she remembered, "turned my perspective around totally." When Elizabeth went to high school that fall, she was "high on acceptance, totally high on [the fact that] it doesn't matter because, whatever, these people love me for who I am." For Elizabeth, the scars may not have disappeared, but her wounds did begin to heal.

There is no question that a new activity can mean the world to an ostracized child. Ideally, you should choose activities where kids are valued more for the contribution they make than for what they're wearing, saying, or watching. The shift in scrutiny, away from what makes a girl popular and on to what makes her a good player or writer or horseback rider or baby sitter, can make the difference. So get your daughter on a team or in a club, on the school newspaper or in an after-school writing workshop. Get her singing, dancing, throwing pottery, tumbling, volunteering: get her with other people who are disconnected from her social misfortune.

Be thoughtful: Don't put your kid on the soccer team if she's got two left feet or in a gymnastics class with a razor-sharp power clique or even in a workshop where most kids come from another school. Take the social temperature before you enroll her by talking to the adult in charge or to other parents. Set your child up to succeed, or at least blend in and enjoy herself.

Activities are exciting gateways to finding a childhood passion, and like falling in love, passion often makes the rest of life bearable. I know that no matter how bad my day was, once I got on the basketball court, it was pure focus and meditation. Nothing could touch me.

In times of crisis, Ellen, a psychotherapist, found role-playing extremely effective in helping her daughter Roma. She asked Roma and her ally to act out different scenarios of confrontation with their tormentor, Jane. "I was encouraging them to speak their truths," Ellen explained, "and to not be afraid of what [Jane] was going to say to other kids, and not let that control them. I would get very, very specific wading through with them—'Yeah but if I say that, she'll say this!'—and I would help them figure out what they would say next. It was how to handle a situation."

Too often we dispense advice to children in a vertical way: "Tell her this!" or "Have you just tried walking away?" Role-playing is more horizontal and interactive. It makes the strategy three-dimensional and real for your daughter, while at the same time giving you a presence in her social world that will comfort both of you. Having a friend engage in the role-playing can shore up your child's sense of moral support and decrease the terror of isolation.

In the meantime, cover all the bases of your child's day and see where you can lighten her load. Find out what she's doing at lunch and recess: If she's alone, where is she? Would it be possible to arrange for her to go to the library or art room or gym twice a week? It's not a permanent solution, nor should she make a habit of escaping every single day, but if she is truly suffering, perhaps you can find her some space to breathe.

Are there any other friends she can play with during the day? Encourage her to join their lunch table or group at recess. If you have good friends with children your daughter can play with, talk to them about it. Be careful: avoid the appearance of trying to force your daughter into friendship with another girl. Be sure to communicate with the parent about the potential for a good fit with her child. Never assume it's the other child's responsibility to help your daughter, no matter how dire your child's straits. To encourage the other child to exercise compassion at the expense of her own social needs would be to reinforce the message that care and self-sacrifice are her priority. At the end of the day, the decision should lie with the two children.

Before taking on the school, cover all of *your* bases. The most effective parent will be able to derail the school's attempts to hand the problem back to the family. This means knowing, to the fullest extent possible, the status of your child's development. What are her social relationships like outside the classroom? Have you spoken to her coaches and other instructors? What kind of disposition is your daughter perceived by peers and others as having? Although no child ever deserves to be bullied, if your daughter is a social butterfly who does not have a history of problems with peers, your argument for school action may be more powerful.

It is easy for an episode of bullying to absorb parents in feelings of desperation, rage, and sadness. It's a serious mistake, however, to let those feelings overcome or even dominate your approach to your child's ordeal. Deciding it's the other child's problem or fault, whether you tell your daughter that "she's just jealous of you" or chalk it up to the bully's own problems in life, is only half the battle. For whatever reason, your child's fallen prey to someone else, but one thing is certain: she needs you to help her be a stronger, more self-loving person.

As a rule, it's not a good idea to call the bully's parents. These conversations tend to go swiftly and woefully awry. It's rarely easy for the approaching parent to conceal her discomfort and anger. It's also important to remember that news of a daughter's aggression can be embarrassing: when a girl isn't nice to everyone, it's a sign of her failure to conform to her sex role. It's like receiving news that your son is too submissive around other boys. On top of this, parents often see comments about their children as a personal affront to their parenting skills, or worse, to themselves. Their responses tend to be angry and defensive as a result, and it's not unusual for the parent to deny the problem altogether.

Even when the parents are friends, problems can crop up. One parent may feel obligated to the other, and resentment can build up between parents and between girls. Also, the accusation that one child is aggressing against another can set off repressed tensions within the relationship. Or the anxiety triggered in one parent can be strong enough to challenge the fabric of the relationship itself. Parents often elect to address the problem directly with other parents because schools lack the infrastructure to help mediate between parties. If parents could feel safe knowing their child's safety was ensured at school, they would probably feel less of a need to take the situation into their own hands.

At the end of the day, be aware of what your daughter sees when she looks at you. Be conscious at all times of how you "present" to your daughter. Parents for whom bullying evokes visceral reactions, beware. Are you reliving your own experience through your daughter's? Losing yourself in the intensity of her pain?

You *can* overempathize. If you've drowned out your child's voice and circumstances, you've entered dangerous territory. It can be extremely uncomfortable for a child if her mother weeps or loses strength at the moment when her daughter needs it most. The message sent is that *you* need to be taken care of, not the other way around. Most worrisome, your response may affect your child's willingness to keep confiding in you. She may believe it's in your best interests not to know the messiest feelings she has, that on some level it is not acceptable for her to share them with you. Remember those times when your daughter was learning to walk: If you showed fear and panic when she slipped and fell on the floor, she'd usually sense it and wail. If you chortled, "Oops! Up you go!" and plucked her up calmly, she probably kept on trucking.

Suzanne Cohen had always struggled to separate her feelings from her daughter's, but when Hannah's torment began, her sense of helplessness nearly broke her. "I didn't know where [my feelings] left off and hers began and vice versa," she told me. With the help of a therapist, she learned that she could not live vicariously through her daughter, and that her behavior suggested to Hannah a need to be parented by her. "I wanted to be able to make it right," she said, but "at a certain point I kind of realized that it's not about anyone doing anything other than just listening. [I had to] give her the shoulder, let her vent, let her get it out of her system, because I am a mother, and then not respond to that in anything but a loving way, and not make it my battle." Eventually Suzanne learned how to play a role in her daughter's experience that would both honor her child's circumstances and afford herself a sense of agency. It was harder than you think, she said, to do it.

So take your own temperature. How are *you* feeling? Like the mothers in chapter eight, most parents bring as much to the bullying situation as their daughters. Your response to your daughter will bear the imprint of your priorities, your fears, your childhood. Linda recalled her response to her daughter with some regret. In hindsight, she said, "I wouldn't have pushed so hard [for her to fight back]. . . . I feel fine about listening and supporting and offering suggestions for actions but not pushing her because it has to come from within. Otherwise it becomes about what I want instead of what she wants, and sometimes I think I made that mistake because it was so painful to watch." Ask yourself, What is the subtext of my strategy, my emotions? Remember that what is best for your child and what you want may not always be the same thing.

"I'd love to hear my daughter come up with some really strong responses," one mother told me. "I don't want to see her be weak. We want our children to be stronger than we were." In spite of this, and in spite of the uniqueness of each bullying episode, most parents find themselves at the doorstep of the age-old question: At what point do we let our children fight their own battles? When parents ask me what the right thing is to do, I ask them to imagine doing nothing at all: Is the teacher aware of what is happening? Will she step in when things go too far? Does the school punish these behaviors? Until alternative aggressions win recognition as real forms of violence in schools, parents should err on the side of intervention. They should assume nothing about their school or their child's ability to fight it. They should understand that their claims are as much about gaining recognition for the problem as they are about redressing it.

HOW TO APPROACH YOUR DAUGHTER:
FOR BETTER AND WORSE

Ten minutes before the last bell, and I was winding up my discussion with ninth-grade girls at Linden. Papers were rustling like leaves, bodies were starting to wriggle and fidget. "Okay!" I said, a little louder than I meant to, "one more question." I asked them if they talk to their parents about bullying, or when a girl is mean to them.

A ripple of "No way!" and "Yeah, right" crested through the room, followed by snorts, muttering, and one girl spitting up her soda.

"Right," I said coolly, trying to look unfazed. "Why? Really," I said, cheerfully. "Come on, you guys."

Mollie piped up, "You can disappoint your parents if you're not friends with everyone."

"You don't want your parents to think badly of your friend because you'd get over it," Lydia added. "You want to stand up for your friend because they reflect you."

"Oh yeah!" Reena cackled. "My mother will go, 'I never liked that friend of yours anyway!'"

"Totally," murmured a voice in the corner.

"My mom's a dork. She says, 'Oh, I'll be your friend,'" Lauren said.

"I don't want to tell her if she thinks I'm wrong. If she's not on my side, it's like I failed and it's terrible because your parents are supposed to be on your side."

"I don't want my friends *and* my parents against me."
And on and on.

Most girls don't tell their parents what's going on in a bullying situation. That's not a sex difference, either; bullying is a deeply humiliating experience for every child. Since alternative aggressions lack a public identity, however, the burden of silence may be heavier. Some girls may not be able to identify what they're experiencing as wrong or punishable. Instead, they may internalize the problem as their fault and never speak of it.

A child might also feel that since there are no rules prohibiting the behavior, and so much of it slips beneath the radar of teachers, that it's somehow not worth mentioning or pursuing. Faith, an eighth grader in Ridgewood who attempted suicide when her friends abandoned her, was too embarrassed to tell her mother what was happening. "I didn't think my mama had went through all this because she never told me about any of it. I didn't want her to know all this because it was really embarrassing telling your mom that a girl was picking on you and bullying you and stuff."

Talking with your children about alternative aggressions is absolutely critical. If you indicate to your child in a nonjudgmental way that you know what goes on at school—that on some level you "get" the hidden culture of girls' aggression—she will feel safe showing you its darkest corners. Asking leading questions can help:

- When girls want to be mean in your class, what kinds of things do they do?
- Does the teacher see it when it's happening? Why or why not? How does she react?
- Are some girls more secret about their meanness? How?
- Can friends be mean to each other? How?

It helps to introduce your questions in the third person. It will give your child the chance to acclimate to talking with you about it.

Girls are socialized to care for others, so they often internalize negative feelings to shield others from the weight of their pain—hence the spike in depression, self-mutilation, and anorexia that can accompany the loss of self-esteem around adolescence. Stephanie, whose silence left an ulcer in her stomach, explained, "I didn't want [my parents] to worry more. I didn't want them to think that I was a freak who couldn't like make the grade." Helping your child understand the messiness and mutuality of relationship will help her be more emotionally honest in other parts of her life. You can't leave the door open unless it swings both ways: living honestly with your children and sharing a moderate amount of your own grief and fears will go a long way.

Once I got them going, the over three hundred girls I met individually and in groups spoke passionately about what their parents did wrong when it came to helping them. Here are some of the most commonly cited responses of parents to their daughters' ordeals, followed by what many girls said they'd prefer (with my own two cents thrown in for good measure).

WRONG: *"It's a phase"* or: *"It happens to everyone, honey."*

This remark is meant to soothe, but it ends up trivializing your daughter's pain. It says, "You're a dime a dozen" when she feels just the opposite—that her pain is the worst she's ever felt, that she is surely the first to feel it this intensely, that she is the only one who's ever endured something so horrible. It may indeed be a phase, but she doesn't know that. This comment only underscores for her how little you get what she's dealing with.

A lot of parent-child communication surrounding bullying is like the children's game of Operator. What sounds like "It happens to everyone" out of your mouth might sound like "It happens to losers like you" in her ears. One of the most common reasons girls don't tell is because of the shame they feel for failing to perform socially. If girls' social identities are built on their relational skills, isolation is a disaster. The feeling of failure is only increased by comments that trivialize what they're going through.

BETTER: *"Oh, honey. That is so terrible. I'm sorry."*

Honor your child's pain as though she were the first to experience it. At the same time, tell her about alternative aggressions. As many parents are well aware, you can tell your child something and she'll turn up her nose, and when she hears it from someone else, she'll nod effusively. Explain what *scientists* have found. Explain that she is not alone.

ADD: *"It happened to me."*

Did it? Can you remember? The most effective listeners empathize. They respect a person's vulnerability and connect to it by showing some of their own. If you can connect to the feelings you had as an adolescent, your daughter is far more likely to keep listening, indeed, to believe you. But don't overdo it: some kids told me they hated it when their mothers insisted they knew exactly how they were feeling. "My mother says, 'I know how you feel,' but she doesn't," they said. "Things are different now."

WRONG: *"I never liked that friend of yours anyway."* Also known as *"Why are you hanging out with those girls to begin with?"* and *"How many times do I have to tell you [fill in the blank]?"*

Ever date someone your friends didn't like? Remember when they told you how awful and immature and insensitive the person was? Did you say, "Oh, that's *right*! Thank you *so* much!" and dump him? The same is true for your daughter. Sure, she's hanging out with girls you may think are terrible, but she's not going to figure it out until she's ready, and you may have little to do with it when she does. At this point, it's wise to remember girls' fear of relational loss and that your child is probably looking for a way to heal the relationship, not end it. Unless it's a cut-and-dried case of serious emotional abuse, when you suggest she lose her friend, all you're doing is invoking her worst nightmare, not to mention making her feel like you've turned on her at the same time others have, too.

BETTER: *"I am really sorry to hear that. Have you considered talking with her about it?"* and/or *"What do you think you want to do next?"*

Empathize, empathize, empathize. Alizah felt let down by her mother's stoic reaction to her problems. If she were herself a mother, she said, "I would probably cry with [my daughter] to start out with. Just because it's so awful." Let your daughter do the talking. She needs you to listen and not much else. If you can, treat her like a friend who's confided a problem. Home should be her sanctuary, and it may be the only place she feels truly loved and respected. Questions and comments should be peaceful, affirmative, and loving, never accusatory, never judgmental: she gets enough of that at school.

WRONG: *"What could you be doing to cause this?"*

If your daughter is being bullied or cast out of her social group, it is highly unlikely anything she does or changes about herself is going to make a difference. There's often no rhyme or reason to the moment a girl or clique finally decides to get angry or even. Moreover, your daughter is probably already cataloging her faults with the efficiency of a Pentium IV computer. No matter what your intention, we have the Operator problem again. You say, "What can you change about yourself?" She hears, "My mother thinks it's my fault and there's something wrong with me." Naomi believes her mother's interpretation of her travails as a social skills problem left a second scar. "I wanted her to be a mother lion and protect me, to treat me as endangered and not as a kid with problems. I wanted her to see a greater, more immediate danger."

BETTER: *"Do you want to brainstorm together about how we got here?"*

This is not to say you or your daughter should embrace victimization. The problem may not always be developmental. Remember Erin: all her friends repressed their problems with her, letting their anger simmer quietly for years until finally it exploded. Remembering the dynamics between herself and her friends during the years leading up to their meltdown helped Erin understand why their anger felt so disproportionate. Erin could see where she inspired anger, competition, and jealousy, and where her friends might have been afraid to talk about it or express anger. Working backward with your child by walking her through memories of tension may be similarly effective.

ALSO: *Ask the guidance counselor or the teacher.*

Perhaps your daughter could improve her social skills; perhaps she's not responding to cues the right way and is drawing the ire of her peers. She's probably too young to tell you that herself. Visit her guidance counselor or teacher for an evaluation. See what resources are available to help your family. Helping your daughter improve her social skills is another way to engage her in bettering her own situation. Asking how she may be triggering the behavior is not an inappropriate question, but as my mother always says, "It's not what you say, it's how you say it." Your approach should be balanced, respectful, and tender, one that reflects a mix of empathy for your child's pain and support for her social success.

WRONG: *"I'm calling that school RIGHT NOW!"*

Unless you just cut a fat check to your school's endowment fund, the I'll-huff-and-I'll-puff approach is generally ineffective. Getting labeled the hysterical parent is a fatal mistake, and the best way to do that is to approach the school up in arms, as though they have never seen this behavior before. Not only have they seen it, but they probably don't have any rules prohibiting it, nor do they have the slightest clue what to do about it. All anger will do is make them defensive and aloof.

More important, however, is what your daughter thinks. Does *she* want to call the school? Unless your child's life is endangered, exploiting parental authority to override your child's desire is, and there's no nice way to say this, unforgivable. She may have little left but her autonomy, and anyway, you're not the one who's going to spend eight hours a day in that classroom. Naomi remembered her parents' panicked response to her distraught behavior: "It was like I really broke down. The stress was too much, and they wanted to take me out of school. They wanted to call the school. I was like, don't,

I'll die, I'll get killed, you don't understand, do not make a case out of it. I thought there was no limit. I can't—how can I emphasize enough that this was *real* to me. These were kids; adults didn't have power. I witnessed every day adults being out of the loop and kids having the power."

Even if you swear the teacher to secrecy, you can't predict what might happen. One teacher promised a girl that she would not mention the bullying in class, then pulled the perpetrating clique into the hallway and made them promise to be nice to her. The girls made a game out of pretending to be sugary sweet for the rest of the year, an agonizing fate.

Obviously there are exceptions. If your child's welfare is seriously endangered, you may have to make an executive decision in her best interests. Alternatively, you may wish to move your child out of the classroom or school altogether.

BETTER: *"Do you want me to talk with your teacher?"*

If she does, remaining calm is everything. As I just mentioned, once you raise your voice and get angry, eyes glaze over and people stop listening. If you're really unlucky, you might get brushed off, or better yet, condescended to. Emotion is weak currency in this market. What you need are the facts about alternative aggressions. What you need is to present the information in a clear, organized manner, to argue that the school community stands to gain a lot in taking this issue on. This is not unlike the way someone might have proposed sex education or college preparatory classes years ago.

Finally, you need other parents. Margaret, who dreaded the idea of others knowing her daughter's problem, found a group of four mothers who met informally for coffee once a week to talk. After a couple of months, Margaret said, "We discovered that we were safe." After a year, the women started opening up about problems and shared tears. Margaret told them about Chloe's trials. "We're there to support each other."

The hidden culture of girls' aggression subsists on silence and isolation. As Mary Pipher[58] has written, "We need to politicize, not pathologize, families." Part of this means that in order to fight the forces that prey on children outside our homes, we must first step forward to publicly acknowledge our questions and fears within them. For it is not just the girls who think they are suffering alone when they are bullied. So do parents. When families don't talk, parents can't learn from one another and it becomes easier to blame themselves for their children's problems. Blaming parents means we focus less on our daughters' peer cultures. It prevents us from realizing collectively as a society that there are systemic social patterns to be resisted and corrected.

Instead of organizing a committee around your child's experience of cruelty, how about a committee to develop and implement a policy on alternative aggressions? Ask teachers and students to join. If you can, ask mothers whose daughters have no direct affiliation with bullying, which can add credibility, reducing, as it does, the appearance of being "hysterical mothers." The point is to ask your school for public consciousness and rules, not attention for your specific child. Anyone interested in the development of her child's assertiveness skills should be concerned, a point I explore in more detail in the next chapter.

WRONG: *"This is the way girls are. You may as well get used to it."*

No matter whom you're talking about, generalizing about a group of people never sets a positive example for your daughter. Teaching her to fear and hate other females, of course, is a mistake. Mothers who were once victims of girls' aggression often voice this sentiment. This is another instance in which the parent's experience may overwhelm the child's.

BETTER: *"Did you know that there is research about why some girls act in these ways when they get angry?"*

Initiate your daughter's journey into self-awareness. Teach her about how girls are socialized, about what being "feminine" means, about the caregiving functions females are expected to perform. Explain how "good girls" are denied direct forms of anger and aggression and feelings of competition and jealousy, and how that affects the specific ways girls show anger. Give her the tools to know she is not alone.

So that she does not come to believe all females are this way, explore how the rules of femininity against anger and fighting affect all her relationships, the healthy and the troubled, so that she begins to understand how conflict avoidance can appear in all kinds of relationships, not just the bad ones. Help her identify her own fears of conflict, even her own acts of alternative aggression. Urge her to distinguish between feeling upset about her own victimization and feeling upset about girls' aggression itself. Be wary of indirectly reinforcing stereotypes about the need for girls to be "nice."

WRONG: *"But you two were such good friends!"*

Remember, appearances can be deceiving. Girls easily tuck bullying into the folds of friendship, making aggression almost invisible. Your child's brief disclosure may be the only warning you get. Faith explained how appearances masked her perpetrator's capacity to injure others. "Nobody knew because Liz was like a straight-A student, and they thought she was friends with all these people. Nobody knew what she'd do to some of her friends." If you find yourself arguing with your daughter, it wouldn't hurt to ask yourself why. After all, we see what we want to see. What do you have to gain or lose if your daughter is no longer friends with this person?

BETTER: *"When did this start? When does it happen? Is there anything you can do to make it stop?"*

Interview your child and figure out just how much trouble her friendship is in. Is the problem isolated, or does it pervade all of her interactions? Does it happen only when they're with other girls, or just at soccer? Pinpoint the trigger moments or situations, and see if you can help your daughter through them either by role-playing or through a counselor's intervention.

If the problem is more serious, or if the perpetrator won't play any other way, it can be a critically important opportunity for you as a parent. The trouble in these situations is that girls confuse friendship with abuse, not unlike the way a battered person might. You are not overreacting. Call the situation what it is; hold a new lens up to the relationship and show your daughter just how unfriendly this friendship is. Talk to her about abuse in a nonjudgmental, loving way. And get professional help if you feel in over your head.

WRONG: *"You're being too sensitive. They don't really mean it!"*

As my grandmother would say, "Oy vey." It would be hard to overstate the resentment adult women still feel about this particular pearl of wisdom. You may think you're toughening up your daughter, teaching her to roll with the punches, but she experiences these remarks as a blatant denial of her feelings.

Naomi grew up in the kind of home where if she fell down, her grandmother would laugh and say, "I hope you didn't break the floor!" When she told her parents how the others were whittling her down, they advised her to act as though it weren't happening. So, she recalled, "I couldn't cry about it. I couldn't ask for help. I couldn't fight back. I didn't have a right to defend myself. You couldn't show your pain. You couldn't react as if someone had done a really bad thing. There was this silence, this you can't speak. And I feel as though I have a right to nothing more than I have a right to my own feelings. . . . You have a right to do whatever you need to do to defend yourself and you have the right to feel dignity. I think that was the greatest thing that I feel was ever taken from me. And only now am I getting it back."

If you weren't present for the episode your daughter is describing, calling her hypersensitive is unfair and judgmental. It's one of the clearest ways to signal you don't understand her or her life. It also perpetuates the silencing and invalidation of girls' aggression.

BETTER: *"How can you tell they're not joking? Are you sure they really mean to make you feel this bad?"*

If your child is recalling a situation her friends insisted was a "joke," beware. As I show in chapter three, girls use humor as a vehicle to convey negative feelings indirectly, and your daughter may be correctly intuiting the subtext. In a culture that denies the anger and meanness girls visit upon one another, it is incumbent upon you as a parent to validate your child's version of events. You may be the only one who ever will. That's not to say you should overreact and overidentify with your child's painful disclosures. But you do have to take her word for it. If you don't, you may risk never hearing from her again.

the road ahead

Assertiveness training is the new "it" program for girls, mostly at the schools that can afford it. The lion's share of these ventures focuses on the link between physical and verbal self-defense. But getting girls to punch a padded perpetrator that looks like an oversized marshmallow misses the point when it comes to alternative aggressions. Anyone can punch a pillow. It's a lot harder to confront rumor spreading, ganging up, or your best friend. To be truly effective, these programs must teach acts of courage that are based on girls' everyday relationships. At the very least, role-playing exercises should simulate real, lived social moments in order to capture the heart of what girls fear. They should address the intense roles that relationships and isolation play in the female life, and integrate that consciousness into self-defense strategies.

I think it is clear by now that alternative aggressions and the motivations girls feel to engage in them are more than an interpersonal problem for girls, more than an unfortunate blip of youth. We will need much more than assertiveness training to reverse the toxic elements of girls' socialization. To begin with, we will need an infrastructure with two main components: regulation and education.

REGULATION

Late last summer, I accompanied my roommate Jenny to a Brooklyn store for educators to help her shop for the new school year. The place was wall-to-wall bulletin boards, stickers, and sentence strips. Near the registers was a huge display of the signs that adorn so many classrooms: groundhogs touching noses beneath the banner RESPECT OTHERS!; butterflies fluttering against a blue sky above the words BE A GOOD FRIEND! I can't argue with teachers who claim they're attractive, stimulating fillers for plain walls. Yet they also seem to be signs of vague, clichéd strategies to teach our children how to behave. It is simply not enough to tell girls to respect others. We must explain clearly what will and will not be tolerated.

The first step is to change the rules. We must introduce new, more inclusive anti-bullying language into school policy. Currently, our regulatory approach to alternative aggressions is at best haphazard, at worst nonexistent. School districts often set broad guidelines for students, allowing some schools to be strict about specific antibullying policies, while others seem to avoid the word "bullying" altogether.

In a culture that denies the alternative aggressions children visit upon one another, it is not enough merely to prohibit harassment or bullying. School antibullying policies and handbooks must be revised to reflect the new research on alternative aggressions. Schools need to define clearly what constitutes aggressive behavior among *all* students. Existing rules should be amended to prohibit *specific* behaviors such as rumor spreading, alliance building, secret telling, and severe episodes of nonverbal aggression. We need reasonable rules that can be applied consistently, without regard to family, social status, race, or gender.

In 2001, Washington State lawmakers introduced legislation requiring schools to adopt detailed antibullying policies. The policy-making process was to include students and members of the school community, and schools were encouraged but not required to form "bullying prevention task forces." Special training for school employees was also required. So far, the law does not ask schools to name the disciplinary consequences for bullying, a mandate the state of Oregon has included in its new antibullying legislation. Oregon, however, defines bullying as a "written, verbal or physical act," emphasizing physical and direct forms of aggression and excluding the nonverbal and relational aggression so prevalent in girls' bullying.

There is some debate about the appropriateness of legislating school behavior. Nevertheless, the cultural momentum is unmistakably strong. As bullying moves to center stage in our collective thinking, now is the time for supporters of girls to join the conversation and advocate its inclusion.

EDUCATION

How can a teacher create a classroom culture that treats alternative and direct aggressions equally? Beginning in preschool, along with how to stand in line, how to be quiet when the teacher asks, how to take care of the pet guinea pig, and how to wait their turn, girls and boys must learn that alternative aggressions are not acceptable. Just as they learn that punching to get what you want is a kind of violence, they must learn that threatening to not be someone's friend anymore is, too. The instruction must begin early and continue year after year. Just because alternative aggressors sigh instead of shout, snort instead of tease, roll their eyes instead of taunt, or turn their backs instead of hit, they shouldn't be let off the hook.

Banning these behaviors and socializing girls *away* from them should become as important as any other lesson in citizenship or morality. We need to be vigilant about the fact that ignorance of girl bullying affects perpetrators as much as victims. Just as there are girls who believe what they're going through is not serious enough, or "not a big deal," there are others who think going behind someone's back is the "nice" thing to do.

Again, I'm not saying girls should efface their anger. Rather, they should not be deceived that silence and indirection are acceptable ways to express negative feelings. At the same time, girls should be held to the same standards of nonaggressive behavior as boys, and they should be entitled to equal protection in the classroom. To do that, however, we need to expand our definition of aggression itself.

A classroom sensitive to alternative aggressions is managed by a teacher who openly discusses its different forms. Like any other classroom priority, an integrated approach is essential. A teacher may use lessons with stories of children who experience alternative aggressions. She may openly discuss her own history with bullying. He may use some instruction time to talk about the social dynamics of the class. She may work with other teachers to share effective discipline strategies and discuss the social climate of the grade. He may take time out to praise acts of truth telling and assertiveness.

We need to create an antibullying curriculum that puts alternative aggressions at its center. For example, we should be exploring with girls the reasons behind alliance building and developing with them strategies that will prevent it. Many of the conflicts that ignite girl bullying are relational, and teachers frequently report that allowing girls to talk their issues out helps dissipate their anger. An antibullying program that attends to relational crises might carve out regular time for conflict resolution. Most importantly, we should involve girls every step of the way and allow them to lead us through their underground. We can get there no other way.

Teachers cannot do this without the support of their principals and superintendents. Teachers must feel that time spent on these issues is neither wasted nor stolen but instead important to their students' days and development.

As long as girls bully covertly, teacher intervention will always be a choice. As we saw in the last chapter, many educators fear singling out behavior they have not witnessed. With so much of girls' aggression invisible, identifying the perpetrators of alternative aggressions is rarely easy. Girls will need different standards of reporting in order to have their injuries redressed. Likewise, teachers should know they will be supported in the event of controversy. For them, the best reassurance is often bureaucratic.

The Ophelia Project, named after Mary Pipher's groundbreaking book, is the country's first organization to develop anti-bullying curricula using research on relational aggression. The Erie, Pennsylvania, organization worked directly with the psychologists who pioneered research on alternative aggression to develop a groundbreaking intervention called "How Girls Hurt Each Other." The program trains high school mentors to teach younger girls to prevent and confront relational aggression. "Creating a Safe Social Climate in our Schools," Ophelia's school-wide training program, works directly with teachers, administrators, and students to guide the school into awareness of relational aggression. Ophelia also works with parents to help them play more influential roles in creating a safer social climate at school.[59]

The Empower Program, based in Washington, DC, has developed cutting-edge programs for girls and boys which focus on interpersonal boundary-setting, conflict management, and relationship violence. Both organizations have undertaken the critical tasks of education and regulation. Their work must be emulated and supported.

for girls especially (but not only): everyday truth telling and conflict

Girls have a critical role to play in changing the culture of their cliques and friendships. After all, most of us hate this way of life. I can't count the number of girls who told me they'd rather be beaten up than ignored or cut down spiritually by their peers. We need to abandon the belief that doing this is natural or unavoidable. It isn't. We can change.

It's like riding in the passenger seat of a car when you're young. You hardly ever pay attention to what the driver's doing. You don't have to. But one day, you get your learner's permit and switch seats. You're going all the same routes, only this time you have to relearn each part of the way. All the turns someone made for you, you now have to make yourself. You have to make sure the wheels don't jump the curb, that you come to a complete stop, that you check your blind spot.

It's the same thing with our relationships: we have to get in the driver's seats and relearn healthier ways of taking the twists and turns. We don't have to give in to the autopilot urge to tell someone else we're angry instead of the person who made us angry in the first place.

The biggest reason we don't talk to each other is because we're afraid we'll lose the friendship with the person we're confronting, or worse, that the person we're talking to will turn everyone against us.

The fear throws up a wall that prevents us from speaking our hearts and minds to each other. As we also know, it also leads to a ton of gossip, rumor spreading, and resentment that mushroom into other kinds of nastiness.

AN EXERCISE FOR
GIRLFRIENDS AND CLIQUES:
THROW THE GEARS OF
OUR CULTURE INTO REVERSE

"I hate the fact that you have to go through all this stuff," Shelley said to me at Starbucks one afternoon. "You can't tell someone you're mad at them, you have no idea what's going on, you're kind of like lost. Or you end up having problems with six people when you're only mad at one person."

It doesn't have to be this way. If we talk openly with our friends about our fears of losing each other, we often discover they share the same feelings. One thing I noticed in my many conversations with groups of girls was the mixture of relief and surprise on their faces when they found their friends felt the same way. Over the three years I researched and wrote this book, I went through some pretty dramatic changes as a person. I suddenly became conscious of how often I avoided being directly angry with people, how much I held things in and acted cold or quiet while my resentment grew. When I had my fight with Jenny, I discovered what can happen when you share hidden feelings of jealousy and competition with a friend. I'm no expert, but for what it's worth, why not try this:

1. Get your closest friends together, or just one friend, and make time to talk. Get comfortable in a quiet space, however you choose to do that.

2. Talk about your fears of conflict. Ask each other, "When I make you angry or upset, do you tell me about it?" If not, talk about what you do instead of talking about it.

3. Talk about what happens when you hold your feelings inside or hide them. Is the buildup of emotion better than dealing immediately with what's happened? Explore specific situations. They can be resolved or ongoing, but think of a time when you feared speaking up. Was it when Joanna made that comment about your shorts, then said she was joking, but you felt pretty sure she wasn't? Was it when Leigh ignored you in front of the guy she liked? Try talking about it to each other and keeping the promise to respect each other's anger, to own the anger as a part of your friendship.

4. Look yourself in the eye and see the face of your own aggression. Talk about times you have felt angry, mean, competitive, or jealous. They can include feelings you've felt in your life or toward each other. Like my roommate Jenny and I, put it out on the table. Show your cards. Stop hiding and start owning your feelings, and see just how little damage they will wreak on your life once you do. See what a relief it is not to be perfect.

5. If some or all of your friends say they're afraid of losing each other or being ganged up on, make some promises. Say you won't do that. Say you'll be there no matter what. Say you'll work it out somehow. Say that you feel that way, too, if you do. This is nothing more than a commitment of friendship, something we're all used to making with each other. It's not that different from promising to keep a secret, or be best friends, or save a seat. We're *good* at this.

If you want to, talk about how girls are socialized to *not* be angry and aggressive and to not tell each other the truth. If you're into girl power, this is ground zero. This is taking your voices and your relationships back from the forces that would divide you from each other. When girls shut each other down, they seal the fate of their own socialization. They tell each other that anger is indeed wrong, that they do not deserve to feel it.

6. Comfort each other. Reassure your friends that their feelings are important, that conflicts bring you closer together, that you *want*

each other to talk about stuff, because all of you know just how much it sucks when you have to keep it in and feel resentful and angry.

In a healthy immune system, the body can tell the difference between the cells it needs to survive and the foreign ones that threaten it. When our immune systems malfunction, our bodies mistake healthy cells for dangerous ones and start to attack. As a result, we actually weaken ourselves. Sadly, this is how many of us are taught to approach conflict: as a foreign event that threatens our very constitution. But that fear, so absurdly false, ends up breaking us down from the inside. It turns us against each other. It makes our fights much, much worse than they really have to be. To strengthen ourselves, we have to learn to recognize aggression as a healthy part of our relationships and lives, something that makes us stronger and more honest individuals.

After spending weeks talking about fears of confrontation with one group of girls, one student began speaking about anger that had been brewing toward a friend. "I decided to go up to that person and I really had to have a lot of courage to do that, and when I told the person, I was like, 'Oh, what if she's not going to be my friend anymore, and she's going to hate me? I'll lose one of my best friends.' And after I told her, she told me some of the things that I was kind of doing that were mean and annoying her. And we solved our problems and then we're like still best friends. It's not always what you think is going to happen."

BULLYING: WHEN YOU'RE IN REAL TROUBLE

"If you could go back in time and talk to yourself at the moment when you were most upset, what would you say?" This was the question I asked every woman and girl I spoke with who was bullied. I wouldn't have written this book if a small piece of me wasn't still eight years old, standing in the darkened community center theater listening to the fading giggles and footsteps running away from me.

I guess I wanted to know what I could have done, what someone might have told me. So I asked.

1. get help.

Try not to do this alone. Find someone who can support you. Eleven-year-old Dina advised, "If something goes wrong and you can't stand up for yourself, then you should make friends with someone you can trust [who can] be on your side. If you don't have a friend, then go to your parent because parents should know what's going on. Maybe they've been through it so they'll know. They can call the school and say what's going on. You shouldn't just stand in the corner and try to deal with it by yourself."

Susie Johnston, also eleven, said she regrets not telling her parents how bad it was for her. "I was afraid to tell my parents because I was afraid they'd call the kids' parents and that would make things worse. I didn't tell them everything," she said. "And I just wish I had sometimes, because if I had maybe I could have gotten out of the school earlier." Once she switched to her new school, she made more friends than she'd ever thought possible.

Talk to a teacher. There may be someone who gets it, who understands how bad this is. Perhaps she'll talk with you after school or at lunchtime. Can she arrange for you to go to the art room or the library at lunch?

Haley said, "You should talk to friends who've either been through this or who are your very true friends, and that's very helpful." One of the worst things about getting bullied is that you feel so alone. Sometimes you feel like you're the only person in the world who's been through it. If you've read any part of this book, you know that's not true. But it does help to see someone in the flesh who gets it, who *knows*, and that, according to many girls, can make you feel a lot better.

2. lose them.

If you're miserable because you're trying to get popular, or it's your friend who's doing this to you, give it up. If you think being popular is going to make you happy, you're wrong. "The only way to get through it," said Stephanie from chapter four, "is to find the people you like because you like them, not because of their position at school, not because they're the prettiest or the most popular or all the boys want to date [them]. Find someone that you have fun with, that you share interests with." If the other girls are ignoring you, aren't inviting you out, are giving you the worst seat, aren't telling you the secrets—if they're using you as a tool to make themselves feel cooler—take the hint. You are putting yourself in emotional danger every minute you spend with them.

3. *get it out.*

Get a diary and write about your feelings. Paint, dance, kickbox, run in the rain, punch a bag, write a song, bang on drums. Don't keep it inside. Don't kick the dog. The culture raises us to swallow our pain until we choke. The way to fight back is to release.

"It helps a lot to get your problems out," eleven-year-old Jill said. Most of the time it's good to write down who's being mean to you or how they're being mean to you. And write down an equals sign next to it [and] what you can do to solve the problem."

4. *do something.*

Join the newspaper, take a workshop, join a team, take an art class, volunteer, get a job. Join a chat room of girls online. Try not to curl into a ball under your blanket, or at least not all day, every day. Finding a different community of people can make the difference. Find what you love to do.

It doesn't necessarily have to be with others. When you find what you love, you come closer to finding yourself. You start putting out a vibe to others, an energy of sorts. It happened to Alizah, and it had a profound impact on her life in high school. She said, "Explore what you like to do by yourself because I really think that's where your strength lies, within yourself. People will come to you because of who you are, and I think we all have gifts."

5. *it* will *end.*

Ever try to tell a screaming three-year-old that her mother will be back in five minutes? She could sooner tell you who the forty-three presidents are than what five minutes from now is. We can get like that when someone's making it her goal in life to ruin ours. But— and you can trust me on this—one day you won't have to wake up and go to school with these people.

"You have no reason to believe me," said Naomi, "but take a leap and trust that this is not the real world. This is school. This structure will never exist again, it will never be possible again.... Things are going to get better because I'll never be defined by just one group of people's opinion of who I am."

The world may feel like it's ending. It isn't. Roma said, "It gets better. These people are the people you're with now and whose opinion matters the most now, but it's not going to be the opinion that lasts. Try and listen to what is most important to you. Try and isolate the fact that you have a whole world of possibilities and things you're going to be interested in and that you'll want to do for you. Try really hard to get in touch with those things. And when you do, hold on to those things that are most important because nobody outside of you is more important."

when it isn't bullying

Is every time a child feels socially rejected a moment of victimization? What makes a girl the "odd girl out"?

In a world without bullying, there will always be exclusion. Exclusion will happen naturally as relationships grow more intimate. Exclusion does not necessarily constitute bullying, even when we account for alternative aggressions. It would be wrong to read this book as an argument against exclusion.

Every case of exclusion is as unique as the child in question and must be evaluated on its own terms. If a child is being left out here and there, or from a certain group, then she is being left out here and there, or from a certain group—nothing more and nothing less.

If she is failing to forge close relationships with others, it bears further investigation before deciding she's been bullied. If her exclusion bothers her or her parents, interrogate the disappointment. The desire to see a child become popular can color the way we view her social universe, can make the everyday rise and fall of friendship look like something else. If the child needs help with social skills, she should get it, but it's not other children's responsibility to compensate for what another girl lacks.

That girls sometimes use relationship as a weapon does not mean that every time a relationship is not offered, the girl is behaving aggressively. We must distinguish between intentional acts of meanness and the reality of children's social order. Like exclusion, popularity will outlast us all, and to cry foul at it will only make a parent appear overinvested and ignorant.

To expect girls to play nice with everyone, despite what they may really want, is to enforce upon them precisely what we are trying to stop: a "tyranny of the nice and kind"[60] that will stifle girls' voices, shuttle them into idealized, alienating relationships, and impress upon them the belief that their own needs should be subverted to others' at any cost. A common situation is one girl who silently trails after another, copying her behavior and appearance as though to absorb by osmosis what she is unable to take independently for herself. The followed girl is annoyed and embarrassed. Is she obligated to spend time with the follower, who has done nothing but hover quietly? I don't think so.

Only when a child has been shunned by most of her peers or suddenly dropped by the friends she once had does exclusion look less like social ordering and more like relational aggression. And even then, discipline may not be appropriate. This isn't to say that when one child lets go of a friendship with another to get popular, she isn't being mean. She is. But could someone have "made" me talk to Anne? Probably not. There will always be cases where we have to let girls negotiate their own social lives. What we can do is provide them with as much emotional support as possible, and let them know that life will get easier.

conclusion

Writing this book brought light to the dark corners of my life. Naming the alternative aggressions allowed me to see myself and my relationships in an entirely new way. It gave me a way to talk with others, to come to peace with what I remembered and what I continue to experience today.

I believe our task now is to give every girl, every parent, and every teacher a shared, public language to address girls' conflicts and relationships. A world that acknowledges the hidden culture of girls' aggression would empower girls not only to negotiate conflict, but to define relationship in new and healthier ways. Girls would learn that relationship is an option and not a mandate. They would understand relationship as a chosen partnership in which care and conflict are comfortably exchanged.

When girls understand that relationship can be chosen and that conflict is natural, their social identities will cease to hinge on how many idealized friendships they can rack up. Conflict will no longer feel like a violation of relationship but rather will be seen as a by-product of relationship, even a worthy skill to be honed. Conflict will not be something to be kept locked out of relationship. It will not feel, as it did to Carmen Peralta, like a bomb, splintering friendship beyond repair.

Parents would show girls that conflict-free relationships do not exist. Instead of believing conflict terminates relationship, girls could learn that *no relationship can survive without conflict.* Girls would learn not to be controlled by fear, understanding that relationships ebb and flow beyond the power of one.

In a world that acknowledges the hidden culture of aggression, girls would cease to play out their own fearful prophecies of loss. Knowing that conflicts are periodic, and that relationships survive them, girls might be less inclined to engage in the repression, back-stabbing, and ganging up that so often rise up to crush friendships. Most of the behaviors mapped out in this book—nonverbal gesturing, ganging up, behind-the-back talking, rumor spreading, the *Survivor*-like exiling of cliques, note passing, the silent treatment, nice-in-private and mean-in-public friends—are fueled by the lack of face-to-face confrontations. If girls could recognize their anger and upset, the intensity and scope of their reprisals might very well subside.

In a world that acknowledges the hidden culture of aggression, girls who are victimized would know they are not alone. They would have a language to assign meaning to what happened to them. They would enjoy protection at school. They could assimilate girl bullying into their lives as a painful, but not earth-shattering, event. Schools would have the resources, research, and strategies to address the wide range of alternative aggressions. Parents would have the confidence to approach their schools and properly protect their children.

the price of alternative aggressions

In the course of writing this book, I watched alternative aggressions and conflict avoidance intersect with three areas of girls' lives: leadership, relationship violence, and the reported loss of girls' self-esteem around adolescence.

GOOD LEADERS, GOOD GIRLS

At a girls' leadership workshop for twenty middle-class teenagers, one third of whom were nonwhite, we were talking about what made us uncomfortable about leadership, what we were calling "danger zones." As the girls began discussing their fears, I was amazed that nearly every concern related to how others would react to what they say or do.

Over and over again, looking bad or stupid—in their parlance, "getting judged"—was their worst fear. Whether meeting new people, speaking in public, reciting, or debating, the girls feared being "shut down"; they worried that people would not give them a chance to explain themselves and that others would shatter their self-confidence. As a result, they worried, people would not like them, would not want to be their friends, would turn their backs on them.

"The most remarkable thing about the socialization of aggression in girls is its absence," writes sociologist Anne Campbell. "Girls do not learn the right way to express aggression; they simply learn not to express it."[61] Many girls at the workshop, for instance, perceived being agreed with or supported as a sign of personal connection and being opposed as relational loss. Intriguingly, the dread they felt toward certain leadership practices was a mirror reflection of the fears so many girls voiced about *personal* conflict. In other words, these girls felt a comparable anxiety toward the "good" aggressions (confidence, competition, assertiveness) as many did toward the "bad" ones (interpersonal confrontation, anger, overt meanness). Like the girl who will not say why she is angry because she is afraid of losing her friend, the workshop participants predicted similar relational loss if they acted as leaders.

Throughout the workshop, more parallels emerged. These girls imagined themselves at work on everything from extracurricular projects to their future ventures as adults. Among the girls' most salient fears was being seen as conceited, which they believed would make them unlikable to coworkers. Girls who would do anything to avoid being seen as "all that" about a boyfriend were similarly alarmed when they envisioned professional conduct. Instead of thinking about how much they could achieve at work, they were wondering how to appear as though they hadn't, or how to look like they didn't think they deserved to.

The same thing happened with competition and desire. Many workshop participants told me they were afraid of being called competitive or bossy at work. What they were thinking about at work was not what they wanted and how to get it, but how to appear as though they didn't care as they maneuvered their way patiently toward their goals.

Finally, the workshop participants confided a fear of "messing up" or losing control by saying the wrong thing. This anxiety would force them to think every little thing through, driving them away from the risk taking and shoot-from-the-hip thinking so critical to success in the workplace.

At the following year's workshop, thirty middle-class teenagers were scattered in a circle on cushions in a recreation room. One-quarter of them were nonwhite. We were talking about what makes a good leader. I asked them to call out the words they thought described her, and I scribbled along on an easel at the front of the room. When I stepped back to look at their list, here is what I saw:

A GOOD LEADER IS . . .

Loving	**Dedicated**	Outgoing
Loud	**Sensitive**	Organized
Good listener	**Cooperative**	**Respectful**
Helpful	Creative	**Open-minded**
Optimistic	Unique	**Understanding**
Flexible	Expressive	Mature
Proud	Talented	**Caring**
Determined	**Willing**	**Patient**
Committed	Bold	Responsible

Thoughtful	**Honest**	**Friendly**	ODD
Supportive	**Trustworthy**	**Kindhearted**	*girl*
Balanced	**Open**	**Well-mannered**	OUT
Independent	**Positive**	Insightful	

Passive, yielding, caring words (in bold) overwhelmed the list. Only four of the words, or less than ten percent of their "good leader" (underlined) words, suggested a person unwilling to be nice.

To these girls, a good leader was a good girl.

Taking charge, saying no, and engaging in conflict were not signs of their good leader. The girls' leader was easy to get along with. She was nice. She was caring. She was someone you'd like to have as your friend. Looking back at the "anti-girl" list the group made the day before, mentioned in chapter four (see page 124), I was shocked by what they believed was wrong in girls: "Brainy," "Opinionated," "Pushy," "Mean," "Professional," "Serious," "Strong," "Independent," "Egocentric," "Unrestrained," "Artsy." The qualities that are the ingredients for a strong leader are the qualities of a bad girl.

Unfortunately, this is not a passing phase. In *Play Like a Man, Win Like a Woman,* CNN Executive Vice President Gail Evans explores why women struggle for equality in the corporate world. After decades of watching women hit the glass ceiling, Evans concludes that a misguided focus on personal relationships is partly to blame.

Evans argues that women struggle when hearing the word no from colleagues or superiors, construing it as a sign of interpersonal conflict. Because of this, women will avoid asking questions they anticipate will end in a no, hearing it as "a sign the relationship between us and our superiors has failed." Many women also avoid risk taking because they fear situations in which they may need to act like they know more than they really do, or bluff. Like the girls who fear being seen as "all that," women workers fear coming off as a person who thinks she's better than everyone else.

Evans notes that girls who wait to be asked "to go out on a date, to get called on in class," turn into women who wait to be asked to do projects rather than get out there and do them. Girls who, like seventh-grader Lily Carter in chapter three, communicate with friends through "hints" turn into women who "assume" the boss knows their work is excellent.

Because women have not been taught to see fighting as a sport or acceptable event, Evans explains that "the concept of a fair fight is an oxymoron. A fight shouldn't take place. If it does, the rules go out the window." Where Evans has watched men buy each other a beer after a conflict at work, a woman often takes it personally. She may storm away angry, reflecting a lifetime association of conflict with relational loss. Women who, as girls, never learned to be comfortable with conflict now as adults have trouble distinguishing normal, day-to-day disagreements from personal attacks.[62]

Evans's observations are not surprising. When girls learn to assert themselves indirectly, or not at all, they claim power similarly as adults. They may become helpers instead of leaders, work behind-the-scenes instead of at center stage, serve as deputies and vice presidents instead of chiefs and presidents.

To be sure, corporate culture does nothing to discourage this view. Women who are confident, who brag, who are assertive, and who fight are often called "manly" or "bitchy," frigid," "castrating," or "aggressive." Their courage is not an asset. It's considered inappropriate. The California-based Bully Broads program is singular evidence: the instructor teaches female executives how to appear less assertive, advising them to stutter and cry in public in order to "soften" their image.[63] Small wonder the very girls who feel comfortable lost in the crowd end up as working women holding the short end of the stick.

BULLYING AND RELATIONSHIP VIOLENCE

Listening to the stories of Vanessa, Natalie, and Annie in chapter two, the word "bullying" sounds hollow. These girls endured protracted emotional abuse at the hands of their closest friends. They refused to give up their friendships, struggling at any cost to remain connected to their bullies. When I spoke to these girls and others, I could not help but ask how they could stay involved with people who were so hurtful. Their responses often sounded like those of battered women.

One girl wanted to leave her friend, but she was afraid of sitting at lunch and recess alone. Another insisted that her friends would be nicer tomorrow, or next week. I was reminded of the way a battered woman refuses to leave an abusive spouse because of her fears of living alone, or because he "said he was sorry." Conventional anti-bullying strategies at school are misplaced in these situations because they are built on the assumption that the perpetrator and victim are not friends. The intimacy of girlfriends is a central component of relational aggression between girls, and current strategies used by relationship violence experts might be more helpful for girls trapped in these situations.

Indeed, the warning signs of relationship violence bear a powerful resemblance to bullying between best friends. Like Lucia in chapter six, abusers "can make you feel like you are the most special person in the whole world." No matter how hard a victim of relationship violence tries, she can never meet her abuser's expectations, a dynamic prominent in Reese's and Natalie's relationship. As in Annie's friendship with Samantha, an abuser can try to cut the victim off from friends, family, or anyone who could help her leave the relationship. The abuser will argue these individuals are "untrustworthy or don't like the abuser."

If we care about teaching girls to choose healthy relationships of all kinds, it is vital that we promote awareness of submissive and aggressive behaviors in girls' relationships. When abusive dynamics are without a language, and when anger cannot be properly voiced, girls may not develop the ability to name what is happening or extract themselves from destructive situations. As a result, girls may be learning submissive behavior they will import, uninterrupted, into intimate adult relationships. In other words, the failure to recognize abuse may not confine itself to girls, or to girlhood. Consciousness of these behaviors is absolutely critical to stopping vulnerability to abuse at the earliest possible ages.

THE BERMUDA TRIANGLE REVISITED

The middle school years are what many would call the epicenter of the crisis of female adolescence. By now well-known, the story of the crisis is often read as a eulogy to the intrepid, authentic girl. Uncovered most famously by psychologists Mary Pipher in *Reviving Ophelia,* and Carol Gilligan and Lyn Mikel Brown in *Meeting at the Crossroads,* the event marks a moment that has by turns been described as a "Bermuda triangle" in which the "selves of girls go down in droves" and a crossroads at which girls undergo a second socialization by the culture into womanhood.

Over the course of a few years, as girls become conscious of the culture around them, they are forced into abrupt disconnection with themselves. Their truthful voices, their fearless capacity to speak their minds, their fierce appetite for food and play and truth, will no longer be tolerated. To be successful and socially accepted, girls must adopt feminine postures of sexual, social, verbal, and physical restraint. They must deny their own versions of what they see, know, and feel. To avoid rejection, they must enter whitewashed relationships, eschewing open conflict and becoming shackled to cultural rules that deny their freedom to know the truth of themselves, their bodies, and their feelings. It is here, in the growing space between what girls know to be true and what they must pretend to feel and know with others, that their self-esteem shrivels.

The crisis of female adolescence has been described mostly in individual terms, its interpersonal consequences largely ignored.[64] In fact, the loss that is taking place is not simply one of the authentic self but of the self that is able to engage with her peers. The crisis, Brown and Gilligan report, is fundamentally relational. Pressure to deny the authenticity of *themselves* robs girls of the ability to communicate sincerely with one another. After all, girls are making Faustian bargains, sacrificing their true selves for damaged, false relationships with others. Disconnecting internally, they fall apart interpersonally, suppressing conflict and anger, adopting facades of the "nice and polite," and striving toward interactions that deny the realities of human relationship. They lose the ability to "name relational violations," or assert feelings of hurt and anger toward another person. "Feelings are felt, thoughts are thought," but they are "no longer exposed to the air and the light of relationship." Instead, they are sequestered in an "underground."

If we look at the crisis as a moment where alternative aggressions intensify, the loss of girls' self-esteem may be seen in a new light. By adjusting the lens we use to examine girls' lives, the underground appears as not just an emotional end point where girls store their true feelings. It may itself be an active medium to communicate conflict, especially alternative aggressions. Further investigation of this link may offer a new portal into the kinds of help we can give girls during this difficult period. If alternative aggressions are a major symptom of girls' loss of self-esteem, perhaps we can strengthen our attack against the onset of this crisis by focusing more resources and research on girls' interpersonal relationships. We might work harder to prohibit girls from engaging in alternative aggressions and instead guide them into more assertive acts of truth telling and direct aggression.

Teach girls to be aggressive? Well, yes. I return again to a major symptom of girls' loss of self-esteem: idealized, or conflict-free, relationships. If we can guide girls into comfort with "messy" feelings such as jealousy, competition, and anger, they will be less likely to take them out of their relationships with others. They will feel free to confess strong feelings, and they will stay in touch with themselves. They will be less likely to repress the feelings that over time simmer into rageful acts of cruelty.

Events of unexplained aggression and loss mark some girls forever. The worry that there is always a hidden layer of truth beneath a facade of "niceness" can leave girls permanently unsure about what they can trust in others and in themselves. These stories in particular haunt me. These are the girls, it seems, who drift away from other girls, who cease to support one other, who mature into mistrust and even hatred toward their peers.

Marcie was one of the first adult women I interviewed. The odd girl out more often than not during elementary and middle school, she confided that her current relationships with other women today are bittersweet. Now in her late twenties, she remarked, "Quite often, I feel like it's me who doesn't fit in with the rest of them. I know it's internal, and that there's a little part of me that will never quite trust them. There's a little part of me that believes they will turn on me at any moment."

Marcie's words were echoed in the voices of many girls and women I later met. Women like Marcie, injured in childhood by their peers, are still speaking in girls' voices. They feel a raw hurt and bewilderment that belies the years that have passed. These women are asking why the people around them, sometimes their closest friends, expressed anger indirectly and at times without warning, leaving them disoriented, alone, and full of self-blame.

When we can agree that nice girls get really angry, and that good girls are sometimes quite bad, we will have plowed the social desert between "nice" and "bitch." When we have built a positive vocabulary for girls to tell each other their truths, more girls will raise their voices. They will pose and answer their own questions and solve their own mysteries of relationship.

What greater gift can we give girls than the ability to speak their truths and honor the truths of their peers? In a world prepared to value all of girls' feelings and not just some, girls will enjoy the exhilarating freedom of honesty in relationship. They will live without the crippling fear of abandonment. It is my hope that as they, and any woman who has ever been the odd girl out, collect their thoughts to speak their minds, they will whisper to themselves, "What I most regretted were my silences. Of what had I *ever* been afraid?"[65]

1. Lyn Mikel Brown and Carol Gilligan, *Meeting at the Crossroads: Women's Psychology and Girls' Development* (Cambridge, MA: Harvard University Press, 1992).

2. Adrienne Rich, "From Women and Honor: Some Notes on Lying," in *On Lies, Secrets, and Silence: Selected Prose, 1966–1978* (New York: W. W. Norton, 1979).

3. Anne Campbell, *Men, Women, and Aggression* (New York: BasicBooks, 1993).

4. Lyn Mikel Brown and Carol Gilligan, *Meeting at the Crossroads*.

5. Peggy Orenstein, *Schoolgirls: Young Women, Self-Esteem, and the Confidence Gap* (New York: Doubleday, 1994). In the first part of this quote Orenstein cites Lyn Mikel Brown and Carol Gilligan, "The Psychology of Women and the Development of Girls," paper presented at the Laurel-Harvard Conference on the Psychology of Women and the Education of Girls, Cleveland, OH, April 1990; Orenstein also advises readers to see Lyn Mikel Brown and Carol Gilligan, *Meeting at the Crossroads*.

6. For other examples, see Beverly I. Fagot and Richard Hagan, "Aggression in Toddlers: Responses to the Assertive Acts of Boys and Girls," *Sex Roles* 12 (1985): 341–51; David G. Perry, Louise C. Perry, and Robert J. Weiss, "Sex Differences in the Consequences that Children Anticipate for Aggression," *Developmental Psychology* 25 (1989): 312–19.

7. Kaj Bjoerkqvist and Pirkko Niemela, "New Trends in the Study of Female Aggression," in *Of Mice and Women: Aspects of Female Aggression,* ed. K. Bjoerkqvist and P. Niemela (San Diego: Academic Press, 1992).

8. Kaj Bjoerkqvist, Kirsti M. J. Lagerspetz, and Ari Kaukiainen, "Do Girls Manipulate and Boys Fight? Developmental Trends in Regard to Direct and Indirect Aggression," *Aggressive Behavior* 18 (1992): 117–27.

9. Lyn Mikel Brown and Carol Gilligan, *Meeting at the Crossroads.*

10. Carol Gilligan, *In a Different Voice: Psychological Theory and Women's Development* (Cambridge, MA: Harvard University Press, 1982).

11. Adrienne Rich, "Compulsory Heterosexuality and Lesbian Existence," in *Blood, Bread, and Poetry: Selected Prose, 1979–1985* (New York: W. W. Norton, 1986).

12. Anne Campbell, *Men, Women, and Aggression.*

13. For example, see Patricia A. Adler and Peter Adler, *Peer Power: Preadolescent Culture and Identity* (New Brunswick, NJ: Rutgers University Press, 1998).

14. Nicki R. Crick, Maureen A. Bigbee, and Cynthia Howes, "Gender Differences in Children's Normative Beliefs about Aggression: How Do I Hurt Thee? Let Me Count the Ways," *Child Development* 67 (1996): 1003–14.

15. For the best overview of research on relational aggression, see Nicki R. Crick, et al., "Childhood Aggression and Gender: A New Look at an Old Problem," in *Gender and Motivation,* ed. Dan Bernstein (Lincoln: University of Nebraska Press, 1999).

16. Nicki R. Crick, "The Role of Overt Aggression, Relational Aggression, and Prosocial Behavior in the Prediction of Children's Future Social Adjustment," *Child Development* 67 (1996): 2317–27; Nicki R. Crick and Jennifer K. Grotpeter, "Relational Aggression, Gender, and Social-Psychological Adjustment," *Child Development* 66 (1995): 710–22; Nicki R. Crick, Maureen A. Bigbee, and Cynthia Howes, "Gender Differences in Children's Normative Beliefs about Aggression: How Do I Hurt Thee? Let Me Count the Ways."

17. Lyn Mikel Brown and Carol Gilligan, *Meeting at the Crossroads.*

18. Ibid.

19. Ibid.

20. Lynn Smith, "Hey, Poo-Poo Head, Let's Be Friends: Childhood Teasing Needn't Be Traumatic," *Los Angeles Times,* 6 December 2000, sec. E, p. 1.

21. Alice H. Eagly and Valerie J. Steffen, "Gender and Aggressive Behavior: A Meta-Analytic Review of the Social Psychological Literature," *Psychological Bulletin* 100 (1986): 309–30; Ann Frodi, Jacqueline Macaulay, and Pauline R. Thorne, "Are Women Always Less Aggressive Than Men? A Review of the Experimental Literature," *Psychological Bulletin* 84 (1977): 634–60.

22. Don E. Merten, "The Meaning of Meanness: Popularity, Competition, and Conflict among Junior High School Girls," *Sociology of Education* 70 (1997): 175–91.

23. Erica Goode, "Scientists Find a Particularly Female Response to Stress," *New York Times,* 19 May 2000, sec. A, p. 20.

24. For example, see Jean Kilbourne, *Deadly Persuasion: Why Women and Girls Must Fight the Addictive Power of Advertising* (New York: Free Press, 1999); Deborah L. Tolman and Elizabeth Debold, "Conflicts of Body and Image: Female Adolescents, Desire, and the No-Body Body," in *Feminist Perspectives on Eating Disorders,* eds. Melanie Katzman, Patricia Fallon, and S. Wooley (New York: Guilford Press, 1994).

25. Peggy Orenstein, *Schoolgirls.*

26. Patrick Welsh, "Bully-Boy Focus Overlooks Vicious Acts by Girls," *USA Today,* 12 June 2001, sec. A, p. 15.

27. Elizabeth Wurtzel, *Bitch: In Praise of Difficult Women* (New York: Doubleday, 1998).

28. A welcome exception to this rule appears to be athletics, where competition among girls is embraced and encouraged. However, the freedom to compete openly has yet to move off the field.

29. Lyn Mikel Brown, *Raising Their Voices: The Politics of Girls' Anger* (Cambridge, MA: Harvard University Press, 1998).

30. Deborah L. Tolman, "Daring to Desire," in *Sexual Cultures and the Construction of Adolescent Identities,* ed. Janice Irvine (Philadelphia: Temple University Press, 1994).

31. Mimi Nichter and Nancy Vuckovic, "Fat Talk: Body Image among Adolescent Girls," in *Many Mirrors: Body Image and Social Relations,* ed. Nicole Sault (New Brunswick, NJ: Rutgers University Press, 1994).

32. Jill McLean Taylor, Carol Gilligan, and Amy M. Sullivan, *Between Voice and Silence: Women and Girls, Race and Relationship* (Cambridge, MA: Harvard University Press, 1995).

33. Nicki R. Crick, et al., "Childhood Aggression and Gender."

34. Perhaps this is because the memory of being victimized buffered these speakers against the feelings that may have deterred others from telling their stories.

35. Adrienne Rich, "From Women and Honor: Some Notes on Lying."

36. Wiseman's Empower Program group in Washington, DC, works to end violence of all kinds between teenagers, and her "Owning Up" curriculum can be found at *www.empowered.org.*

37. Lyn Mikel Brown and Carol Gilligan, *Meeting at the Crossroads.*

38. Patricia A. Adler and Peter Adler, *Peer Power.*

39. Carolyn G. Heilbrun, *Writing a Woman's Life* (New York: Ballantine, 1988).

40. Lyn Mikel Brown and Carol Gilligan, *Meeting at the Crossroads.*

41. *Ibid.*

42. American Association of University Women, *Shortchanging Girls, Shortchanging America: A Call to Action* (Washington, DC: American Association of University Women, 1991).

43. Niobe Way, "Between Experiences of Betrayal and Desire," in *Urban Girls: Resisting Stereotypes, Creating Identities,* ed. Bonnie J. Ross Leadbeater and Niobe Way (New York: New York University Press, 1996).

44. bell hooks, *Bone Black: Memories of Girlhood* (New York: Henry Holt & Co., 1996).

45. Dorothy Allison, *Two or Three Things I Know for Sure* (New York: Dutton, 1995).

46. Lyn Mikel Brown, *Raising Their Voices.*

47. Jill McLean Taylor, Carol Gilligan, and Amy M. Sullivan, *Between Voice and Silence.*

48. Janie Victoria Ward, "Raising Resisters: The Role of Truth Telling in the Psychological Development of African-American Girls," in *Urban Girls: Resisting Stereotypes, Creating Identities,* ed. Bonnie J. Ross Leadbeater and Niobe Way (New York: New York University Press, 1996).

49. *Ibid.*

50. Patricia Hill Collins, "The Meaning of Motherhood in Black Culture and Black Mother-Daughter Relationships," in *Double Stitch: Black Women Write about Mothers and Daughters,* ed. Patricia Bell-Scott, et al. (Boston: Beacon Press, 1991).

51. Lyn Mikel Brown and Carol Gilligan, *Meeting at the Crossroads.*

52. Jill McLean Taylor, Carol Gilligan, and Amy M. Sullivan, *Between Voice and Silence.*

53. Tracy Robinson and Janie Victoria Ward, "'A Belief in Self Far Greater Than Anyone's Disbelief': Cultivating Resistance among African American Female Adolescents," in *Women, Girls, and Psychotherapy: Reframing Resistance,* ed. Carol Gilligan, Annie Rogers, and Deborah Tolman (New York: Harrington Park Press, 1991).

54. Ena Vazquez-Nuttall, Zoila Avila-Vivas, and Gisela Morales-Barreto, "Working with Latin American Families," in *Family Therapy with School Related Problems,* ed. James Hansen and Barbara Okun (Rockville, MD: Aspen Systems Corp., 1984).

55. Janie Victoria Ward, "Raising Resisters: The Role of Truth Telling in the Psychological Development of African-American Girls."

56. Jill McLean Taylor, Carol Gilligan, and Amy M. Sullivan, *Between Voice and Silence.*

57. Peggy Orenstein, *Schoolgirls.*

58. Mary Pipher, *Reviving Ophelia: Saving the Selves of Adolescent Girls* (New York: Ballantine, 1995).

59. The Ophelia Project is based in Erie, PA, and can be visited at *www.opheliaproject.org.*

60. Lyn Mikel Brown and Carol Gilligan, *Meeting at the Crossroads.*

61. Anne Campbell, *Men, Women, and Aggression.*

62. Gail Evans, *Play Like a Man, Win Like a Woman* (New York: Broadway Books, 2000).

63. Neela Banerjee, "Some 'Bullies' Seek Ways to Soften Up; Toughness Has Risks for Women Executives," *New York Times,* 10 August 2001, sec. C, p. 1.

64. For example, see Lyn Mikel Brown and Carol Gilligan, *Meeting at the Crossroads;* Mary Pipher, *Reviving Ophelia.*

65. Audre Lorde, "The Transformation of Silence into Language and Action," in *Sister Outsider: Essays and Speeches* (Trumansburg, NY: Crossing Press, 1984).

Adler, Patricia A., and Peter Adler. *Peer Power: Preadolescent Culture and Identity.* New Brunswick, NJ: Rutgers University Press, 1998.

———. "Dynamics of Inclusion and Exclusion in Preadolescent Cliques," *Social Psychology Quarterly* 58, no. 3 (1995): 145–62.

Allen, LaRue, et al. "Acculturation and Depression among Latina Urban Girls." In *Urban Girls: Resisting Stereotypes, Creating Identities,* edited by Bonnie J. Ross Leadbeater and Niobe Way. New York: New York University Press, 1996.

Allison, Dorothy. *Two or Three Things I Know for Sure.* New York: Dutton, 1995.

American Association of University Women. *Shortchanging Girls, Short-changing America: A Call to Action.* Washington, DC: American Association of University Women, 1991.

Angier, Natalie. *Woman: An Intimate Geography.* New York: Houghton-Mifflin, 1999.

Anzaldúa, Gloria. *Borderlands—La Frontera: The New Mestiza.* San Francisco: Aunt Lute Books, 1987.

Atwood, Margaret. *Cat's Eye.* New York: Doubleday, 1988.

Banerjee, Neela. "Some 'Bullies' Seek Ways to Soften Up: Toughness Has Risks for Women Executives." *New York Times,* 10 August 2001, sec. C, p. 1.

Bell-Scott, Patricia, et al., eds. *Double Stitch: Black Women Write about Mothers and Daughters.* Boston: Beacon Press, 1991.

Bjoerkqvist, Kaj, Kirsti M. Lagerspetz, and Ari Kaukiainen. "Do Girls Manipulate and Boys Fight? Developmental Trends in Regard to Direct and Indirect Aggression." *Aggressive Behavior* 18 (1992): 117–27.

Bjorkqvist, Kaj, and Pirkko Niemela, eds. *Of Mice and Women: Aspects of Female Aggression.* San Diego: Academic Press, 1992.

Borg, Mark G. "The Emotional Reaction of School Bullies and Their Victims." *Educational Psychology* 18, no. 4 (1998): 433–44.

Bosworth, Kris, Dorothy L. Espelage, and Thomas R. Simon. "Factors Associated With Bullying Behavior in Middle School Students." *Journal of Early Adolescence* 19, no. 3 (1999): 341–62.

Brook, Judith S., Martin M. Whiteman, and Steven Finch. "Childhood Aggression, Adolescent Delinquency, and Drug Use: A Longitudinal Study." *Journal of Genetic Psychology* 153, no. 4 (1992): 369–83.

Brown, Lyn Mikel. *Raising Their Voices: The Politics of Girls' Anger.* Cambridge, MA: Harvard University Press, 1998.

Brown, Lyn Mikel, and Carol Gilligan. *Meeting at the Crossroads: Women's Psychology and Girls' Development.* Cambridge, MA: Harvard University Press, 1992.

Brown, Lyn Mikel, Niobe Way, and Julia L. Duff. "The Others in My I: Adolescent Girls' Friendships and Peer Relations." In *Beyond Appearance: A New Look at Adolescent Girls,* edited by Novine G. Johnson, Michael C. Roberts, and Judith Worell. Washington, DC: American Psychological Association, 1999.

Brumberg, Joan Jacobs. *The Body Project: An Intimate History of American Girls.* New York: Vintage, 1997.

Campbell, Anne. *Men, Women, and Aggression.* New York: BasicBooks, 1993.

Chodorow, Nancy J. *The Reproduction of Mothering: Psychoanalysis and the Sociology of Gender.* Berkeley, CA: University of California Press, 1978.

Claiborne, Liz, Inc. "What You Need to Know about Dating Violence: A Teen's Handbook." New York: Liz Claiborne, Inc., 2000.

Coie, John D., John E. Lochman, Robert Terry, and Clarine Hyman. "Predicting Early Adolescent Disorder from Childhood Aggression and Peer Rejection." *Journal of Consulting and Clinical Psychology* 60, no. 5 (1992): 783–92.

Corsaro, William A., and Donna Eder. "Children's Peer Cultures." *Annual Review of Sociology* 16 (1990): 197–220.

Cott, Nancy F. *The Bonds of Womanhood: "Woman's Sphere" in New England, 1780–1835.* New Haven: Yale University Press, 1977.

Craig, Wendy M., and Debra J. Pepler. "Observations of Bullying and Victimization in the School Yard." *Canadian Journal of School Psychology* 13, no. 2 (1997): 41–59.

Crick, Nicki R. "Engagement in Gender Normative Versus Nonnormative Forms of Aggression: Links to Social-Psychological Adjustment." *Developmental Psychology* 33, no. 4 (1997): 610–17.

———. "The Role of Overt Aggression, Relational Aggression, and Prosocial Behavior in the Prediction of Children's Future Social Adjustment." *Child Development* 67, no. 5 (1996): 2317–27.

———. "Relational Aggression: The Role of Intent Attributions, Feelings of Distress, and Provocation Type." *Development & Psychopathology* 7, no. 2 (1995): 313–22.

Crick, Nicki R., et al. "Childhood Aggression and Gender: A New Look at an Old Problem." In *Gender and Motivation,* edited by Dan Bernstein. Lincoln: University of Nebraska Press, 1999.

Crick, Nicki R., and Maureen A. Bigbee. "Relational and Overt Forms of Peer Victimization: A Multiinformant Approach." *Journal of Consulting & Clinical Psychology* 66, no. 2 (1998): 337–47.

Crick, Nicki R., and Nicole E. Werner. "Response Decision Processes in Relational and Overt Aggression." *Child Development* 69, no. 6 (1998): 1630–39.

Crick, Nicki R., Juan F. Casas, and Monique Mosher. "Relational and Overt Aggression in Preschool." *Developmental Psychology* 33, no. 4 (1997): 579–88.

Crick, Nicki R., Maureen A. Bigbee, and Cynthia Howes. "Gender Differences in Children's Normative Beliefs about Aggression: How Do I Hurt Thee? Let Me Count the Ways." *Child Development* 67, no. 3 (1996): 1003–14.

Crick, Nicki R., and Jennifer K. Grotpeter. "Relational Aggression, Gender, and Social-Psychological Adjustment." *Child Development* 66, no. 3 (1995): 710–22.

Davis, Angela Y. *Women, Race, and Class.* New York: Vintage, 1981.

Debold, Elizabeth, Marie Wilson, and Idelisse Malave. *Mother Daughter Revolution: From Betrayal to Power.* Reading, MA: Addison-Wesley, 1993.

Dolan, Deirdre. "How to Be Popular." *New York Times Magazine,* 8 April 2001, sec. 6, pp. 44–46.

Eagly, Alice H., and Valerie J. Steffen. "Gender and Aggressive Behavior: A Meta-Analytic Review of the Social Psychological Literature." *Psychological Bulletin* 100, no. 3 (1986): 309–30.

Eder, Donna. "Serious and Playful Disputes: Variation in Conflict Talk among Female Adolescents." In *Conflict Talk: Sociolinguistic Investigations of Arguments in Conversations,* edited by Allen D. Grimshaw. Cambridge, MA: Cambridge University Press, 1990.

Eder, Donna, and David A. Kinney. "The Effect of Middle School Extracurricular Activities on Adolescents' Popularity and Peer Status." *Youth & Society* 26, no. 3 (1995): 298–324.

Eder, Donna, and Janet Lynne Enke. "The Structure of Gossip: Opportunities and Constraints on Collective Expression among Adolescents." *American Sociological Review* 56, no. 4 (1991): 494–508.

Evans, Cathy, and Donna Eder. "No Exit: Processes of Social Isolation in the Middle School." *Journal of Contemporary Ethnography* 22, no. 2 (1993): 139–70.

Evans, Gail. *Play Like a Man, Win Like a Woman: What Men Know about Success That Women Need to Learn.* New York: Broadway Books, 2000.

Fagot, Beverly I., Mary D. Leinbach, and Richard Hagan. "Gender Labeling and Adoption of Sex-Typed Behaviors." *Developmental Psychology* 22, no. 4 (1986): 440–43.

Fagot, Beverly I., and Richard Hagan. "Aggression in Toddlers: Responses to the Assertive Acts of Boys and Girls." *Sex Roles* 12 nos. 3/4 (1985): 341–51.

Fein, Ellen, and Sherrie Schneider. *The Rules: Time-Tested Secrets for Capturing the Heart of Mr. Right.* New York: Warner Books, 1995.

Fine, Michelle. "Sexuality, Schooling, and Adolescent Females: The Missing Discourse of Desire." *Harvard Educational Review* 58, no. 1 (1988): 29–53.

Friedan, Betty. *The Feminine Mystique.* New York: W. W. Norton, 1983.

Frodi, Ann, Jacqueline Macaulay, and Pauline R. Thorne. "Are Women Always Less Aggressive Than Men? A Review of the Experimental Literature." *Psychological Bulletin* 84, no. 4 (1977): 634–60.

Galen, Britt Rachelle, and Marion K. Underwood. "A Developmental Investigation of Social Aggression Among Children." *Developmental Psychology* 33, no. 4 (1997): 589–600.

George, Thomas P., and Donald P. Hartmann. "Friendship Networks of Unpopular, Average, and Popular Children." *Child Development* 67, no. 5 (1996): 2301–16.

Gilligan, Carol. *In a Different Voice: Psychological Theory and Women's Development.* Cambridge, MA: Harvard University Press, 1982.

Gilligan, Carol, Nona P. Lyons, and Trudy J. Hanmer, eds. *Making Connections: The Relational Worlds of Adolescent Girls at Emma Willard School.* Cambridge, MA: Harvard University Press, 1990.

Goode, Erica. "Scientists Find a Particularly Female Response to Stress." *New York Times,* 19 May 2000, sec. A, p. 20.

Green, Laura R., Deborah R. Richardson, and Tania Lago. "How Do Friendship, Indirect, and Direct Aggression Relate?" *Aggressive Behavior* 22, no. 2 (1996): 81–86.

Groneman, Carol. *Nymphomania: A History.* New York: W. W. Norton, 2000.

Grotpeter, Jennifer K., and Nicki R. Crick. "Relational Aggression, Overt Aggression, and Friendship." *Child Development* 67, no. 5 (1996): 2328–38.

Hanley, Robert. "Girl in Shooting Was Seen as Dejected." *New York Times,* 9 March 2001, sec. A, p. 16.

Harris, Judith Rich. *The Nurture Assumption: Why Children Turn Out the Way They Do.* New York: Touchstone, 1998.

Heilbrun, Carolyn G. *Writing a Woman's Life.* New York: Ballantine, 1988.

Henington, Carlen, Jan N. Hughes, Timothy A. Cavell, and Bruce Thompson. "The Role of Relational Aggression in Identifying Aggressive Boys and Girls." *Journal of School Psychology* 36, no. 4 (1998): 457–77.

Hey, Valerie. *The Company She Keeps: An Ethnography of Girls' Friendship.* Bristol, PA: Open University Press, 1997.

hooks, bell. *Bone Black: Memories of Girlhood.* New York: Henry Holt & Co., 1996.

Hudson, Barbara. "Femininity and Adolescence." In *Gender and Generation,* edited by Angela McRobbie and Mica Nava. London: MacMillan, 1984.

Hughes, Linda A. "'But That's Not Really Mean': Competing in a Cooperative Mode." *Sex Roles* 19, nos. 11/12 (1988): 669–87.

Ialongo, Nicholas S., Nancy Vaden-Kiernan, and Sheppard Kellam. "Early Peer Rejection and Aggression: Longitudinal Relations with Adolescent Behavior." *Journal of Development & Physical Disabilities* 10, no. 2 (1998): 199–213.

Irvine, Janice M., ed. *Sexual Cultures and the Construction of Adolescent Identities.* Philadelphia: Temple University Press, 1994.

Jarrell, Anne. "The Face of Teenage Sex Grows Younger." *New York Times,* 2 April 2000, sec. 9, p. 1.

Jones, Jacqueline. *Labor of Love, Labor of Sorrow: Black Women, Work and the Family from Slavery to the Present.* New York: Vintage, 1985.

Kantrowitz, Barbara, and Pat Wingert. "The Truth About Tweens." *Newsweek,* 18 October 1999, 62–72.

Kaukiainen, Ari, et al. "The Relationships Between Social Intelligence, Empathy, and Three Types of Aggression." *Aggressive Behavior* 25, no. 2 (1999): 81–89.

Kerber, Linda K., et al., "On *In a Different Voice:* An Interdisciplinary Forum: Some Cautionary Words for Historians." *Signs: Journal of Women in Culture and Society* 11, no. 2 (1986): 304–10.

Kerns, Kathryn A., Lisa Klepac, and AmyKay Cole. "Peer Relationships and Preadolescents' Perceptions of Security in the Child-Mother Relationship." *Developmental Psychology* 32, no. 3 (1996): 457–66.

Kilbourne, Jean. *Deadly Persuasion: Why Women and Girls Must Fight the Addictive Power of Advertising.* New York: Free Press, 1999.

Kindlon, Daniel, and Michael Thompson. *Raising Cain: Protecting the Emotional Life of Boys.* New York: Ballantine, 1999.

Kumpulainen, Kirsti, Eila Raesaenen, and Imeli Henttonen. "Children Involved in Bullying: Psychological Disturbance and the Persistence of the Involvement." *Child Abuse & Neglect* 23, no. 12 (1999): 1253–62.

Lagerspetz, Kirsti M., Kaj Bjoerkqvist, and Tarja Peltonen. "Is Indirect Aggression Typical of Females? Gender Differences in Aggressiveness in 11- to 12-Year-Old Children." *Aggressive Behavior* 14, no. 6 (1988): 403–14.

Laurence, Patricia. "Women's Silence as a Ritual of Truth: A Study of Literary Expressions in Austen, Brontë, and Woolf." In *Listening to Silences: New Essays in Feminist Criticism,* edited by Elaine Hedges and Shelley Fisher Fishkin. New York: Oxford University Press, 1994.

Lees, Sue. *Losing Out: Sexuality and Adolescent Girls.* London: Hutchinson, 1986.

Lever, Janet. "Sex Differences in the Complexity of Children's Play and Games," *American Sociological Review* 43, no. 4 (1978): 471–83.

Lorde, Audre. *Sister Outsider: Essays and Speeches.* Trumansburg, NY: Crossing Press, 1984.

Maccoby, Eleanor Emmons. "Gender and Relationships: A Developmental Account." *American Psychologist* 45, no. 4 (1990): 513–20.

Maccoby, Eleanor Emmons, and Carol Nagy Jacklin. *The Psychology of Sex Differences.* Vol. 1. Stanford, CA: Stanford University Press, 1974.

Magner, Carolyn. "When They Were Bad." Salon.com., 9 October 2000 (http://www.salon.com/mwt/feature/2000/10/09/freeze_out).

McMillan, Carol. *Women, Reason, and Nature: Some Philosophical Problems with Feminism.* Princeton, NJ: Princeton University Press, 1982.

Menesini, Ersilia, et al. "Cross-National Comparison of Children's Attitudes towards Bully/Victim Problems in Schools." *Aggressive Behavior* 23, no. 4 (1997): 245–57.

Merten, Don E. "Enculturation into Secrecy among Junior High School Girls." *Journal of Contemporary Ethnography* 28, no. 2 (1999): 107–37.

———. "The Meaning of Meanness: Popularity, Competition, and Conflict among Junior High School Girls." *Sociology of Education* 70, no. 3 (1997): 175–91.

———. "The Cultural Context of Aggression: The Transition to Junior High School." *Anthropology & Education Quarterly* 25, no. 1 (1994): 29–43.

Miller, Jean Baker. *Toward a New Psychology of Women.* 2nd ed. Boston: Beacon Press, 1986.

Neary, Ann, and Stephen Joseph. "Peer Victimization and Its Relationship to Self-Concept and Depression among Schoolgirls." *Personality & Individual Differences* 16, no. 1 (1994): 183–86.

Nichter, Mimi, and Nancy Vuckovic. "Fat Talk: Body Image among Adolescent Girls." In *Many Mirrors: Body Image and Social Relations,* edited by Nicole Sault. New Brunswick, NJ: Rutgers University Press, 1994.

Oesterman, Karin, Kaj Bjoerkqvist, Kirsti M. J. Lagerspetz, Ari Kaukiainen, et al. "Peer and Self-Estimated Aggression and Victimization in 8-Year-Old Children from Five Ethnic Groups." *Aggressive Behavior* 20, no. 6 (1994): 411–28.

———. "Cross-Cultural Evidence of Female Indirect Aggression." *Aggressive Behavior* 24, no. 1 (1988): 1–8.

Okin, Susan Moller. *Women in Western Political Thought.* Princeton, NJ: Princeton University Press, 1979.

Orenstein, Peggy. *Schoolgirls: Young Women, Self-Esteem, and the Confidence Gap.* New York: Doubleday, 1994.

Paquette, Julie A., and Marion K. Underwood. "Gender Differences in Young Adolescents' Experiences of Peer Victimization: Social and Physical Aggression." *Merrill-Palmer Quarterly* 45, no. 2 (1999): 242–66.

Pateman, Carole. *The Sexual Contract.* Cambridge, England: Polity Press, 1988.

Pepler, Debra J. "Aggressive Girls: Development of Disorder and Outcomes." Report #57, La Marsh Research Centre Report. Toronto: York University, 1999.

Perry, David G., Louise C. Perry, and Robert J. Weiss. "Sex Differences in the Consequences that Children Anticipate for Aggression." *Developmental Psychology* 25, no. 2 (1989): 312–19.

Pipher, Mary. *Reviving Ophelia: Saving the Selves of Adolescent Girls.* New York: Ballantine, 1995.

Pollack, William. *Real Boys: Rescuing Our Sons from the Myths of Boyhood.* New York: Random House, 1998.

Raymond, Janice G. *A Passion for Friends: Toward a Philosophy of Female Affection.* Boston: Beacon Press, 1986.

Rhodes, Jean E., and Anita B. Davis. "Supportive Ties between Nonparent Adults and Urban Adolescent Girls." In *Urban Girls: Resisting Stereotypes, Creating Identities,* edited by Bonnie J. Ross Leadbeater and Niobe Way. New York: New York University Press, 1996.

Rich, Adrienne. *On Lies, Secrets, and Silence: Selected Prose, 1966–1978.* New York: W. W. Norton, 1979.

———. *Of Woman Born: Motherhood as Experience and Institution.* New York: W. W. Norton, 1986.

———. "Compulsory Heterosexuality and Lesbian Existence." In *Blood, Bread, and Poetry: Selected Prose, 1979–1985.* New York: W. W. Norton, 1986.

Rigby, Ken. "The Relationship between Reported Health and Involvement in Bully/Victim Problems among Male and Female Secondary Schoolchildren." *Journal of Health Psychology* 3, no. 4 (1998): 465–76.

Robinson, Tracy, and Janie Victoria Ward. "'A Belief in Self Far Greater Than Anyone's Disbelief': Cultivating Resistance among African American

Female Adolescents." In *Women, Girls, and Psychotherapy: Reframing Resistance,* edited by Carol Gilligan, Annie Rogers, and Deborah Tolman. New York: Harrington Park Press, 1991.

Rogers, Annie G. "Voice, Play, and a Practice of Ordinary Courage in Girls' Lives and Women's Lives." *Harvard Educational Review* 63, no. 3 (1993): 265–95.

Rotheram-Borus, Mary Jane, et al. "Personal and Ethnic Identity, Values, and Self-Esteem among Black and Latino Adolescent Girls." In *Urban Girls: Resisting Stereotypes, Creating Identities,* edited by Bonnie J. Ross Leadbeater and Niobe Way. New York: New York University Press, 1996.

Rys, Gail Summers. "Children's Moral Reasoning and Peer-Directed Social Behaviors: Issues of Gender and Development." Ph.D. diss., University of Delaware, 1998. Abstract in *Dissertation Abstracts International* 58 (1998): 5167B.

Rys, Gail Summers, and George G. Bear. "Relational Aggression and Peer Relations: Gender and Developmental Issues." *Merrill-Palmer Quarterly* 43, no. 1 (1997): 87–106.

Sadker, Myra, and David Sadker. *Failing at Fairness: How America's Schools Cheat Girls.* New York: Scribner's, 1994.

Salmivalli, Christina, Arja Huttunen, and Kirsti M. J. Lagerspetz. "Peer Networks and Bullying in Schools." *Scandinavian Journal of Psychology* 38, no. 4 (1997): 305–12.

Sheldon, Amy. "Conflict Talk: Sociolinguistic Challenges to Self-Assertion and How Young Girls Meet Them." *Merrill-Palmer Quarterly* 38, no. 1 (1992): 95–117.

Silver, Marc, and Joellen Perry. "Hooked on Instant Messages." *U.S. News and World Report,* 22 March 1999, 57–58.

Simon, Robin W., Donna Eder, and Cathy Evans. "The Development of Feeling Norms Underlying Romantic Love among Adolescent Females." *Social Psychology Quarterly* 55, no. 1 (1992): 29–46.

Slee, P. T. "Situational and Interpersonal Correlates of Anxiety Associated with Peer Victimization." *Child Psychology & Human Development* 25 (1994): 97–107.

Smith, Elsie J. "The Black Female Adolescent: A Review of the Educational, Career, and Psychological Literature." *Psychology of Women Quarterly* 6, no. 3 (1982): 261–88.

Smith, Lynn. "Hey, Poo-Poo Head, Let's Be Friends: Childhood Teasing Needn't Be Traumatic." *Los Angeles Times,* 6 December 2000, p. 1.

Smith, Peter K., Helen Cowie, and Mark Blades, eds. *Understanding Children's Development.* 3rd ed. Oxford, England: Blackwell, 1998.

Smith-Rosenberg, Carroll. "The Female World of Love and Ritual: Relations between Women in Nineteenth-Century America." *Signs: Journal of Women in Culture and Society* 1 (1975): 1–29.

Spelman, Elizabeth. "Anger and Insubordination." In *Women, Knowledge, and Reality: Explorations in Feminist Philosophy,* edited by Ann Garry and Marilyn Pearsall. Boston: Unwin Hyman, 1989.

Stack, Carol B. *All Our Kin: Strategies for Survival in a Black Community.* New York: Harper, 1974.

Stanley, Lisa, and Tiny (C. M. J.) Arora. "Social Exclusion Amongst Adolescent Girls: Their Self-Esteem and Coping Strategies." *Educational Psychology in Practice* 14, no. 2 (1998): 94–100.

Sutton, Jon, and P. K. Smith. "Bullying as a Group Process: An Adaptation of the Participant Role Approach." *Aggressive Behavior* 25, no. 2 (1999): 97–111.

Sutton, Jon, P. K. Smith, and J. Swettenham. "Social Cognition and Bullying: Social Inadequacy or Skilled Manipulation?" *British Journal of Developmental Psychology* 17, no. 3 (1999): 435–50.

Tanenbaum, Leora. *Slut! Growing Up Female with a Bad Reputation.* New York: Seven Stories Press, 1999.

Taylor, Jill McLean, Carol Gilligan, and Amy M. Sullivan. *Between Voice and Silence: Women and Girls, Race and Relationship.* Cambridge, MA: Harvard University Press, 1995.

Thompson, Kevin M., Stephen A. Wonderlich, Ross D. Crosby, and James E. Mitchell. "The Neglected Link between Eating Disturbances and Aggressive Behavior in Girls." *Journal of the American Academy of Child & Adolescent Psychiatry* 38, no. 10 (1999): 1277–84.

Thompson, Michael, Lawrence J. Cohen, and Catherine O'Neill Grace. *Best Friends, Worst Enemies: Understanding the Social Lives of Children.* New York: Ballantine, 2001.

Thorne, Barrie. *Gender Play: Girls and Boys in School.* New Brunswick, NJ: Rutgers University Press, 1993.

Tolman, Deborah L. "Daring to Desire." In *Sexual Cultures and the Construction of Adolescent Identities,* edited by Janice Irvine. Philadelphia: Temple University Press, 1994.

Tolman, Deborah L., and Elizabeth Debold. "Conflicts of Body and Image: Female Adolescents, Desire, and the No-Body Body." In *Feminist Perspectives on Eating Disorders,* edited by Melanie A. Katzman, Patricia Fallon, and S. Wooley. New York: Guilford Press, 1994.

Tracy, Laura. *The Secret between Us: Competition among Women.* Boston: Little Brown, 1991.

Tronto, Joan C. *Moral Boundaries: A Political Argument for an Ethic of Care.* New York: Routledge, 1993.

Vasquez-Nuttall, Ena, Zoila Avila-Vivas, and Gisela Morales-Barreto. "Working with Latin American Families." In *Family Therapy with School Related Problems,* edited by James Hansen and Barbara Okun. Rockville, MD: Aspen Systems Corp., 1984.

Walkerdine, Valerie. *Schoolgirl Fictions*. London: Verso, 1990.

Ward, Janie Victoria. "Raising Resisters: The Role of Truth Telling in the Psychological Development of African American Girls." In *Urban Girls: Resisting Stereotypes, Creating Identities*, edited by Bonnie J. Ross Leadbeater and Niobe Way. New York: New York University Press, 1996.

Way, Niobe. " 'Can't You See the Courage, the Strength That I Have?' Listening to Urban Adolescent Girls Speak about Their Relationships." *Psychology of Women Quarterly* 19, no. 1 (1995): 107–28.

———. "Between Experiences of Betrayal and Desire: Close Friendships among Urban Adolescents." In *Urban Girls: Resisting Stereotypes, Creating Identities*, edited by Bonnie J. Ross Leadbeater and Niobe Way. New York: New York University Press, 1996.

Welsh, Patrick, "Bully-Boy Focus Overlooks Vicious Acts by Girls." *USA Today*, 12 June 2001, sec. A, p. 15.

White, Jacquelyn W., and Robin M. Kowalski. "Deconstructing the Myth of the Nonaggressive Woman: A Feminist Analysis." *Psychology of Women Quarterly* 18, no. 4 (1994): 487–508.

Wolf, Naomi. *Promiscuities: The Secret Struggle for Womanhood*. New York: Ballantine, 1997.

———.*The Beauty Myth: How Images of Beauty Are Used Against Women*. New York: Random House, 1991.

Wurtzel, Elizabeth. *Bitch: In Praise of Difficult Women*. New York: Doubleday, 1998.

Zollo, Peter. *Wise Up to Teens: Insights into Marketing and Advertising to Teenagers*. Ithaca, NY: New Strategist Publications, 1999.

acknowledgments

It would be hard to overstate how much this book owes its life to the help of others.

From the first moment we met, R. K. had faith in me and this project. She put her reputation on the line for me, opened doors for *Odd Girl Out,* and became a supervisor, confidante, and friend. Lynn Arons, Bernice Berke, Tamika Ford, Rabbi Reuven Greenwald, Marti Herskovitz, Rudy Jordan, Eloise Pasachoff, Rebecca Prigal, Sherie Randolph, Laura Rebell, Kate Sussman-Reimer, Joan Vander Walde, Toby Weinberger, and Claire Wurtzel provided me with the critical resources and access I needed to interview girls.

Stella Connell and Andrew Mullins believed in my project and led me to Ridgewood, where I had one of the most special experiences of my life. I am especially grateful to the Superintendent's staff, C. H., S. B., and M. V.; and the teachers of Ridgewood. M. F., P. P., S. P., and G. P., gave me as authentic a Southern experience as a woman could wish to have and friendships I will cherish for a lifetime.

For reasons I will never quite understand, the wonderful people at Harcourt never blinked when my brief residence at Twenty-sixth Street turned into a six-month stay. Their companionship eased the solitude of writing, and I am deeply grateful for their hospitality. For their support and hard work, I thank Susan Amster, Jennifer Gilmore, Jennifer Holiday, David Hough, Arlene Kriv, and Jacqueline Murphy. Kent Wolf provided me with much needed comic relief during my stay. Jennifer Aziz was a brilliant editorial assistant and friend. Rachel Myers was a superb copyeditor.

I am grateful to an extraordinary group of friends and colleagues who supported me throughout this journey. Many of them reached out to their friends on my behalf and enabled the project to go forward. I wish to thank Elaine and Lydia Amerson, Peter Antelyes, Julie Barer, Jill Erlitz, Frances Fergusson, David Gmach and Sally Friedman, Zoe Holiday Grossman, Sula Harris, Jane Hanson, Judith Holiber and Kim Warsaw, Sandra Hershberg, Kari Hong, Karen Maxwell, Rhonda Kleiner and Alizah and Elana Lowell, Ilana Marcus, Terri McCullough and Howard Wolfson, Danielle Merida, Noa Meyer, Heather Muchow, Nancy Needle, Carmen Peralta, Sid Plotkin and Marjorie Gluck, Rose Polidoro, Elana Waksal Posner, Lisa Sacks, Robert and Stacy Skitol, Freyda Spira Slavin, Leigh Silverman, Taije Silverman, Elizabeth Stanley, Linsey and Kelly Tully, Diane Tunis, Annie Weissman, Susan Wellman and the Ophelia Project, and Rosalind Wiseman and Empower.

Special thanks to Abdul Aziz Said and the Center for Global Peace at American University; Paulette Hurwitz, whose generous care and counsel helped me find the strength to embrace risk; Molly Shanley, a steadfast friend, colleague, and mentor who talked me down from the proverbial ledge more times than I can count; Senator Charles Schumer and Iris Weinshall for their friendship and support; Sandy Kavalier, who captured me perfectly in the photograph for this book; and Ashleigh May, Ilana Sichel, and Virginia Wharton, who provided me with excellent research assistance.

I will always be indebted to Maryana Iskander, who helped me make the hardest decision of my life and believed in me at every turn, especially when I didn't. It was over lunch in London that Jeremy Dauber became the first person to hear about a book on bullying and girls. Back in New York, on my most frantic days, he ministered carefully to my thinking and prose.

It is hard for me to put into words how much the support of my closest friends has meant. Jenny Bender and Josh Mecham, Maggie Bittel, Luke Cusack and Denis Guerin, Ellen Karsh, Astrid Koltun, Cathie Levine and Josh Isay, Lissa Skitol, and Daniella Topol are my family. The force of their faith, listening, love, and laughter guided me through every day of this challenge. I could not have survived it without them.

Odd Girl Out would not have been possible without the unflinching support of my family. My wise brother Joshua was my comic savior and the best friend I could call twenty times a day. My grandfather Bernard Simmons astonished me with his swift acceptance of the changes I made in my life, and he immediately became a devoted press secretary. My grandmother Lia Simmons peppered my computer screen with supportive instant messages and stuck bills in the mail with notes begging me to "stop eating burritos." My Bubby Frances Goldstein is a true inspiration, and my Aunt Sylvia Brodach never forgets me. Finally, my Uncle Bill Goldstein's support has been invaluable, and my inimitable cousins Sergei and Ziggy, who joined our family during the writing of this book, have made spirited additions to our family.

Finally, and most importantly, I thank the extraordinary group of women and girls who trusted me with their stories. I continue to be awed by your courageous voices. Above all, you are the ones who will show the readers of this book they are not alone. I hope your stories touch girls' lives as profoundly as you have touched mine, and that *Odd Girl Out* makes you proud to have spoken up.

abandonment, fear of, 30–33, 270
abusive relationships, 32, 161–67, 217,
    219–20, 222, 241, 246–47, 266–68
academic performance, 95, 98, 99–100,
    193
acceptance, importance of, 32–33
advertisements, 117, 118
African Americans, 11, 178–81, 183–88,
    189, 194–97, 200–201
aggression
    in analysis of self, 254
    as barometer of social values, 16–17
    of boys versus girls, 2, 3, 4–5, 8, 9–10,
        15–16, 84, 196–97, 200
    direct, 11, 20
    of "good girls," 20
    physical, 18, 23, 26–27, 179–83, 195–97,
        200
    recognizing, 255
    types of, 21
    See also girl bullying
Alizah (student), 198–99, 242, 257
alliance building, 25–30, 50–52, 75,
    79–84, 88–101, 137–38, 196–97,
    212–16, 248, 249, 251, 262
Allison, Dorothy, 179

alternative aggressions. *See* girl bullying
Amber (student), 229
American Association of University
    Women, 106, 177–78, 226
anger
    fear of expressing, 69–74, 101, 209–10,
        269
    hiding, 152, 153
Anne (adult), 129–30, 135, 151, 259
Annie (student), 36, 56–62
anorexia, 240
antibullying curriculum, 251
antibullying language, 249
antibullying policies, 249–50
antibullying strategies, 34–35
anti-girl qualities, 124–26, 127, 264–65
anxiety, 98, 110, 133–34, 264
apologies, 75–77
Asian Americans, 139–43
assertiveness, 115, 127, 151, 177, 178–79,
    201. *See also* resistance
assertiveness training, 248
attachment, 30
Atwood, Margaret, 21–22
authenticity, 111, 173–75, 183–89, 199, 201,
    268–69

backbiting and backstabbing, 3, 262
Bank, Pam (principal), 47, 184
Barbara (mother), 213–16
Best Friends, Worst Enemies
   (Thompson), 9
betrayal, 139–43
bitch, 18
blame, 36–37, 42, 91, 111–12, 204, 205–6,
   207–11, 270
body language, 44, 47–48, 227–28
body slamming, 23, 26–27
Bonnie (student), 180–83
boundary maintenance, 35
bragging, 104, 120
Brown, Lyn Mikel, 6–8, 17, 23, 62, 76,
   78, 80, 83, 122, 153, 174, 177, 179,
   186–87, 268
Bully Broads program, 266

Campbell, Anne, 16–17, 31, 148, 263
Canter, Debbi (teacher), 47
caregiver role, 11, 17, 18, 30–31, 220,
   221–22, 239–40, 245–46, 265
Carter, Lily (student), 73–74, 157, 158,
   174–75, 266
Cassie (student), 40–42, 44
Cat's Eye (Atwood), 21–22
classroom culture, 225–26, 250–51
cliques, 87–101, 262
   bait for, 133
   exclusion from, 3, 44–45, 134, 135–36,
      212–16, 258–59
   expulsions, 88–101, 130–31
   silent treatment, 107–13
code names, 26–29, 172
code words
   ideal girl versus anti-girl, 124–28
   nature of, 120–24
   "she's all that," 10–11, 103–28
Cohen, Suzanne (mother), 203–4, 205,
   237
communication with daughters
   active listening, 232, 242
   children's resistance in, 12
   methods of, 238–48
competition, 90, 117–20, 123–24, 126–27,
   152, 156–60, 172, 193, 253, 264, 269
compliments, 123
conceitedness, 10–11, 120

confidence, 95, 110, 114, 115, 118, 185, 201,
   224, 263
conflict
   direct, 11, 20, 37
   fear of, 163, 253
   making peace with, 231, 261–62
   negotiating, 31–32
   stockpiling of, 81
   truth telling and, 252–55
   unresolved, 69–74
confrontations, 37, 48
connection, importance of, 9, 10, 32–33,
   171–73
control, 143–46
copying, 123–24, 259
Corinna (student), 173–74
counseling, 96, 111–12, 204, 219, 243
covert aggression, 10
covert looks, 22, 44–47
Cruel Intentions (film), 23, 175

Danielle (student), 144–46
depression, 53, 73, 95, 98, 209, 218–19,
   240
desire, 126–27
diaries, 58, 158, 257
DiFranco, Ani, 106
direct conflict, 11, 20, 37
dirty looks, 94
disciplinary practices, 226–27, 251
distance, 75
duplicity, 16, 46–47, 116–17, 169–73, 187,
   246

egalitarian ethos, 127
Elaine (mother), 220–21
Elizabeth (adult), 167–69, 232, 233
e-mail messages, 32, 93, 95, 97, 158
empathy, 241, 242, 243
Empower Program, 252
Erin (student), 88–101, 103, 135–36, 176,
   222, 242–43
Evans, Gail, 265–66
exclusion, 3, 44–45, 134, 135–36, 212–16,
   258–59
expulsions from cliques, 88–101, 130–31

Faith (student), 246
false exterior, 46–47

"Fat Talk" (study), 122–23
fault, 74–75, 91
fear
    of abandonment, 30–33, 270
    of being called "all that," 118–20
    of conflict, 163, 253
    of expressing anger, 69–74, 101,
        209–10, 269
    of isolation, 69–70, 74, 80, 135–36, 146
    of parents, 211–16
    of reprisal, 78
feelings of others, 70–71, 86
femininity
    middle-class notions of, 179, 201,
        245–46
    niceness and, 13, 17, 18–19, 67–68,
        106–7, 150, 269–70
    passivity in, 124–26
    rules of, 115
    sexual modesty and, 122
feminism, 171–72
Fields, Laura (superintendent), 62–63
"fight or flight" response, 87
flirting, 104, 108, 120, 121–22
frigidity, 18, 127

ganging up, 25–30, 50–52, 75, 79–84,
    88–101, 137–38, 196–97, 212–16, 248,
    249, 251, 262
Gilligan, Carol, 6–8, 17, 23, 30, 62, 76,
    78, 80, 83, 153, 174, 177, 186–87,
    268
girl bullying, 11, 15–37, 43–44
    boys' aggression versus, 2, 3, 4–5, 8,
        9–10, 84, 196–97, 200
    confronting, 229–30
    cost of, 262–70
    defined, 8–9
    forms of, 3, 22
    ignoring, 204
    lack of public awareness of, 4, 42
    parents' responses to, 33, 111–12,
        232–35
    prevalence of, 1–3
    public strategies for handling, 34–35
    as rite of passage, 33–35
    self-awareness of own, 129–53
    as social skills deficit of victims, 35–37
glares, 46

"good girls," 17–18, 20–21, 24, 115, 123,
    245–46, 264–66
gossip, 35, 73, 82, 83, 152
grades, 95, 98, 99–100
guilt, 77, 142–43
gun violence, 4

Haley (student), 161–64, 256
Hannah (student), 237
Harrigan, Diane (mother), 88–89,
    95–100
Heathers (film), 48–49, 159, 175
helplessness, 11–12, 219, 220–23, 237
hints, 74, 266
Hispanic Americans, 11, 188–97
hooks, bell, 178
humiliation, 239
humor, 51–52, 77–79, 111, 132–33, 138, 149,
    171, 174, 247–48
hypersensitivity, 247
hysterical parents, 243, 245

ideal girl, 124–26
independence, 185, 206
indirect aggression, 21
indirection, 115–17
Instant Messenger (IM), 158
intimacy, 30–31, 48–66, 101, 171
isolation, 30, 31, 32, 60, 61, 217, 222,
    240
    fear of, 69–70, 74, 80, 135–36, 146
    imposed, 76, 80, 88–101
    self-imposed, 183

Janet (student), 164–67
Jasmine (student), 190–94
Jawbreaker (film), 79, 175
jealousy, 16, 100, 114, 115, 117–21, 123–24,
    127, 142, 145, 152–53, 192, 253, 269
Jennifer (student), 71
Jenny (student), 25–30, 197
Jessica (student), 164
Joanna (student), 220–21
Johnston, Jessie (student), 157, 160
Johnston, Paula (mother), 22–23
Johnston, Susie (student), 22–23, 256
joking, 51–52, 77–79, 111, 132–33, 138, 149,
    171, 174, 247–48
journals, 58, 158, 257

Kaplan, Chloe (student), 169–71, 223–25
Kaplan, Margaret (mother), 169–71, 206, 209, 223–25, 244
Keisha (student), 184–85
Keller, Tasha (student), 78–79, 117–18
Keltner, Dacher, 79
Kendra (teacher), 229–30
kin networks, 186

Latinas, 11, 188–97
leadership traits, 263–66
lesbianism, 18
Lexie (student), 157
Lisa (student), 136–39
listening, active, 232, 242
Liu, Kathy (student), 139–43
love
    romantic, 92–94, 100
    unconditional, 232
Lucia (student), 267
Lynn (counselor), 229

manipulation, 3, 22, 43, 116–17, 126, 137–38, 146
manliness, 18
Marcie (adult), 270
Marilyn (teacher), 226–28
Maryann (teacher), 229
meanness
    as part of friendship, 56–62
    repression of, 149–53
    self-awareness of own, 129–53
mediators, 69, 84–87, 197
Meeting at the Crossroads (Gilligan and Brown), 268
Megan (student), 131–34
Melanie (student), 72
Melissa (daughter), 211–16
mentors, 13
Michelle (student), 88–101, 135–36
middle-class communities, 179, 201, 245–46
middlegirls, 69, 84–87, 197
middle school years, 268–69
Molly (student), 146–49

name-calling, 3, 26–29, 32
Naomi (adult), 242, 243–44, 247, 258
Natalie (student), 62–63, 173, 267
new activities, 233–34, 257
new students, 25–30, 88–101, 113–14
nice-in-private and mean-in-public, 262
niceness, 13, 17, 18–19, 67–68, 106–7, 150, 269–70
nonverbal gesturing, 44, 47–48
note passing, 22, 25, 32, 59, 137, 141, 262

Ophelia Project, 251–52
oppression, 186
Oregon, 249
Orenstein, Peggy, 17, 106, 226

parents, 44, 203–25, 232–48
    active listening and, 232, 242
    blame and, 205–6, 207–11
    communicating with daughters, 238–48
    demands on teachers, 204, 226, 227
    empowering of children, 194
    fear of, 211–16
    helplessness of, 220–23, 237
    hysterical, 243, 245
    involvement with other parents, 33, 235–36, 244
    perceptions of children and, 216–20
    and physical aggression in girls, 18
    responses to girl bullying, 33, 111–12, 232–35
    as role models, 236
    sense of fate and, 223–25
    support groups for, 206, 244
    of victims, 11–12, 52–54, 59–60
passion, 30–31
passivity, 124–28
Patricia (mother), 207–10
Patterson, Susan (mother), 206
Peralta, Carmen (student), 71–72, 77
perfectionism, 32, 36–37, 99, 124–26, 174–75
petitions, 4, 28–29
Petra (mother), 59–60
physical aggression, 18, 23, 26–27, 179–83, 195–97, 200
Pipher, Mary, 244–45, 251–52, 268
Play Like a Man, Win Like a Woman (Evans), 265–66
popularity, 11, 135, 155–76
    competition and, 156–60, 172
    loss of close friend to, 160–64
    nature of, 82

price of, 164–69

secrets and lies in, 169–73

sex differences in, 156

truth about, 173–76, 256–57

privacy, 228

professionalism, 127, 264

psychological scripts, 185

punching, 20

punking out, 188–89, 195

racism, 186

recognition, 9

Reese (student), 62–63, 173, 267

regulation of bullying, 248–50

relational violations, 62

relationships

    abusive, 32, 161–67, 217, 219–20, 222, 241, 246–47, 266–68

    caregiver role of girls, 11, 17, 18, 30–31, 220, 221–22, 239–40, 245–46, 265

    as chosen partnerships, 261

    competition for, 156–60

    connection and, 9, 10, 32–33, 171–73

    fears and questions about, 13

    of "good girls," 17–18

    importance of, 10, 131, 146, 158–59

    loss and, 30–33

    sex in service of, 122

    as weapons, 43–44

repression, 146–53, 262

    of hurt feelings, 88–101, 146–49

    of meanness toward others, 149–53

resentment, 103, 152

resistance, 177–201

    African-American, 178–81, 183–88, 189, 194–97, 200–201

    assertiveness training, 248

    in authenticity, 183–89, 199, 201

    confronting girl bullying, 229–30

    education, 250–52

    Latina, 188–97

    parental role in, 194

    physical aggression, 179–83, 195–97, 200

    regulation, 248–50

    unbidden, 197–201

    working-class, 177–83, 190–94

respect, 161, 199, 225

retaliation, 29–30, 137–39, 150–51, 197

Reviving Ophelia (Pipher), 268

Rich, Adrienne, 16, 146

rite of passage, 33–35

role models, 13, 113, 118, 126, 186, 222–23, 236

role-playing, 234, 248

Roma (adult), 143–44, 234, 258

romantic love, 92–94, 100

Ruiz, Jacqueline (student), 188–89

rumors, 3, 32, 35, 43, 45, 83, 85, 171, 172, 195, 248, 249, 262

sadness, 221–22

Samantha (student), 36, 56–62, 267

school culture, 114–15

Schoolgirls (Orenstein), 17, 226

secrets, 31, 49–50, 83, 169–73, 228, 249

self-actualization, 185

self-awareness, 245–46

self-blame, 36–37, 42, 91, 111–12, 270

self-confidence, 95, 110, 114, 115, 118, 185, 201, 224, 263

self-defense, 248

self-esteem, 12, 34, 43, 78, 101, 110, 166, 168, 173–76, 177–78, 186, 189, 197–98, 210–11, 240, 269

self-hatred, 16

selflessness, 127–28

self-mutilation, 240

self-reliance, 193, 222

self-respect, 161

sexual abuse, 166

sexuality, 51, 116–17, 122

shame, 11–12, 204–5, 240

Shelley (student), 73, 158, 198, 253

She's All That (film), 175

silence

    burden of, 3–4, 239, 250

    ending of, 4–9

    of families, 205–6

    silent treatment, 43, 44–47, 75, 97, 102, 107–13, 192, 262

skank, 122

sleep problems, 110

sluts, 122

Smith, Cassie, 40–42, 44

socialization

    of African Americans, 11, 178–81, 183–88, 189, 194–97, 200–201

    of aggression, 263

    of girls, 11

    of Latinas, 11, 188–97

social skills, 35–37
solitude, 30, 31, 32, 60, 61, 135–36, 197–98
Stacy (student), 49–56
staring, 46
Stephanie (student), 107–13, 121, 240, 257
subordination, 185
suicidal thoughts, 53–54, 96, 97, 219, 239
superiority, 103–28
    being called "all that," 10–11, 105–6, 114–15, 118–20
Survivor (television show), 87–88
suspicion, 159
Sussman, Susan (mother), 206

Taylor, Jill McLean, 183, 200
teachers, 225–30
    classroom culture and, 225–26, 250–51
    disciplinary practices, 226–27, 251
    expectations of girls, 19–20, 23, 24, 25
    and girl bullying, 34–35, 44
    misunderstanding between students and, 228–29
    parent demands on, 204, 226, 227
    and physical aggression in girls, 18
teasing, 20
Thompson, Michael, 9
threatening, 20
Tolman, Deborah, 122

trust, 98, 110, 112, 127, 138, 143, 152, 168, 169–70, 172, 174, 188, 223, 224, 269–70
truth telling, 11, 153, 178, 183–88, 189, 252–55, 270
Twister (game), 115–16

ulcers, 111, 240
unconditional love, 232
University of California at Berkeley, 79
University of California at Los Angeles, 87
University of Michigan, 18

Vanessa (student), 49–56
Vernon, Ashley (student), 158
voices of girls, 6, 44, 226, 259

Ward, Janie, 185
Washington State, 249
Way, Niobe, 178
weight problems, 53–54, 214–15
whispering, 22, 25, 108
Wiseman, Rosalind, 152
Wood, Donna (mother), 216–20
Wood, Tracy (daughter), 216–20
working-class communities, 11, 177–83, 190–94
Wurtzel, Elizabeth, 116